TRANSACTIONS OF THE

AMERICAN PHILOSOPHICAL SOCIETY

HELD AT PHILADELPHIA

FOR PROMOTING USEFUL KNOWLEDGE

VOLUME 73, PART 6, 1983

# Ripon Minster
# The Beginning of the Gothic Style in Northern England

M. F. HEARN

Professor of Fine Arts, University of Pittsburgh

THE AMERICAN PHILOSOPHICAL SOCIETY

INDEPENDENCE SQUARE: PHILADELPHIA

1983

Copyright © 1983 by The American Philosophical Society

Library of Congress Catalog
Card Number 83-71300
International Standard Book Number 0-87169-736-X
US ISSN 0065-9746

To Jean Bony

Ripon Minster, general view from the south. Drawing by Beresford Pite, from *The Builder*, Feb 4, 1893.

## CONTENTS

| | Page |
|---|---|
| List of Illustrations | vii |
| Acknowledgments | xiii |
| Introduction | 1 |
| Part One—Archaeological Interpretation | |
|   1. The Actual and Intended Forms | 9 |
| Part Two—Historical Interpretation | |
|   2. The Dates of Construction | 63 |
|   3. The Patron and His Purposes | 80 |
|   4. A Search for the Origin of the Ripon Master | 102 |
|   5. The English Concept of the Gothic Style | 122 |
| Appendix | 136 |
| Bibliography | 138 |
| Plates | 141 |
| Index | 195 |
| Plans 1 and 2 | Inside back cover |

# List of Illustrations

*Plates*

| | | |
|---|---|---|
| Frontispiece | Ripon Minster, general view from the South. Drawings by Beresford Pite, from *The Builder*, Feb. 4, 1893 | iv |
| 1 | Ripon Minster, east end. | 141 |
| 2 | Ripon Minster, choir, looking east | 142 |
| 3 | Ripon Minster, choir, west bays of north elevation. | 143 |
| 4 | Ripon Minster, choir, east bays of north elevation. | 144 |
| 5 | Ripon Minster, choir, second freestanding pier of north elevation. | 145 |
| 6 | Ripon Minster, choir, capital of first freestanding pier of north elevation (with impost replaced in the late thirteenth century). | 145 |
| 7 | Ripon Minster, choir, capital of third freestanding pier of north elevation. | 146 |
| 8 | Ripon Minster, choir, scar of original plinth on east bay of south aisle wall, at the juncture with the chapter house apse. | 146 |
| 9 | Ripon Minster, choir, detail of east wall showing scar of relieving arch. | 147 |
| 10 | Ripon Minster, choir, north flank showing set-back late-thirteenth-century bays to left. | 147 |
| 11 | Ripon Minster, choir, triforium arcade in the fourth bay of the north elevation. | 148 |
| 12 | Ripon Minster, vaults in north choir aisle. | 148 |
| 13 | Ripon Minster, vault respond shafts in south choir aisle. | 149 |
| 14 | Ripon Minster, chapter house south flank. | 149 |
| 15 | Ripon Minster, chapter house apse. | 150 |
| 16 | Ripon Minster, juncture of chapter house and south transept showing continuous courses of ashlar masonry. | 150 |
| 17 | Ripon Minster, chapter house, vaults of undercroft, showing inserted ribs. | 151 |
| 18 | Ripon Minster, chapter house, vaults of upper chamber. | 151 |
| 19 | Ripon Minster, north transept, east flank. | 152 |
| 20 | Ripon Minster, north transept, north and east elevations. | 152 |
| 21 | Ripon Minster, north transept, eastern chapel vault (inner bay). | 153 |
| 22 | Ripon Minster, north transept, clerestory arcade in west elevation. | 153 |
| 23 | Ripon Minster, north transept, west elevation. | 154 |

| | | |
|---|---|---|
| 24 | Ripon Minster, north transept, north elevation showing detached shafts and revised arch decoration. | 154 |
| 25 | Ripon Minster, south transept facade. | 155 |
| 26 | Ripon Minster, south transept, west flank. | 156 |
| 27 | Ripon Minster, south transept, south elevation. | 157 |
| 28 | Ripon Minster, south transept, west elevation. | 158 |
| 29 | Ripon Minster, south transept, eastern chapels, showing cluster of detached shafts for vault responds. | 159 |
| 30 | Ripon Minster, crossing, showing lantern tower. | 160 |
| 31 | Ripon Minster, crossing seen from nave, showing original crossing pier. | 161 |
| 32 | Ripon Minster, nave, looking east. | 162 |
| 33 | Ripon Minster, nave, south elevation, west bays, lower stories. | 162 |
| 34 | Ripon Minster, nave, south elevation, west bays, upper stories. | 163 |
| 35 | Ripon Minster, nave, north elevation, west bays. | 164 |
| 36 | Ripon Minster, south west tower, blind arcade behind triforium of nave west bay. | 165 |
| 37 | Ripon Minster, juncture of south and west elevations. | 165 |
| 38 | Ripon Minster, south west tower, arch opening from the nave. | 166 |
| 39 | Ripon Minster, nave, south elevation, penultimate bay. | 166 |
| 40 | Ripon Minster, nave, south elevation, east bay. | 167 |
| 41 | Ripon Minster, nave, north elevation, east bay. | 167 |
| 42 | Ripon Minster, nave north flank, buttress scar (located in north aisle of the early-sixteenth-century nave). | 168 |
| 43 | Ripon Minster, juncture of nave south flank and south west tower, showing original wall buttress (located in south aisle of the early-sixteenth-century nave). | 168 |
| 44 | Ripon Minster, west front, south tower from the south. | 169 |
| 45 | Ripon Minster, west front, south tower interior. | 169 |
| 46 | Ripon Minster, west front, juncture of north tower and nave north flank at plinth, showing continuous courses of ashlar masonry above the plinth. | 170 |
| 47 | Ripon Minster, west front, juncture of north tower and nave north flank, showing continuous courses of ashlar masonry up to the top of the nave wall buttress. | 170 |
| 48 | Ripon Minster, west front, north tower north east face showing lack of correspondence between ashlar masonry courses of the left and right window jambs. | 171 |
| 49 | Ripon Minster, west front, north tower showing corbel table which corresponds to the original ceiling level in the nave. | 171 |
| 50 | Ripon Minster, west front, north tower from the northeast. | 172 |
| 51 | Ripon Minster, west front, north tower, showing corbel table at the top of the upper story. | 172 |

## ILLUSTRATIONS

| | | |
|---|---|---|
| 52 | Ripon Minster, west front, facade. | 173 |
| 53 | Fountains Abbey, south transept, windows of eastern chapels. | 174 |
| 54 | Preuilly Abbey, choir east elevation. | 174 |
| 55 | Laon Cathedral, choir, looking east. | 175 |
| 56 | Roche Abbey, north transept, east elevation (with remains of west elevation plinth in foreground). | 176 |
| 57 | Canterbury Cathedral, south (east) transept, upper stories. | 177 |
| 58 | Noyon Cathedral, south transept, east elevation. | 177 |
| 59 | Selby Abbey, west front before the remodeling of 1935, but with modern gable. | 178 |
| 60 | Kirkstall Abbey, north transept, east elevation. | 179 |
| 61 | Kirkstall Abbey, nave, north elevation. | 179 |
| 62 | Roche Abbey, nave, north elevation, remains of pier. | 180 |
| 63 | Byland Abbey, south transept, east elevation, detail of main arcade. | 180 |
| 64 | Byland Abbey, south transept, east elevation, upper stories. | 181 |
| 65 | Byland Abbey, choir aisle, vault responds. | 181 |
| 66 | Byland Abbey, south transept, eastern chapel, vault arches. | 182 |
| 67 | Byland Abbey, south transept, east elevation, remains of pier. | 182 |
| 68 | Furness Abbey, south transept, east elevation. | 183 |
| 69 | Furness Abbey, south transept, east elevation, detail of main arcade. | 183 |
| 70 | Whitby Abbey, choir, looking north. | 184 |
| 71 | Lanercost Priory, detail of north choir elevation. | 185 |
| 72 | Jedburgh Abbey, nave, looking west. | 185 |
| 73 | Wells Cathedral, nave, south elevation. | 186 |
| 74 | Bertaucourt-les-Dames, nave south elevation, pier. | 186 |
| 75 | Bellefontaine Chapel, arcade of north aisle chapel. | 187 |
| 76 | Soissons Cathedral, south transept, detail of main arcade. | 187 |
| 77 | Laon Cathedral, north transept, east elevation. | 188 |
| 78 | Laon Cathedral, north transept, vaults. | 188 |
| 79 | Laon Cathedral, north transept, wall passage at gallery level in north elevation. | 189 |
| 80 | Noyon Cathedral, south transept, east flank. | 189 |
| 81 | Lillers Abbey, nave, south elevation. | 190 |
| 82 | Canterbury Cathedral, choir. | 191 |
| 83 | Canterbury Cathedral, choir aisle, Romanesque capital. | 192 |
| 84 | Canterbury Cathedral, Trinity Chapel main arcade, Gothic capital. | 192 |
| 85 | Chichester Cathedral, retrochoir. | 193 |
| 86 | Lincoln Cathedral, nave, looking east. | 194 |
| 87 | Lincoln Cathedral, north choir aisle, blind arcade. | 194 |
| Plans 1 and 2 | Inside back cover. | |

*Figures*

| | | |
|---|---|---|
| 1 | Ripon Minster, plan of G. G. Scott's reconsitution of the original scheme. Reproduced from *Archaeological Journal*, 21, (1874). | 3 |
| 2 | Ripon Minster, choir elevation as reconstituted by G. G. Scott, Reproduced from *Archaeological Journal*, 21, (1874). | 4 |
| 3 | Ripon Minster, nave elevation as reconstituted by G. G. Scott, Reproduced from *Archaeological Journal*, 21, (1874). | 4 |
| 4 | Ripon Minster, plan. Reproduced from *The Builder*, February 1893. | 10 |
| 5 | Ripon Minster, choir, reconstitution of original juncture of north and east elevations. | 15 |
| 6 | Ripon Minster, choir interior reconstitution according to the intended scheme. | 18 |
| 7 | Ripon Minster, choir elevation reconstitution (based, with emendations, on that of G. G. Scott) showing intended scheme. | 22 |
| 8 | Ripon Minster, choir interior reconstitution according to the revised scheme actually constructed. | 25 |
| 9 | Ripon Minster, north transept reconstitution according to the intended scheme. | 34 |
| 10 | Ripon Minster, nave reconstitution according to revised scheme actually constructed. | 43 |
| 11 | Ripon Minster, reconstitution of intended nave exterior and west front. | 46 |
| 12 | Ripon Minster, west front, reconstitution of intended scheme. | 53 |
| 13 | Ripon Minster, extent of construction in Stage One. | 56 |
| 14 | Ripon Minster, extent of construction in Stage Two. | 57 |
| 15 | Ripon Minster, extent of construction in Stage Three. | 58 |
| 16 | Ripon Minster, as completed at the end of Stage Four. | 59 |
| 17 | Byland Abbey, south transept east elevation, reconstituted by Peter Ferguson. Reproduced with permission from *Journal of the British Archaeological Association*, 37 (1975). | 70 |
| 18 | Byland Abbey, plan reproduced with permission of Oxford University Press from Alfred Clapham, *English Romanesque Architecture after the Conquest*, Oxford, 1934. | 71 |
| 19 | Rochester Cathedral, plan of choir by St. John Hope. Reproduced from *Archaeologia Cantiana*, 23 (1898). | 83 |
| 20 | York Minster, plan of the church as it stood after completion of Roger of Pont l'Evêque's choir and transepts. Adapted from various plans published by Robert Willis, Alfred Clapham, Eric Gee and Derek Phillips—not drawn to scale. | 83 |
| 21 | Canterbury Cathedral, plan of Romanesque choir. Reproduced from Robert Willis, *The Architectural History of Canterbury Cathedral*, London, 1845. | 91 |
| 22 | Daméry Church, tower arcade. | 114 |

ILLUSTRATIONS

\* \* \*

## Credits

I. Plates

Author/Courtauld Institute of Art: 1, 5, 6, 7, 8, 9, 10, 11, 12, 13, 14, 15, 16, 17, 19, 20, 22, 23, 24, 25, 26, 27, 28, 29, 31, 36, 37, 38, 39, 40, 41, 42, 43, 44, 45, 46, 47, 48, 49, 50, 51, 53, 58, 60, 61, 62, 63, 64, 65, 66, 67, 68, 69, 70, 72, 76, 77, 78, 79, 80, 84.
Courtauld Institute of Art: 18, 52, 55, 56, 57, 73, 82, 83, 85, 86, 87.
F. H. Crossley: 2, 3, 4, 21, 32, 35, 71.
Peter Fergusson: 30, 54, 74, 75, 81.
Arnold Klukas: 33, 34.
National Monuments Record, Royal Commission on Historical Monuments, England: 59, 85.

II. Figures

Gary Cirrincione, with author: 5, 6, 7, 8, 9, 10, 11, 12, 13, 14, 15, 16, plans 1 and 2.
Matthew Roper: 1, 2, 3, 4, 17, 18, 19, 21, 22.

# ACKNOWLEDGMENTS

The research for this book would never have been possible without the enthusiastic hospitality for my project extended by the Rev. James B. Ashworth, then Residentiary Canon of Ripon Cathedral, who granted me access to all parts of the structure and all materials in the Library during two study campaigns, in 1972 and 1977. The cathedral stonemason, Jack Yarker, placed ladders wherever I needed them, guided me through the various passages of the structure, and provided useful data concerning both repairs of the fabric and soundings around the foundations and the crypt in recent decades. John Miller, architect, of Harrogate, joined me at the cathedral to discuss his own archaeological observations, particularly of the chapter house. Arnold Klukas, then researching his dissertation under my direction and now teaching at Oberlin College, assisted me in taking measurements during my 1977 visit. At York Minster, Derek Phillips explained all the excavations he had directed there through 1972 and showed me the relevant excavation reports and drawings.

The drawings, which confer much of the value this book may have, were patiently executed by Gary Cirrincione, architect, of Pittsburgh, over a long period and with diligence beyond the normal call of duty. Earlier versions of the nave elevation were drawn by Patricia Pepin and Arnold Klukas. Peter Fergusson, of Wellesley College, has generously provided several photographs (and listened to hours of discourse supporting my conclusions) and Matthew Roper, slide curator of the Fine Arts Department, has made numerous photographs for me.

Reprinting of an extended passage from my 1972 article on the nave elevation in the *Journal of the British Archaeological Association* has been kindly permitted by the Editorial Board of the learned society. Earlier versions of different portions of this text have been presented as scholarly papers to the College Art Association of America, in San Francisco, 1972; to the Courtauld Institute of Art, London, 1977; to the British Archaeological Association in Durham, 1977; and to the Medieval Institute, Kalamazoo, 1980 and 1982.

Financial support for this project has been provided in the form of research and travel grants from the Faculty of Arts and Sciences, University of Pittsburgh, in 1969; from the American Council of Learned Societies, the American Philosophical Society, and the University Center for International Studies, University of Pittsburgh, all in 1977; and from the Research Development Fund, University of Pittsburgh, in 1982. I also had the benefit of sabbatical leaves from the Fine Arts Department, University of Pittsburgh, in 1972 and 1978.

M. F. Hearn<br>
University of Pittsburgh<br>
November 1982

# INTRODUCTION

Ripon Cathedral, anciently one of the four minsters of the archdiocese of York, was designated a cathedral when the new diocese of Ripon was created in 1836. In the history of architecture it is properly known as Ripon Minster, a collegiate foundation of secular canons who maintained the daily cycle of liturgical offices but who also ministered to the laity. Initially a monastery, established at an unknown date, it was reorganized and dedicated to St. Peter under the aegis of (St.) Wilfrid shortly after the English church was unified under the Roman observance (largely due to Wilfrid's urging) at the Synod of Whitby in 664. The monastery was probably converted to a minster about the time of the Norman Conquest in 1066, but construction of a new church did not occur for another century. This new church is now a patchwork of architecture dating from the late twelfth to the early sixteenth centuries, built over the small crypt which survives from Wilfrid's seventh-century structure. For architectural history the important portion is the remainder of the twelfth-century building, the basic outlines of which governed the later modifications. Begun by Roger of Pont l'Evêque, archbishop of York from 1154 until 1181, this church has been known ever since by its joint dedication to SS. Peter and Wilfrid.[1]

Twelfth-century Ripon Minster was one of the earliest Gothic structures in England and was probably the first fully Gothic building in the North. To make this assertion, though, is to displace Roche Abbey, which has long been considered either proto-Gothic or the first Gothic building in England.[2] Roche, to be sure, has most of the hallmarks of the Gothic

---

[1] The institutional history of Ripon Minster, by J. T. Fowler, appears in the prefaces to *Memorials of Ripon*, vols. 1–3. The Publications of the Surtees Society, vols. 74, 78, and 81, (London, 1881, 1884, 1886). The early history of the foundation is in the preface to vol. 3. After the monastery was refounded by (St.) Wilfrid ca. 670, a new church was built. Burned by King Eadred in 948, it was putatively rebuilt by (St.) Oswald before 1000, although no reliable traces of this church have been discovered. Ripon's conversion to a minster with a chapter of canons is attributed to Eadred, archbishop of York from 1060 to 1069, chiefly because the prebends of the canons were mentioned in the Domesday Book. The number of canons was specified as seven at various times after 1100 (2: 2, 8, 33).

[2] John Bilson (in "The Architecture of the Cistercians, with Special Reference to Some of Their Earlier Churches in England," *Archaeological Journal* 66, 1909: 277–78.) regarded the introduction of the Gothic style into the north of England to have been accomplished by the Cistercians, beginning with Roche. He characterized Roche as Gothic with something lacking, but Gothic nevertheless. This position is maintained in the present generation by Nikolaus Pevsner when he terms Roche "truly Gothic" (*Yorkshire: The West Riding* The Buildings of England, Harmondsworth, 1959, 415). In the same volume, p. 407, in connection with Ripon, he distinguishes between kinds of Gothic when he states that ". . . Ripon is rather the Cistercian Gothic of Roche than the cathedral Gothic of Sens or Noyon or Laon." A less

style—specifically, the pointed arch, the high ribbed vault, and, for the most part, a rationalized composition. It lacks, however, a consistent use of shafts and arch moldings in the articulation of all its stories, in consequence of which its stylistic effect is rather static, a very incomplete version of Gothic. Accordingly, historians usually hedge their estimate of Roche's significance with modifiers such as "harbinger," "prefiguration," or "proto-Gothic," but without acknowledging that another building must then be recognized as the first fully Gothic one. Because Ripon was constructed with pointed arches and with the appropriate shafts and moldings but without high ribbed vaults, despite intentions otherwise, it, too, has appeared to lack something necessary—as have other possible candidates, such as Byland Abbey. The matter of what really constituted the Gothic style in the North has thus unwittingly been left undefined, despite its undisputed presence. One of the central purposes of this study is to sort out these problems and to demonstrate that Ripon was the first building in the North that was meant to be fully Gothic and, as the English saw it, actually fulfilled the indispensible criteria.

Despite its importance, the church of Ripon Minster has never been systematically studied and it has been inaccurately placed within the history of English medieval architecture. Well before 1850, it was classified on formal grounds as an example of early "Pointed" architecture by J. R. Walbran, who gave it for the first time a correct approximate date by identifying it with the documented patronage of Roger of Pont l'Evêque.[3] But after this good beginning the historical account of Ripon veered off on the wrong path. In 1874, reconstitutions of the twelfth-century plan (fig. 1) and elevations (choir and nave, figs. 2, 3), were published by Sir George Gilbert Scott,[4] who had restored the church in the 1860s. His work on the fabric of the church apparently imbued his reconstitutions with a special aura of authority—despite mistakes that could have been easily proven—for they were repeated uncritically until recent times. Cecil Hallett's archaeological description of the whole church in its present state, published in 1901,[5] provided a reliable guide to analytical observation but

---

definite stance has been adopted by others. Jean Bony (in "French Influences on the Origins of English Gothic Architecture," *Journal of the Warburg and Courtauld Institutes* 12 1949: 6) notes that ". . . the style of Roche resembles the Gothic architecture of northern France, especially Picardy," without stipulating whether or not it should be regarded as a Gothic building. Geoffrey Webb follows Bony's lead (*Architecture in Britain: The Middle Ages*, The Pelican History of Art, Harmondsworth, 1956, 82). Peter Kidson (in "Part One," *A History of English Architecture*, Harmondsworth, 1962, 62–64) spells out explicitly what this influence means: "When it comes to the point we call Roche Gothic only because, in a superficial way, it reminds us of real Gothic works." Yet these equivocations have not prompted a recognition of the superior claims of another church, be it either Ripon or Byland Abbey. Indeed, as we shall see in chap. 2, such a claim cannot be vaunted until Ripon's anteriority *vis-à-vis* Byland is established.

[3] John Richard Walbran, *A Guide to Ripon, Harrogate, Fountains Abbey, Bolton Priory, and Several Places of Interest in Their Vicinity*, 5th ed. (Ripon, 1851).

[4] George Gilbert Scott, "Ripon Minster," *Archaeological Journal* 31 (1874): 309–18.

[5] Cecil Hallett, *The Cathedral Church of Ripon, A Short History of the Church and a Description of Its Fabric* (Bell's Cathedral Series). (London. 1901).

# INTRODUCTION

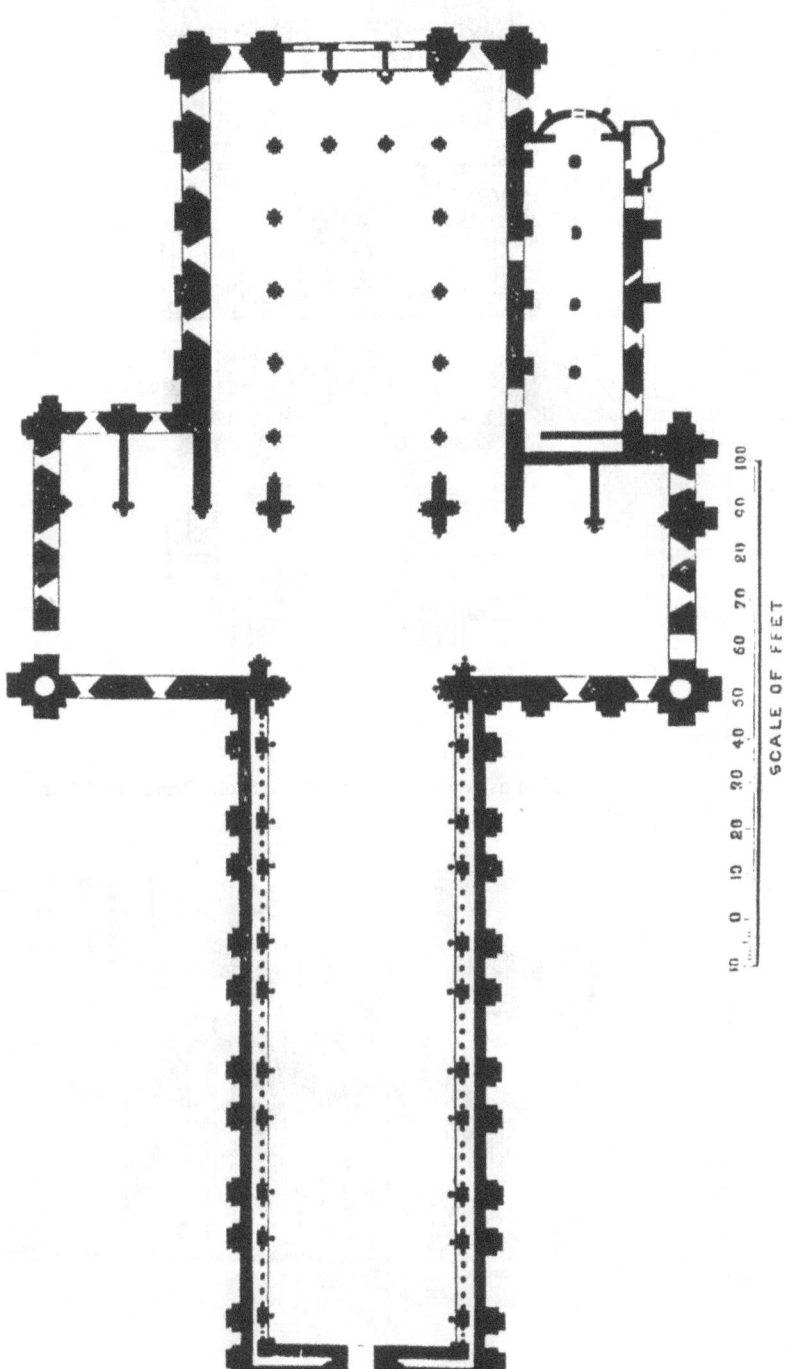

FIG. 1. Ripon Minster, plan of G. G. Scott's reconstitution of the original scheme. Reproduced from *Archaeological Journal*, 21, (1874).

FIG. 2. Ripon Minster, choir elevation as reconstituted by G. G. Scott, Reproduced from *Archaeological Journal*, 21, (1874).

FIG. 3. Ripon Minster, nave elevation as reconstituted by G. G. Scott, Reproduced from *Archaeological Journal*, 21 (1874).

his own conclusions were skewed by an uncritical acceptance of Scott's reconstitutions. These errors were compounded when, in the epilogue to his famous article of 1909 on English Cistercian architecture, John Bilson ascribed the introduction of the Gothic style in the North to the Cistercians and identified Ripon as the earliest non-Cistercian building in the region to reflect the new mode.[6] Since that time there has been no study devoted to the twelfth-century design of Ripon nor to its significance in the development of English medieval architecture. Its historical context—the importation of the Gothic style from France into England—was correctly defined by Jean Bony in 1949,[7] but without detailed discussion of Ripon or its role in this artistic phenomenon. My work, the first of which was published in 1972,[8] is intended to build on this new beginning with a systematic study of the twelfth-century church, first from an archaeological and then from a historical point of view.

For the archaeological study no new documents have come to light and no soundings beneath the fabric in recent decades have indicated the need for further excavation.[9] Evidence obtainable through careful observation and from numerous measurements has been sufficient to reconstitute almost all the twelfth-century church as it was actually constructed and to circumscribe the lacunae so closely as to let us predict the lost parts with a high degree of probability. Through this means it is possible to have a clearer idea of the place of Ripon in English medieval architecture. Beyond this stage, the inconsistencies in the twelfth-century fragments have been analyzed in order to identify the modifications made during construction, thereby to deduce the intended design. Indeed, it is possible to recover the intended design almost as completely as the scheme which was actually constructed. Since it was unrealized, the original design exerted no direct influence upon later buildings; but its composition is valuable to the historian because it reveals the builder's true aesthetic aims and permits us to trace more reliably the sources of his design.

---

[6] Bilson, "Cistercians," 277–80.
[7] Bony, "French Influences," 1–12.
[8] M. F. Hearn, "On the Original Nave of Ripon Cathedral," *Journal of the British Archaeological Association*, 3rd ser., 35 (1972): 39–45; and "Postscript," ibid., 3rd ser., 129 (1976): 93–94.
[9] C. R. Peers (in "Recent Discoveries in the Minsters of Ripon and York," *The Antiquaries Journal* 11, 1931, 114) reported that two large stone drums, crudely molded, were found (during excavations made while installing a heating system) in close proximity to very thick walls running east to west beneath the crossing. He surmised that they belonged to a structure built after Wilfrid's and before Roger's. It is difficult to imagine what kind of tenth or early eleventh-century building could have used column bases of such a scale. Moreover, one of the drums is cut from gritstone, the material of the twelfth-century church, and the other from limestone. Also, the stones are not well finished and show no signs of having been actually used in masonry construction. Almost certainly, then, they were not part of a previous church. The wall foundations on which they were found were surely intended to keep the present tower piers from shifting in their sandy bed.

More recently, R. A. Hall (in "Rescue Excavations in the Crypt of Ripon Cathedral," on *Yorkshire Archaeological Journal* 49, 1977: 59–62, with an appendix by L. A. S. Butler) reported additional excavations in the crossing and transepts during which no evidence of a church of intermediate date was found.

My historical analysis specifies the dates of the design, the purposes of the patron, the background of the builder, and Ripon's significance for the beginnings of the Gothic style in England. This sequence of investigation permits us to distinguish between those parts of the design which were prescribed by the patron and those contributed by the builder. As a rare instance, the patron's purposes and his contributions to the scheme can be detected: his career is well documented and it permits us to justify the choice of models and to explain the liturgical rationale of the highly peculiar plan. While tracing the sources for the various features of the Ripon design we can discern a coherent geographical and chronological pattern that reveals far more about the builder's prior architectural experiences than is normally known. Moreover, because the new church is discovered to have been not only contemporary with the Gothic choir of Canterbury Cathedral but also interrelated with Canterbury in the background of its patronage, it is possible to assess Ripon's version of the Gothic style in the light of the eyewitness description of Canterbury by the monk Gervase. This document, unique in its implications of the quirky English perception of the Gothic style, has previously defied analysis because there was no legitimately comparable building to provide a control for identifying the significant features and stylistic qualities. In view of all these special advantages it has been possible, despite the fragmentary state of the twelfth-century church, to learn more about Ripon Minster as a monument of human aspiration in the Middle Ages than about most other medieval churches.

The methods of this study have been determined by the character of the material at hand. Although current standards for rigorous, scientific investigations of individual buildings now virtually require detailed analyses of masonry courses and structural composition, the fragmentary and modified state of the fabric has made it more appropriate for me to address several different questions in studying the whole group of fragments surviving from the original church. Therefore, following the reconstitution, the investigation has been developed as a series of essays which treat at the same time specific aspects of the church and larger issues of interpretation. For example, the dates are discussed in the context of the relationship of Ripon's design to Cistercian architecture and the sources of the design in terms of the intentions of the patron and the professional background of the designer.

# PART ONE

# ARCHAEOLOGICAL INTERPRETATION

# 1. THE ACTUAL AND INTENDED FORMS

Ripon Cathedral today is a structural patchwork with portions dating from the twelfth to the sixteenth centuries, not counting the small crypt surviving from the seventh-century church and the many small alterations made from the sixteenth century to the present. Yet it retains, or clearly recalls, the basic outlines of its original twelfth-century form. It consists (fig. 4) of an aisled choir of six bays with rectangular chevet, transepts with a pair of eastern chapels in each arm but no western aisles, a crossing (slightly trapezoidal in plan) which culminates in a lantern tower, an aisled nave of six bays (formerly, an aisleless nave), and a west front with two towers flanking the nave. In the southeast quadrant, set into the corner between the south choir aisle and the south transept chapels, is an integral structure of three stories which serves various auxilliary functions but is generally known as the chapter house.

The portions remaining from the original church are as follows:

1. the choir—the three west bays of the north elevation, the three west bays and much of the fourth of both side aisles, including the vaults, and portions of the main arcade of the three east bays of both the north and south elevations (pls. 2-13);
2. the chapter house—the basic perimeter wall of the two lower stories and the vaulting of the ground story (pls. 14-18);
3. the transepts—all of the north transept (pls. 19-24) and its chapels with two minor sixteenth-century alterations and much of the south transept (pls. 25-29) except for the east elevation and the vaults of the eastern chapels;
4. the crossing—the northwest crossing pier (pl. 30) and the north and west sides of the lantern tower (pl. 31);
5. the nave—fragments of the north and south elevations at both the east and west ends (pls. 32-43);
6. the west front—all of the two towers, flanking the nave together with the west wall of the nave (pls. 44-52).

From the evidence available in these portions it is possible to discover how most of the church looked when it was completed early in the thirteenth century and even how it was intended to look when it was designed late in the twelfth century. There are, however, some areas where the original form is problematic, where opinion as to the original form differs, or where it is clear that a modification was introduced during the course of construction. These areas require detailed examination. They are: the plan and elevation of the east end, the intended form of the clerestory

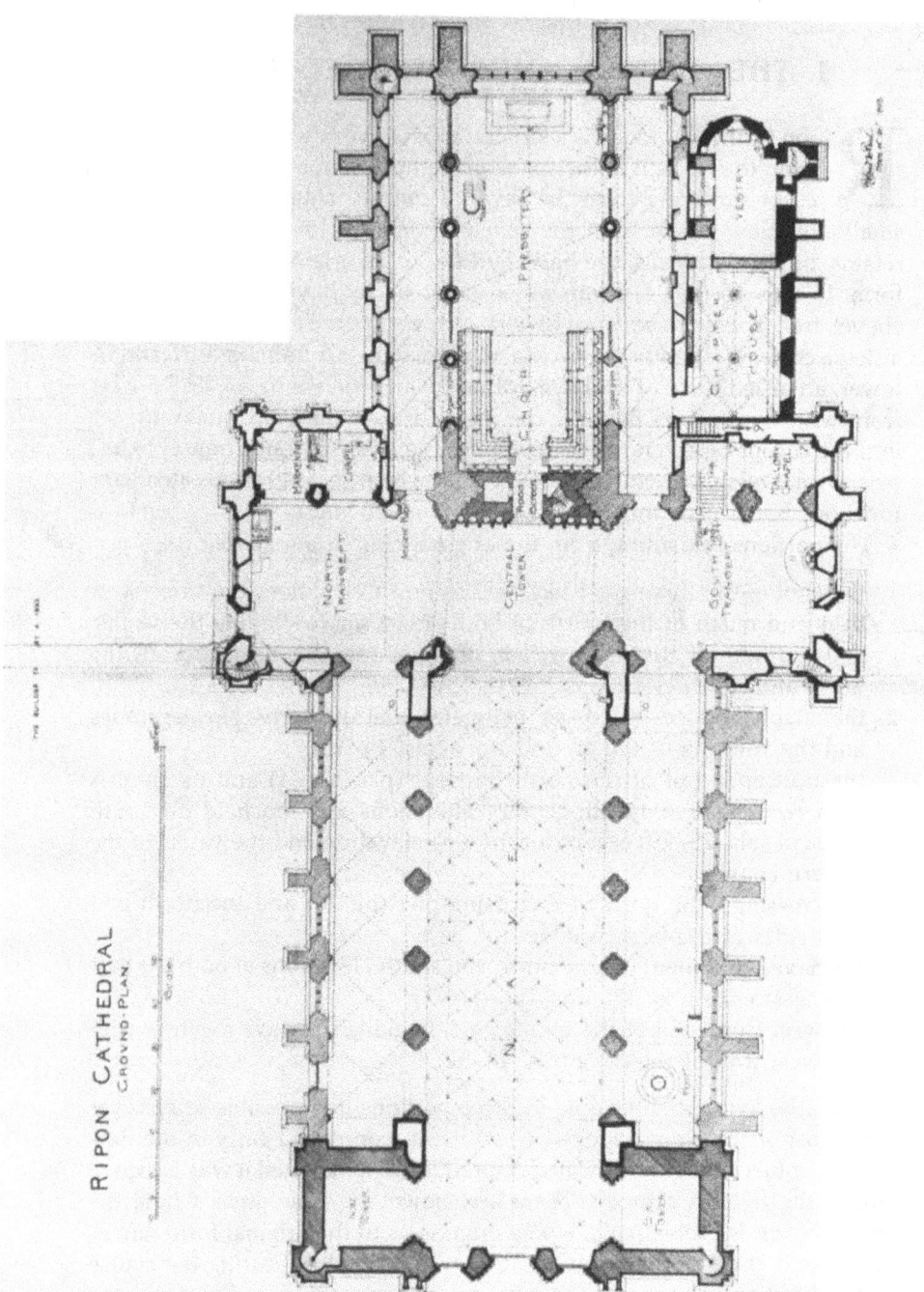

FIG. 4. Ripon Minster, plan. Reproduced from *The Builder*, February 1893.

and high vaults in the choir and transepts, the place of the chapter house in the cathedral's building history, the intended form of the transept terminal elevations, the actual and intended form of the nave elevation, and the intended form of the west front.

## A. The Choir Plan

The original east end of the choir was substantially remodeled toward the end of the thirteenth century[1] (pls. 1, 2). Despite documentary testimony that the chancel was ruinous, it is not fully clear on archaeological grounds whether this project was undertaken to repair structural damage, to provide a different space appropriate to some change in liturgical requirements, or simply to modernize the area around the high altar. In any event, this campaign produced most of what we see in the three east bays of the choir and aisles. Some remnants of the twelfth-century work remain in this eastern zone, though, and they provide the basis for reconstituting most of the lost portion of the original choir. Although the three west bays of the south elevation were rebuilt in the late fifteenth century, the corresponding portion of the north elevation represents the norm for the design of the twelfth-century lateral elevations (pl. 3).

The twelfth-century remnants in the east bays are identifiable by form, type of stone, structural context, or combinations of these factors. Most of these older structural elements are formally recognizable because those in the twelfth-century bays are themselves so rigorously standardized. In determining that a given element was not simply copied from the older work at some later period, it is helpful that the type of stone varies between the two campaigns: the twelfth-century church was built of gritty, yellowish sandstone while the later work was constructed of fine-grained light gray limestone. Unfortunately for identification of material in locations where natural light never illuminates the stones sufficiently, another type of evidence—the tooling pattern on the stones—has been obscured by roughening of the surfaces. Yet for structural elements without analogues in the twelfth-century bays, or for which the evidence is ambiguous, the context of the feature within the structure can usually provide the basis for a reliable attribution.

Cecil Hallett was the first to discern the virtually complete survival of the main arcade of both elevations in the three east bays, even including the soffits of most of the great arches.[2] However, intrusions of thirteenth-

---

[1] The York Registers of Archbishop John Romanus note in 1286 that the chancel was ruinous, in 1288 that funds were needed for repairs, and in 1297 that construction was underway; recorded in (*Memorials of Ripon*, ed., J. T. Fowler, 2: 14, 15, 23). The Publications of the Surtees Society, vol. 78 (London, 1884). The dates of these documentary notations agree with the style of the remodeled bays, especially the great traceried window in the east elevation.

[2] Hallet,*The Cathedral Church of Ripon, A Short History of the Church and a Description of Its Fabric*, Bell's Cathedral Series (London, 1901), 98–102, 113–17. The original twelfth-century elements which survive in the east bays of the main arcade are as follows:

century capitals, imposts, or arch soffits at various points among these remnants frustrate any straightforward explanation of the original east end. Although twelfth-century main-arcade soffits remain in the north elevation right up to the east wall, implying that the choir had the same composition as at present, the half-pier at the east wall and the first freestanding pier (pl. 6) both have thirteenth-century imposts, leaving open the possibility that the voussoirs of the first bay soffit were reused, perhaps even adapted from earlier use in another location. Should that have been the case, the eastern arm may well have had a rectangular ambulatory, one bay deep, to the east of a choir of five bays.[3] There are two other zones of evidence, however, only one of which has been adduced before, that make possible the resolution of the ambiguity.

The first of these, which Hallett has noted,[4] confirms that the eastern limit of the original ground plan was located where it is today. This evidence is located on the exterior wall of the east bay of the south aisle, at the point where the east end of the chapter house is joined to the aisle wall. There a portion of the twelfth-century plinth, its profile clearly outlined on the chapter house wall, stands above the thicker thirteenth-century plinth (pl. 8). Because the twelfth-century aisles projected into the

---

1) all the round molded plinths of the freestanding piers and also the equally tall cluster of polygonal plinths supporting each of the half-piers that abut the east wall (the type repeated in the north transept chapels, supporting the vault respond shafts);
2) all the attic-type bases of the freestanding pier shafts and also the flatter molded bases of the half-piers (despite the repetition of this type for the vault respond shafts in the remodeled east bays of the choir aisles);
3) all the shaft-bundle pier shafts, both freestanding and half-piers, the outer shafts of which have been partially obscured by the thirteenth-century resurfacing of the east wall (compare with the analogous situation at Byland Abbey, pl. 63, where the wall was never altered);
4) all the capitals of the freestanding piers of the north elevation and the capital of the second freestanding pier of the south elevation;
5) the imposts of all the capitals just cited except that of the first freestanding pier of the north elevation;
6) all the main arcade soffits of the north elevation and that of the third bay of the south elevation.

To summarize: In the north main arcade all elements are original through the half-pier against the wall except the capital and impost of the half-pier (easily replaced with the main arcade standing) and the impost of the first freestanding pier. Replacement of the latter was possible because all the wall above the ground story had been removed for the remodeling and much of the spandrel area of the main arcade was also likely removed. It was probably not too difficult an operation to prop up the arch soffits sufficiently to permit insertion of the single stone of the impost.

[3] A rectangular ambulatory plan was hypothesized by Sir George Gilbert Scott (in "Ripon Minster," *Archaeological Journal*, 31, 1874: 311) largely to correspond with the conjectural plan of the twelfth-century choir of York suggested by the Rev. Robert Willis, *The Architectural History of York Cathedral* (London, 1846), 11. Hallett (in *Ripon*, 63) repeats this formulation, which he (erroneously) says Scott accepted from Walbran, even though he cites considerable archeological evidence (see note 2 above) for the flat east end. John Richard Walbran (in *A Guide to Ripon, etc.*, 5th ed., 1851: 44) justified his assumption of a rectangular ambulatory upon the general similarity of Ripon and Byland.

[4] Hallet, *Ripon*, 102.

present easternmost bay, the plan of the original eastern arm of the church was indisputably as long at least as the renewed one.

The other zone of evidence is on the interior of the east wall, above the great traceried window, where a round-headed arch spans the entire width of the choir. Because the crown of this arch is broken by the apex of the east window (pl. 2) it is clear that the arch ceased to serve its intended function when the thirteenth-century remodeling was executed. Undoubtedly, then, it is earlier than the window. Close examination from the clerestory permits several significant observations (pl. 9): the face of the arch has been chipped off to make it flush with the wall surface, so it was originally a more conspicuous feature than at present; the wall surface beneath the arch protrudes about an inch beyond the surface of the arch and the wall above it, the stones beneath the arch have been cut to fit its curvature, and the surface of this lower zone of masonry undulates in an abnormal fashion. These observations permit us to conclude that the masonry beneath the arch is later than both the arch and the wall zone above it and was inserted to create a new wall mass around the traceried window. This arch and the east wall will be discussed more fully later; but suffice it at this point to acknowledge the arch as evidence that the church had a high flat east end before the choir was remodeled.

As we have seen, the twelfth-century fragments remaining in the east bays of the choir indicate that the original choir had the same composition as at present—six aisled bays with a high flat east end. The only functional features that may have been new in the remodeled version were the stair vices located in the aisle buttresses at the east end; but there is no sign of chapels at an upper level to which these might have led. Clearly, the thirteenth-century remodeling was not inspired by the need for a different liturgical arrangement. The surviving twelfth-century elements in the east bays indicate that more of the south choir elevation was replaced than of north, but more of the north aisle than of the south, and that the high east wall was only remodeled. Consequently, there is no pattern in the reconstruction that suggests the repair of major damage caused by some specific disaster. One must conclude, finally, that the principal purpose of the rebuilding was to modernize the area around the high altar, especially to introduce the great traceried window into the east wall and perhaps also to make the decor of the adjacent bays more congenial to this feature. Unless there were numerous cracks in the masonry, randomly distributed in the portions replaced, the documentary notice of a ruinous state may have been more an excuse or justification for rebuilding than a factual explanation.

*The East Wall*

The only feature of the original high east wall that remains in view is the slightly-stilted round arch which spans the whole width of the choir above the great traceried window (pl. 2). Given this paucity of evidence, an attempt to reconstitute the original wall design would seem to be nothing more than a speculative exercise. Yet there are certain parameters, inherent in the overall scheme of the church as it survives in the twelfth-century fragments, which make possible a fairly reliable general description of the basic elements of such an elevation. To be sure, such a reconstitution must depend substantially upon the interpretation of the arch in the east wall.

The arch has long been noted but no special significance was attached to it because it was always assumed to have belonged to a vaulting system, hence not to the original unvaulted choir but to one of the several vaulting systems which are presumed to have preceded the present one.[5] That it could have been the transverse wall arch of the high vault is a physical possibility because the apex of the arch is the same height as the lateral choir walls. Although round transverse arches would have been incongruous in a structure where all the arches in the aisle vaults are pointed, such an incongruity existed already between the round arches of the crossing (pl. 30) and the pointed arches of the main arcade (pl. 3), not to mention the mixture of both types in the choir elevations. Indeed, it would be difficult to employ any other kind of transverse arch in vaults over bays which are more than twice as wide as they are long and still keep the keystones of all the arches at the same height. A pointed arch that low would not be structurally feasible.

Yet it is precisely when such a high vault is constructed in the imagination that its existence becomes doubtful. For one thing, it is unlikely that high vaults over the Ripon choir would have been planned with all keystones at the same level. In a contemporaneous and parallel situation, the transepts of Laon Cathedral, the keystones of the very oblong quadripartite vaults are much higher in the center than along the lateral walls. Even the aisle vaults at Ripon (pl. 12) are slightly lower along the outer walls. A transverse wall arch on the east elevation that would have been consistent with the other vaults at Ripon and in parallel situations elsewhere, would have had a much higher apex than that of the arch in question. Had there been an earlier vault at this level it would have left its mark in the clerestory of the lateral elevation and it could even be roughly dated by observing which of the variously dated bays bore its mark, but there is no such evidence. Since this arch is broken at its apex by the frame of the great traceried window it would have had to pertain to a twelfth-century vault and, as will be discussed later, no vault was erected over the original choir.

More telling than any of the foregoing impediments is the fact that the imposts (or corbels?) from which this arch springs are set too far out from the lateral elevations to have functioned with the wall arch of a vault. In this connection it is important to recall that in the thirteenth-century remodeling the lateral walls were centered forward of the vertical axis of the piers so that they displaced the clusters of five shafts at the bay di-

---

[5] Ibid., 103.

FIG. 5. Ripon Minster, choir, reconstitution of original juncture of north and east elevations.

visions (pls. 4, 10). In the original disposition three shafts would have risen from the half-piers at the east wall (fig. 5), the outermost of which would have been intended to receive the terminal wall arch of the high vault. Yet the imposts or corbels from which the actual arch springs are set still one plane farther forward. Physically disqualified for a place in a vaulting system, the arch can only have been constructed as a relieving arch,[6] related to the composition of the wall itself. This interpretation of its function also accords with the building history. Since the upper portion of the east wall was probably completed after the decision was made not to raise high vaults, an intended relieving arch related to the elevation design would still have been built, but not a wall arch for vaults. There is every reason to assume, then, that the surviving feature in the east wall was built as a relieving arch and that such an arch was included as a necessary feature of the original composition of the east wall.

The hypothetical reconstitution of the east wall design must proceed from this point on an analysis of the circumstances posited by the rest of the church and parallel circumstances in other churches. For the ground story, corresponding to the main arcade, this task is not difficult. The three tall round-headed windows in the ground story of each of the transept terminal elevations (pls. 20, 27) suggest the most apt analogue for the east wall, especially since the widths of the choir and of the transept arms are nearly the same. Indeed, no other arrangement would even be plausible, for every subsequent example of the same type of east elevation, prior to the introduction of bar tracery in the mid-thirteenth century, has its equivalent.[7] For the upper zone, corresponding to the triforium and clerestory of the lateral elevations, the transept terminal elevations are less useful as models. Although structurally the east wall could have included a band triforium with wall passage and a clerestory like those of the transepts, such a composition would have lacked the visual unity appropriate to the focal elevation of the sanctuary. Moreover, the introduction of a band triforium here would have had no precedent in tradition to give it meaning.[8] Whatever this zone contained was undoubtedly compatible with the

---

[6] I am indebted to Arnold Klukas for the observation that this arch is analogous to the relieving arch of the east elevation at Laon Cathedral and therefore probably served the same function at Ripon.

[7] Parallel examples are Hexham Priory, Whitby, and Rievaulx Abbeys, and Ely Cathedral, all built between 1200 and 1240.

[8] The band triforium in English architecture first appeared in aisleless transepts of the early twelfth century (Hereford Cathedral, Pershore Abbey) where it provided access from stair vices in the outer western corners of the transepts to the upper chapels on the eastern side of the transepts. As the middle story of a choir elevation it made a precocious appearance on both the lateral and eastern elevations of the church of St. Cross Hospital, Winchester (ca. 1160), where the aisled choir with a high, flat east end is parallel in form to that of Ripon. When the two types were combined in the Salisbury Cathedral choir, soon after 1220, it was in a situation in which the band triforium masked a wall zone backed by the sloping roof of a rectangular ambulatory. Similarly, in the earlier retrochoir (ca. 1187) of Chichester Cathedral, the triforium passage in the east wall (which was articulated in the manner of the lateral elevation gallery) was backed by the gabled roof of the axial chapel. Yet in none of the churches with a high, flat east end, such as Beverley Minster and the new choir of

compositional limits imposed by the relieving arch and by the configuration of the high vaults above it which had been intended when the elevation was designed. In all likelihood, the highly unusual presence of the relieving arch indicates the structural provision for a large-scale feature, occupying both stories, which was not possible in an ordinary elevation.

Within the context of English church architecture from the mid-twelfth to the mid-thirteenth century, especially in the North, the usual feature for such an upper zone would be a second range of three tall windows, staggered in height to follow the roof or (rarely) the vault line.[9] Such windows might well be set in a double-shell wall with a passage at triforium level, the interior arcade ornamented on the choir side with colonnettes and arch moldings. Yet no matter how typical or plausible this composition would be it offers no justification for the relieving arch. Albeit relieving arches are not entirely unknown above groups of lancet windows,[10] they are neither normal nor necessary. The most likely alternative to lancet windows and one which would amply justify the relieving arch is a large round window, or oculus (fig. 6). Less familiar in the North than the east end with double rows of lancet windows, the east end composition of three lancets and a large oculus, surprisingly, is historically just as plausible.[11]

Since the middle decades of the twelfth-century, round windows had begun to play a significant role in both French and English architecture. Oculi of conspicuous dimensions appeared between 1135 and 1160 in west fronts (Saint-Denis), transepts (Saint-Etienne of Beauvais), east fronts (Barfreston, Kent), and even clerestories (Southwell). More relevant to the point in question was the use of oculi in compositions with two or more arch-headed vertical windows, as in the transept east chapels of Fountains Abbey (1140s) (pl. 53), or in the much later bishop's chapel (ca. 1180) adjacent to Noyon Cathedral. From the last quarter of the twelfth-century and well into the thirteenth, such compositions were sometimes magnified

---

Ely Cathedral (both 1230s) nor in those with a high east end projecting beyond the aisles, such as the new choirs of Worcester Cathedral and Southwell Minster, both also built in the second quarter of the thirteenth century, was there a triforium in the east elevation. From this pattern of inclusion and exclusion it is reasonable to infer that the band triforium was regarded as a specialized functional feature, associated primarily with transepts and only secondarily with choirs (where a complex eastern structure justified its adoption).

[9] Surviving examples from the period after Ripon are Hexham Priory and Whitby and Rievaulx Abbeys, all built between 1200 and 1230. Also from the beginning of this period is Tynemouth Priory, in which the choir aisles did not continue all the way to the east elevation.

[10] Examples are the west ends of Fountains and Kirkstall Abbeys, both built in the third quarter of the twelfth century, and the Archbishop's Chapel, now the Minster Library, at York (ca. 1200).

[11] At Beverley Minster (ca. 1230), there is a relieving arch above the inserted, traceried window in the east elevation. Since all four of the transept terminal elevations have two ranges of lancet windows but no relieving arches, it is plausible that the original east elevation of the choir had a composition of lancets and a large oculus similar to that envisioned here for Ripon (an observation I owe to Eric Cambridge).

FIG. 6. Ripon Minster, choir interior reconstitution according to the intended scheme.

to dominate terminal elevations, especially in Cistercian churches where a flat east or west end was preferred to elaborately articulated terminations. Particularly puissant examples of such east ends, all designed between 1150 and 1175, are in the Cistercian churches at Preuilly (pl. 54), Noirlac, and Silvacane, each of which employs an oculus (plain or lobed) above three lancet windows.[12] But more important for Ripon was the east end of Cistercian Kirkstall Abbey Church, designed 1152, where evidence remains beyond the frame of the ruined traceried window to indicate a similar composition of three tall round-headed windows surmounted by a large oculus.[13] Located in southern Yorkshire, Kirkstall was sufficiently proximate to Ripon in both situation and date to have provided the actual prototype. It is more likely, but unprovable, that this composition passed to Ripon from Kirkstall through an intermediary at Roche Abbey.[14]

However appropriate this composition of apparent Cistercian origin may have been regarded for the east wall at Ripon, there were significant differences from the Cistercian architectural tradition in Ripon's composition which necessarily would have affected the adaptation of this design for the Minster. Unlike Cistercian churches, Ripon was planned with an aisled choir so that two complex, three-storied lateral elevations were terminated and conjoined by the east wall. Since these elevations included passages in both of the upper stories, it was necessary to connect them by one or more passages in the east wall. For this reason, the east wall at Ripon was almost certainly of double-shell construction at some point above the ground story. In such a situation the oculus would be set in the outer shell and the inner shell must be virtually voided in order not to obscure the oculus with some sort of inner arcade. Hence, the inner shell would require a substantial relieving arch, as that at Ripon appears to have been (figs. 5, 6).

The only surviving east end that appears to be a true analogue of the structural situation at Ripon is the later choir of Laon Cathedral, itself a remodeling, done after 1200 (pl. 55). At Laon, there are three tall lancet

---

[12] Frederic van der Meer, *Atlas de l'ordre cistercien* (Paris and Brussels, 1965), illus. 10, 139, 201, and notes on 292, 290, and 297, respectively. John Bilson (in "The Architecture of the Cistercians, with Special Reference to Some of Their Earlier Churches in England," *Archaeological Journal*, 66 (1909): 229–230) identified these examples.

[13] William Henry St. John Hope, "Kirkstall Abbey," *The Publications of the Thoresby Society*, 16 (1907): 26, fig. 18, accepted by Bilson ("Cistercians," 229–30).

[14] This hypothesis that Roche had an east end with three lancets and a large oculus is based in part on the fact that the intermediate story of windows in the eastern portion of the lateral choir walls have no wall passage like that in their counterparts in the transept terminal walls. Since no access from north to south was provided in the upper zones of the east elevation there was little or no reason to build a repetitious triple range of windows. Moreover, with a vaulted choir the effectiveness of the oculus at Kirkstall could be repeated. Another basis for this hypothesis is the observation by Peter Fergusson that Roche is closely based on Preuilly (1160s) "Roche Abbey: The Source and Date of the Eastern Remains," *Journal of the British Archeological Association*, 3rd ser., 34 (1971): 36. As we have already seen (note 12), Preuilly is one of the prime precedents for an east elevation with three lancets and an oculus. Roche, then, had available both a continental and an English model for such an elevation.

windows surmounted by a huge oculus set in the outer shell of a double-shell wall. The inner shell is voided and replaced by a large round relieving arch, supported by shafts set one plane further in than the vault shafts. (There is a separate transverse wall arch but its absence would not alter the character of the relieving arch). A passage beneath the oculus and above the lancets connects the two lateral elevations. The value of the example at Laon, however, is limited to tentative confirmation of the interpretation of evidence at Ripon.

The plausibility of this proposed east wall composition increases considerably when we recall that the east wall was designed for high vaults, under which an oculus would show to advantage. The double rows of lancet windows that became standard for later flat east ends in the North of England were more appropriate for the unvaulted schemes that predominated until the second quarter of the thirteenth century. Short of stripping the surface masonry from both faces of the east wall, there is no way to obtain additional evidence for a reconstitution of the east elevation. We cannot be completely certain, then, that the elevation was composed of three tall round-headed windows and a large oculus, but given the available evidence no other arrangement is equally plausible.

An attempt to deduce the decorative treatment of such a composition, of course, merely piles conjecture on conjecture. Yet the character and type of the decorative details can be circumscribed as closely as for the elevation design, assuming that the general reconstitution is correct. In the lower story the three tall windows would doubtless have been unmolded, like those of the transept terminal elevations (pls. 20, 27), contrasting the simplicity of the enclosing wall with the elaboration of the subdividing main arcades. On the other hand, for an oculus in the upper story there are three plausible options, each with historical precedents that are proximate to Ripon. The great circular opening could have been braced with a wheel armature, as at Saint-Etienne of Beauvais or Barfreston, although this type was not used in later English oculi and appeared on a grand scale in France only decades after Ripon was designed. Accordingly, it seems inconsistent with English Gothic architecture and thus inappropriate for the reconstitution. Alternatively, a virtually unobstructed glazing could have been supported by a geometric or rectangular iron frame, as in the Canterbury transepts (pl. 57) and the Byland west front. While plans for the Canterbury oculi might possibly have been known when Ripon was being designed and while the Byland scheme was directly related to that at Ripon, this treatment of a very large oculus would contrast too strongly with the lateral elevations. Such an extreme differentiation would be inappropriate in the reconstitution in view of the fact that the upper stories of the transept terminal elevations were elaborately articulated in a manner similar to that of the lateral elevations. The third option is a plate tracery composition of circles, like those used in the choir of Preuilly (pl. 54), the Laon transepts and the west front of Vaux-de-Cernay. Although these French examples are geographically the most remote from Ripon, Laon was—as we shall see in chapter 4—directly and closely related to Ripon's design. Moreover, this decorative treatment of an oculus would have, among the three, the virtue of mediating most happily between the terminal and lateral elevations. Indeed, just such a treatment was adopted a few decades later in a similar situation in the Lincoln Cathedral transepts. In the final analysis, then, the likeliest scheme for Ripon's east elevation would include unmolded tall windows in the lower story and a plate-traceried oculus in the upper.

*The Clerestory and the High Vault*

The three west bays of the north choir elevation (pl. 3) preserve intact the choir wall as it was actually constructed, even though some details must be sought behind the severies of the present wooden ribbed vaults.[15] There is clear evidence that the original elevation design was revised when the clerestory was begun, as Hallett was the first to describe in detail and attempt to explain.[16]

The revision is manifest most distinctly in the shafts that articulate the bay divisions (pl. 3, fig. 2). Rising from the imposts of the main arcade piers there are five attached shafts, formed of regular ashlar courses engaged with the wall, terminating with their own capitals and imposts at the base of the clerestory. Both in number and in form these shafts indicate their intended purpose as responds for the transverse, diagonal, and wall arches of quadripartite high ribbed vaults. Above this level, however, the diameter of the shafts set upon them is reduced markedly and, what is more important, the shafts are detached and cut *en délit*.[17] The upper shafts differ from the lower, then, in form, size, and technique. Moreover, these upper shafts serve no purpose other than wall articulation, for which they are too numerous. The modification in the shafts can only represent a decision not to build high vaults and a revision of the elevation design (fig. 7), aimed at resolving the resultant awkwardness as deftly as possible.

In consequence of the decision against building vaults, the triple arcade of the clerestory bays (pl. 3), meant to be ornamented with single shafts and arch moldings like the triforium, received an additional order of shafts and moldings. This additional order was projected forward of the wall plane in order that the shafts could be received by the outer pair of respond shafts below, that is, those intended as wall arch responds. Accordingly,

---

[15] Scott was the first to publish the data for the form of the choir and transept clerestory as it was actually constructed ("Ripon Minster," 312–13).

[16] For the transepts, Hallett, *Ripon Cathedral*, 88–89, for the choir: ibid., 98.

[17] For readers unfamiliar with this term, a shaft cut *en délit* is one cut horizontally in the quarry so that, installed, the grain of the stone runs vertically rather than horizontally as it does in normal ashlar blocks. This technique affects the surface appearance of the stone, making it smoother, and also its structural effectiveness, making it capable of supporting heavier loads than would be feasible with stone cut and laid with a horizontal grain. This technique has been defined and described by Jean Bony in "Origines des piles gothiques anglaises à fûts en délit," *Gedenkschrift Ernst Gall* (Munich and Berlin, 1965): 95, and n.l.

FIG. 7. Ripon Minster, choir elevation reconstitution (based, with emendations, on that of G. G. Scott) showing intended scheme.

the wall surface above this additional order was itself projected forward of the wall plane below. A blind arch constructed in this same plane was devised to fill the interval remaining between the clerestory bays, an interval intended to have been covered by the vaults. In this arrangement, the shafts were set on the responds designed for the diagonal arches. It was necessary, however, to continue the vertical articulation of the bays up to the flat wooden roof, so a single shaft was set on the transverse arch respond and hence projected to a plane forward of the blind arch behind it. Because the shafts of the clerestory arcade were flush with the wall plane and the other shafts were projected, as we have seen, in two planes, the group of shafts at each bay division had a convexity congenial to that of the cluster of shaft responds below it. It is unlikely that such a composition would have been devised for an unvaulted elevation.

Although no portion of the clerestory was constructed before the design was revised, in all other respects the clerestory was probably built as originally intended (fig. 7). First, the tripartite arcade, composed of a wide round-headed arch flanked by two lower and narrower pointed arches, not only expressly reflects the triforium design but also represents the norm for the articulation of a clerestory with wall passage in late twelfth-century England.[18] Second, the technique of constructing the wall passage (pls. 3, 22) albeit new to England in Ripon,[19] is in no way incongruous with the earlier work and there is no evidence to indicate that the technique might have been modified for the revised scheme. Finally, there is good reason to suppose that the height of the clerestory was intended to be the same as at present. To explain that point requires a short digression concerning the measurements and proportions of the stories in the choir elevation.

The whole elevation (fig. 2), measured from the floor to the top of the wall arches of the present high vault, the same point where the flat wooden ceiling was set, is about 64 feet. The main arcade, measured from the floor to the top of the triforium string-course, is about 32 feet, half of the total height. The main arcade piers, from the shaft bases to the top of the imposts, are 17 feet high, while the main arcade arches, from springing to apex, are 11 feet high. The triforium, significantly, is 11 feet high, measured from the top of its lower string course to the top of the clerestory string course, while the clerestory arcade is 17 feet high. (An additional 4 feet, compensatory for the main arcade plinth and the wall above the arches, extends above the clerestory arcade). The correspondence between

---

[18] This tri-partite arcade was usual for clerestory passages in vaulted structures, e.g., the normal bays in the eastern arm of Canterbury Cathedral, in the remodeling of Chichester Cathedral and in the new Lincoln Cathedral, all designed between 1174 and 1192. It was also standard in unvaulted structures with vertical bay articulation, such as Byland Abbey and Hexham Priory (1177 and shortly after 1200). The principal exception was Wells Cathedral (ca. 1185) with its single arch opening in each bay.

[19] See the discussion of the various configurations employed in wall passages in twelfth-century English architecture, below in chapter 3.

the heights of the main arcade arches and the triforium on the one hand and of the main arcade piers and the clerestory arcade on the other can scarcely be fortuitous in an elevation divided in half by the total heights of the main arcade and of the combined two upper stories respectively.

From this proportional harmony it is reasonable to conclude that the intended height of the clerestory, like the articulation of the arcade and the technique of the wall passage, discussed above, was not altered by the decision not to construct high vaults. Except for the arrangement of shafts and the additional layer of wall and its accompanying order of ornamentation on the arcade, the actual clerestory probably represents the design intended (fig. 7) to complete that seen on the lower stories. All that remains to be envisioned is the system of high vaults.

The intended composition of the high vaults (fig. 6), as we have seen in the clusters of five shaft responds at the bay divisions, was a regular succession of quadripartite ribbed vaults with wall arches in addition to transverse arches and diagonal ribs. The wall arches would have sprung from a point well above that for the other arches, as was the usual procedure in high vaults elsewhere, and most probably from the impost level of the clerestory arcade. In all likelihood the transverse arches and diagonal ribs would also have been pointed arches. Also, the respective profiles of the three categories of arches would probably have repeated those in the aisle vaults.[20] While it is possible that the vaults, like those at Canterbury, could have been supported by flying buttresses there is no evidence in the pilaster buttresses of the aisle wall and main wall that flyers were anticipated in the earliest work.[21] Since flying buttresses were seldom used in churches with a double-shell clerestory, probably they were not intended in the design of Ripon. Indeed, the use of engaged rather than detached shafts at the bay divisions may have been calculated to add strength to the wall on the interior, equivalent to the pilaster buttresses on the exterior, thus making flying buttresses unnecessary.

In summary, it is possible to determine that the choir (pl. 2, figs. 4, 6, 8) retains its original composition of six bays with a high flat east end. Twelfth-century remnants located in the east bay of the south aisle, in the three eastern bays of the main arcade, and in the east elevation above the great traceried window confirm its length, interior spatial disposition,

---

[20] The profiles of the aisle vault arches are as follows: a) diagonal ribs—three tori, the center one slightly thicker and keeled, on a square dosseret; b) transverse arches—a keeled torus flanked by hollow chamfers on a thick square dosseret; c) wall arches—a slender torus flanked by a hollow chamfer on the wall edge and set on the diagonal of a square dosseret.

[21] The pilaster buttresses of the aisles are too thin to support flyers and their containment within the outline of the supporting plinth implies that they were meant to be minimal. In the triforium story, the buttresses show no sign of quadrant arches or other supporting members perpendicular to the wall beneath the aisle roof. Such devices were the prototype of flying buttresses and in the earliest developed examples, as at Canterbury, they were used in conjunction with exposed flyers. The lack of any evidence of an additional support device at Ripon in the portions that were probably built before the scheme for high vaults was cancelled is a reliable indicator that no flying buttresses were ever intended.

FIG. 8. Ripon Minster, choir interior reconstitution according to the revised scheme actually constructed.

and its height. Interpretation of the relieving arch in the east wall and of comparative evidence in the transepts leads to the hypothetical reconstitution of the east elevation with a lower story of three tall round-headed lancet windows and an upper story with a giant oculus window. Evidence in the three western bays of the choir elevation indicates that quadripartite high vaults were intended but not built and that the clerestory was constructed basically according to the original design. The intention for the elevation was virtually the form we see today.

## B. The Chapter House

The chapter house of Ripon Minster is an adjunct of the church itself, located in the southeast angle between the choir and transept (pl. 14, fig. 4). Presently composed of three stories, it has been much altered and enlarged during the course of its existence; even so, it certainly never conformed to the architectural types associated with chapter houses. That this structure served in part, or chiefly, as a chapter house can only be inferred from indirect evidence. There are no remains of another structure that could be identified as a chapter house, particularly not of the characteristically English polygonal type built at the other three Yorkshire minsters in the late thirteenth and the early fourteenth centuries.[22] Moreover, when John Leland described the Minster on the occasion of his visit in 1538, he listed the structures near the church, mentioning the houses of the prebends, the archbishop's palace and the quadrangle of vicars' houses but no separate chapter house.[23]

Probably the most important single piece of evidence is documentary, a notice in a Duchy of Lancaster roll, recording a trial which took place before the king's judges in the chapter room (*aula capituli*) of Ripon, in 1228.[24] At the least, this document affirms the existence of such a facility of Ripon soon after the original church was probably completed; at most, it refers to a portion of the structure in question. Much later, in 1535, a document of the prebendaries of Stanwick (the chief appointment in the Ripon Chapter) mentions that the chapter house is in a "very ruinous state."[25] It is difficult to measure the intensity of this assessment or even to be certain that the account refers to the same structure as that cited in 1228. However, assuming that it does, which seems reasonable, the dilapidations cited were probably subsidence cracks in the lower walls that made necessary the heavy buttresses which reinforce the adjacent portions of the south flank. Considered together, these bits of evidence concerning the identity of the adjacent structure of Ripon Minster provide sufficient

---

[22] Between 1280 and 1310, polygonal chapter houses were designed, in chronological order, for the minsters of York, Southwell, and Beverley (destroyed 1550).
[23] "Leland's Description of Ripon," *Memorials of Ripon*, ed. J. T. Fowler, 1: 85, The Publications of the Surtees Society, vol. 74 (London, 1881).
[24] "Duchy of Lancaster Records, Roll A, 23, *"Memorials of Ripon*, 1: 51.
[25] *Fasti Riponienses*, compiled by John Ward, *Memorials of Ripon*, 2: 251, The Publications of the Surtees Society, vol. 78 (London, 1884).

grounds to regard it as having been built for a chapter house and related auxiliary facilities such as a vestry and a treasury. To be sure, the chapter house does not contribute much to the architectural significance of the church, but the chronology of its construction is important because the older portion has long been regarded as a fragment of an earlier church on the same site which in turn presumedly determined the placement of the new Minster.

Whether the chapter house was old or new, the topography of the site was admirably suited to juxtaposing it to the new church without marring the formal regularity or the functional utility of the church. From the west front to the crossing the site is virtually level. Then it drops away toward the east but much more on the south side than on the north. The ground story of the chapter house, accordingly, serves as the undercroft for a middle story at the same level as the choir aisle. These two stories comprise the original structure and the third, serving as a library since the Reformation, was added much later to provide a Lady Chapel. Only then was the exterior light blocked from the south choir aisle and transept chapel windows.

In its lower stories, the chapter house is much simpler in detail than the church, leading nineteenth-century archaeologues to attribute it to the Romanesque, or "Norman," period. Walbran placed it in the late eleventh century;[26] Scott, in the early twelfth.[27] Because the middle story consisted of a sequence of straight bays with an apse at the east end, and because the wall adjacent to the choir aisle clearly was that of the new church, Walbran interpreted the "chapter house" to be a surviving south aisle from a former church of the Norman three-apse type. The undercroft was accepted as a foundation necessary to support the aisle at the level of the putative church, hence not part of a larger crypt. Hallett noted that the location of this structure was too far to the south of the axis of the church to have been an aisle but he nevertheless regarded it as a subsidiary component of an earlier church complex.[28]

That the internal width of more than twenty feet in the chapter house would constitute an aisle implausibly broad in Norman architecture was not noted. Neither was there any great concern over the lack of any other evidence, archaeological or documentary, to prove the existence of a Romanesque church at Ripon. Twentieth-century scholars, however, were prepared to examine the stonework more critically and soon discovered that the archaeological evidence pointed to a date coeval with the church. The case for this conclusion has been constructed at least three times, each independent of the others, but in the two earlier instances it was never published.[29] Consequently, the tradition that the chapter house is part of

---

[26] Walbran, *Ripon*, 47.
[27] Scott, "Ripon Minster," 310.
[28] Hallett, *Ripon Cathedral*, 121–23.
[29] John Bilson presented his case to a meeting of the Royal Archaeological Society in Ripon in 1922, but only his conclusion was reported (*Archaeological Journal*, 29, 1922, 363). In 1966,

an earlier structure has persisted in all but the most specialized circles.[30] The observations gathered in the third investigation—my own—are set forth here to lay the matter to rest but with full acknowledgment that others before me have observed the same evidence and reached the same conclusions.

The exterior wall provides most of the relevant data (pl. 14). Although two thick pilaster buttresses have been added to the south flank and another to the polygonal stair-tower at the southeast corner, most of the masonry of the wall is obviously original and continuous. The ashlar courses are even and the decorative details—including the simple chamfered plinth, the molded string-course, and the corbel table at the former roof line—are uninterrupted. At the east end, where the apse meets the wall of the choir aisle wall, the masonry courses are not continuous and are not even bonded to the aisle wall (pl. 8). On the other hand, at the west end, where the chapter house wall meets the east wall of the south transept chapel, the masonry courses are continuous and bonded (pl. 16). Moreover, the simple plinth continues from the chapter house along the base of the south transept. This two-story structural adjunct, then, was begun after the choir aisle wall was underway but before work started on the south transept wall. From every available point of observation, the stair (connecting the undercroft and the chapter house) which is built in the thickness of this wall appears to be original and was intended to be built there when the wall was laid out. Even the choir aisle was not in a very advanced state of construction when the chapter house was conceived because two doors with simply molded round arches were provided from the third and fifth bays of the aisle. Confirmation of the contemporaneity of the chapter house with the church is provided by several details. Both the string course and the corbel table on the exterior, noted above, are remarkably similar to corresponding details on the surviving twelfth-century portions of the church proper (pl. 19). On the interior, in the undercroft, the impost used on the low square piers is molded with exactly the same profile as that used on the imposts of the choir main arcade (pl. 17 cf pl. 7).

Since this structure was part of the twelfth-century minster it is appro-

---

John S. Miller, an architect in Harrogate, wrote a paper setting forth evidence to support this same position. Dr. Eric A. Gee of the Minstry of Works wrote a commentary on this paper, confirming the conclusion and making additional observations, but neither was published. While completing my own investigation in 1977, assisted by my (then) doctoral student, Arnold Klukas, I reported my findings to the Rev. James Ashworth, then Residentiary Canon of the cathedral. He informed me of the earlier Miller-Gee study and, with their permission, showed me copies of the papers. Subsequently, Mr. Miller and I reviewed the evidence together on the site.

[30] The most widely disseminated publication on Ripon, Canon W. E. Wilkinson, *The Pictorial History of Ripon Cathedral*, The Pitkin "Pride of Britain" Books (London, 1969), 4, is based primarily on Hallett, *Ripon Cathedral*. While Nikolaus Pevsner (in *Yorkshire: The West Riding*, The Buildings of England (Harmondsworth, 1959), 407) cites Bilson's opinion that the chapter house is not earlier than the church, he only implies that he may prefer that assessment and does not explain why.

priate to describe its original state. The undercroft was divided by a stone wall into two chambers, each two bays wide. The western chamber is three bays long; the eastern has two and one-half straight bays and the apse. The plain chamfered ribs in the present vaults have significant amounts of masonry above the extrados to bind them to the rubble groins (pl. 17). Upon inspection it is obvious that the ribs are a later addition, having been neatly fitted to the pier imposts by cutting away the groined rubble at the corners of each bay. The original vaults, then, were simple rubble groined vaults. Examination of the outer wall confirms that there was initially no door to the outside; the only entries were from the upper story through the stairs in the south transept wall and in the turret by the apse (see plan 1). The undercroft was lighted by one deeply-chamfered, narrow window in each of the five full bays and one more window on axis in the apse. The extreme simplicity of the decor and the highly restricted accessibility of this lower story suggest that it served no public purpose.

The upper story, the chapter house proper, has been modified much more than the undercroft and thus requires more detailed scrutiny in order to reconstitute its original or intended form. The north wall of the interior (the south aisle wall) is articulated by four pilaster buttresses, of which the two eastern ones were substantially enlarged during the late thirteenth-century remodeling of the choir. These buttresses very naturally serve to articulate the interior space into four bays, to which the apse is added at the east end. Although the eastern half of this story was separated from the rest by a wall and was remodeled with a flat ceiling in the seventeenth century, its original disposition clearly continued that in the western half. That is, the chapter house had four short columnar piers (standing on round plinths and supporting round molded capitals and imposts) along its longitudinal axis, which divided the width into two bays and supported the ribbed vaults. On the walls, the plain chamfered ribs sprang from molded polygonal corbels. This arrangement of corbels was ideal for an unarticulated south wall but the protruding pilaster buttresses on the north wall, from which the vault ribs sprang, created a difficulty in joining the vaults to the wall surface. This difficulty was overcome by spanning the interval between the buttresses with arches, creating a mural arcade along the top of the wall. The result was a double-aisled, four-bay space oriented toward an apse and entered by doors from the third and fifth bays of the choir aisle. A door in the west wall and another beside the apse provided access to the stairs leading down to the two chambers of the undercroft. The round windows in the two west bays undoubtedly represent the means of lighting once employed in all four bays of the south wall. However, both the intermediate courses of the wall masonry and the round window frames have been so much renewed that it is entirely possible this was not the initial window arrangement. The apse retains its original axial window, similar to the vertical window below it in the undercroft; but the tiny window at the juncture of the apse and the stair-turret was probably cut later (pl. 15). Since the apse has a piscina and an aumbry (both apparently original) recessed in the wall, there was some liturgical use of this upper story, whether or not it was restricted to the clergy.

This composition of the upper story undoubtedly represents its ultimate medieval state, but not necessarily its twelfth-century state. Although the western bays may appear to provide the material for a simple reconstitution of the whole story, there are several discrepancies in the structure which, as soon as they are recognized, raise doubts about such an attribution. If the composition of the upper story is original, why is the bay system of the two stories so discrepant that the piers of the upper story stand virtually over the middle of the bays below them? If the ribbed vaults of the upper story (pl. 18) are original, why was the undercroft built with plain groined vaults? If both stories were not vaulted in immediate succession, why do the ribs have virtually identical chamfered profiles? If the upper story was initially intended to be vaulted, why were there no pilaster buttresses articulating the exterior of the south wall? The most likely answer to all these questions is that the upper story was not originally vaulted or even divided into bays. It was probably an unarticulated space, perhaps divided into two chambers like the undercroft (since it was entered by two doors from the aisle), with a flat wooden ceiling under a gabled roof, which was low enough not to interfere with the aisle windows. The disposition of windows in the south wall probably would have complemented the arrangement in the undercroft with its five small vertical windows. Construction of the roof would have been much easier if the north wall had already been straightened in its upper region through the insertion of the mural arcade. Since the voussoirs of these arches are not regularly integrated with the ashlar courses of the buttresses and since the arches do not all spring from the same course of the masonry, it is possible that not even the mural arcade is original. However, suffice it to acknowledge that the original form of the chapter house and vestry was almost certainly very simple indeed.

If the vaults were originally neither intended nor built, under what circumstances were they most likely to have been constructed? Since, as we saw earlier, the ribs of the undercroft vaults (pl. 17) were later additions and also appear to have been contemporaneous with those of the chapter house, it is virtually certain that the vaults of the upper story (pl. 18) were built after the completion of the chapter house. An otherwise anomalous characteristic of these vaults tends to confirm this deduction: all the arches of the vaults are round rather than pointed, even though all other vaulting arches in the church are pointed. This apparent anachronism was introduced because ribbed vaults with pointed arches would require a roof much higher than one constructed over an unvaulted chamber. Only the use of round-arched vaults constructed in two aisles could have permitted this insertion of vaults without raising the walls externally and rebuilding the roof. Even if the vaults were built when the new story was added to provide a Lady Chapel, the restriction of height was still highly desirable so that the new chapel would not block the light from the south clerestory of the choir. Indeed, the only situation in which vaults with pointed arches would have been likely would be the initial construction project when no third story was anticipated and when the roof could be designed accordingly.

If the vaults of the chapter house were built only as a modification of the original scheme, what is their relative position in the sequence of construction? They could have been built at any time following completion of the chapter house and before construction of the Lady Chapel, or Lady Loft as it is known locally. This chapel of St. Mary is expressly mentioned in a document of about 1358 as being in the chapter house and in another of 1391 as being above the vestry.[31] The vaults, then, could have been built at any time between ca. 1185 and ca. 1350. Unfortunately, the features of these vaults which are most nearly susceptible to dating by formal comparison—the use of round molded plinths, bases, capitals, and imposts on the piers; of polygonal molded capitals and imposts on the corbels; and of ribs with a simple chamfered square profile—can occur at any time during this period, especially in auxiliary structures where details tend to be plainer than in church interiors and less subject to changing fashion.[32] The general appearance of these features suggests a date reasonably early in the thirteenth century. On the other hand, the lack of differentiation in thickness between the transverse and diagonal ribs and the use of diagonal arches whose arcs are considerably less than semi-circular are both usually indicators of later dates. Lacking some more precise evidence, the date of the vaults must remain open. The most likely occasion for installing them was when other construction made this work feasible or appropriate. One such period was when the east bays of the choir were being remodeled, beginning in the late 1280s; another, more plausible, was when Lady Loft was added to the chapter house, in the first half of the fourteenth century.[33]

---

[31] Chapter Acts recorded in the Ingilby Ms., *Memorials of Ripon*, ed. J. T. Fowler, 4: 125 and 109 respectively. (The Publications of the Surtees Society, 108 (London, 1908).

[32] While round molded plinths, bases, capitals, and imposts are possible anytime after ca. 1180, beginning with the crypt of the Trinity Chapel at Canterbury, and polygonal molded corbels and imposts are also possible from the same time, making an early appearance in the Kirkstall Abbey gatehouse, they remained in use for two centuries or more, especially in combination with square chamfered arches. Examples are the undercrofts of the abbot's solar, built at Peterborough between 1222 and 1226 (C. R. Peers, "Peterborough: Cathedral," *The Victoria History of the Counties of England, Northamptonshire*, 2 (London, 1906), 454 and of the Wells Cathedral chapter house, built in the early fourteenth-century.

The polygonal molded corbels, combining impost and capital, are similar in profile to the round molded capitals and imposts of the freestanding piers. Although there are twelfth-century polygonal imposts in the vault responds of the choir aisles, these other examples much more nearly resemble the polygonal molded corbels found in the tower reinforcement work of ca. 1500 in the vaults of the choir aisle west bays. Similar examples elsewhere belong to the fourteenth century, as in the remodeled ambulatory of Tewkesbury Abbey and the remodeled nave of Winchester Cathedral.

[33] Walbran (Ripon, 48) placed the Lady Chapel in 1482, to correspond with the last phase of rebuilding in the church. Scott ("Ripon Minster," 315) dated the chapel to the mid-

From the examination of the chapter house it is possible to draw several conclusions. First and most important, it was built as an adjunct to the present church and was probably conceived shortly after the church was begun, so it exerted no influence whatever upon the siting of the twelfth-century Minster. In its original form it consisted of groin-vaulted undercroft and an unvaulted main floor, each divided into two chambers. The chambers on the main floor were used for a vestry and a chapter house; those on the undercroft, probably for a treasury and other similar storage purposes. The ribs of the undercroft vaults and the ribbed vaults of the chapter house level were added sometime after this structure was initially completed, probably when a third story was added to create a chapel of St. Mary in the first half of the fourteenth century.

## C. The Transepts

The transepts, particularly the north arm, survive almost in the state in which they were completed. Even the virtually flat wooden ceiling (a nineteenth-century replacement in the manner of the late Middle Ages) reflects the basic form of the original covering. More than in any other part of the church, we are able to appreciate here the visual effect of the original repertory of forms. The close affinity of the transept and choir designs is immediately apparent. The width of the main space is almost exactly that of the choir and each arm has three bays. If both arms were placed end to end they would be spatially equal to the central vessel of the choir (plan 1). Also, the east elevation closely resembles the lateral walls of the choir (pls. 3, 20). We sense, then, that the transepts should also have had high vaults.

The appropriateness of high vaults is announced explicitly by the triple bay-division shafts on the wall, intended as responds for quadripartite vaults. The purpose of these shafts is manifest in the placement of capitals at the base of the clerestory, anticipating the springing of the vault arches (pl. 22). The modification, as in the choir, is represented by the change at this point from attached shafts, laid in courses, to detached monolithic shafts cut *en délit*[34] and also by a considerable reduction in their thickness. This modification was accommodated somewhat more neatly than in the choir because there were only three respond shafts: the projecting outer order of the clerestory arcade could utilize the shafts immediately flanking the bay division shaft without leaving an awkward interval. Because there were only three respond shafts, it is clear that the intended high vaults were not meant to have wall arches. This inconsistency with the scheme of the choir vaults was not important in the 1170s, for the use of wall arches was not yet standard practice, but in itself the variation seems strange for a church in which all other vaults had, or were meant to have,

---

fourteenth century for reasons unstated but probably related to the tracery of the windows, Hallett, *Ripon Cathedral*, 54, cited both opinions, favoring the latter.

[34] See note 17.

this feature. The deviation is clearly due to the reduction in the number of respond shafts and to the use of a different type of pier in the transepts. The change acknowledged a distinction in function between the choir and transept piers—the difference between a row of columnar supports for an arcade and a series of openings into individual subsidiary spaces (the transept chapels). Despite this inconsistency, the transept high vaults were intended to be similar to the quadripartite vaults planned for the choir (fig. 9).

Besides the modification in the clerestory of the east and west elevations made when the vaulting scheme was abandoned, there is evidence of another change in the transepts, beginning in the triforium of the terminal and west elevations (pls. 23, 27, 28). In this case the triforium arcade is markedly larger in scale than that of the east elevation and the choir. Moreover, the triforium and clerestory in the terminal elevations are articulated as three bays, a division that would be inappropriate in the intended scheme with high vaults where a single arch would have oversailed all three bays.[35] As in the east and west clerestory, these bays are defined by detached monolithic shafts, cut *en délit* (pl. 24). Hence the modified portions of the terminal and west elevations include all of the triforium and clerestory, a substantial change in the original design.

In reconstituting the intended scheme for the walls, it is helpful to recall that, because high vaults were anticipated, the west elevation was necessarily coordinated with the east. Since this elevation opened to no subsidiary spaces, it had tall round-headed windows rather than a main arcade in the ground story (pl. 23). For the same reason, it had a triforium wall passage rather than a reduced false gallery in the intermediate story. Presumably because it had no piers in the ground story, the vault respond shafts were corbeled out at the window sills (as in the choir aisles). But the clerestory and the bay articulation, including the type of vault response, were necessarily the same. Consequently, we may safely conclude that the only modification of the west walls not related to suppression of the vaulting scheme was in the scale of the triforium arcade. That change was instigated by the arcade of the terminal elevation.

The principal revision in the transept, when the scheme for high vaults was rejected, concerned the terminal elevations (pls. 20, 27). The ground story, with its three tall round-headed windows, was already built, as we have seen, and so was unquestionably a part of the original scheme. For the middle story a wall passage of some sort was required. Even though the triforium above the choir aisles and the chapels was not a liturgical

---

[35] Transept terminal walls with bay division shafts applied to the full length of the elevation and in which there was never any intention to build high vaults included those at Norwich Cathedral (begun ca. 1096) and Romsey Abbey (begun ca. 1120). A similar arrangement for double bays was employed at Ely Cathedral (ca. 1100), and bay division shafts rising from the main arcade piers were used at Peterborough Cathedral (begun ca. 1118). An exception was Fécamp Abbey, in Normandy, where the transept high vaults (before 1187) have extra ribs to correspond with the bay division shafts of the terminal walls.

FIG. 9. Ripon Minster, north transept reconstitution according to the intended scheme.

space, it did require a means of access and in English churches this access was usually provided across the terminal elevation from stair vices in the outer western corners of each transept arm. Moreover, since the aisleless nave was to include a major wall passage in the middle story, there was every reason to make the passage continuous, extending through the west elevation of the transept arms. In aisleless transept elevations in England, such passages were usually provided with a band triforium, especially if there was no intermediate range of transept windows corresponding to choir or nave galleries (or to both).[36] The middle story, then, was undoubtedly intended to have virtually its present form. One important difference, though, is that there would have been no vertical bay articulation when the transept was to be spanned by a high vault. The triforium arches, accordingly, would either have been isolated in pairs or planned in greater number. Because the scale of the present triforium arcade is so much larger than that of the east elevation, the scheme which would have been most consistent with the initial design would specify both shorter and narrower units in the arcade. Although no exact correspondence to the width of the pointed arches of the east elevation would have been feasible, the number in the terminal wall would probably have been nine (fig. 9) rather than the present six.[37] Correspondingly, the west elevation bays would have been variously well-matched with three or four arches rather than two for each bay.

For the upper story there is no evidence available to assist a reconstitution. We can be reasonably sure that it would have included a wall passage to connect the east and west clerestories and equally confident of some form of lighting. Also, we can safely surmise that the respond shafts in the outer corners of the transepts were intended for the diagonal ribs of the high vault, since there were to be no wall arches. Moreover, the conditions that fostered a relieving arch in the east wall of the choir do not obtain in the actual terminal walls of the transepts, so there is no reason to envision such an arch in the intended design. With no wall arch or relieving arch, there was almost certainly a clerestory arcade, albeit a staggered one that could follow the arc of the high vault. The arcade articulation, however, would be determined by the format of the windows. For the windows, there are two plausible arrangements: three vertical windows of staggered height (placed somewhat closer together than in the ground story), or a fairly large oculus. England offered a contemporaneous example of each type in a vaulted transept, the former at Roche

---

[36] The most notable, and earliest, examples are at Hereford Cathedral (begun ca. 1110) and Pershore Abbey (begun ca. 1120).

[37] The pointed triforium arches of a normal choir or transept east elevation bay are about three feet wide. An arcade composed of exactly equivalent units in the transept terminal elevation would consist of twelve arches. However, without the scale modulation provided by the embracing round-headed arches, such an arcade would be too petty and monotonous. It seems to me by visual estimate that nine arches would have made the most harmonious arcade for a terminal elevation with no bay articulation.

and the latter at Canterbury. Neither provides an exact parallel for the Ripon transepts; Roche had neither a triforium nor a clerestory passage and the oculus in the Canterbury clerestory was in a fourth story superimposed in the terminal elevation upon a remodeled three-story elevation (pls. 56, 57). Circumstantial evidence at Ripon for an oculus in the east wall of the choir begs for a consistent window arrangement in the transept terminals (even though this consistency was not observed at Kirkstall and—if applicable, as surmised—at Roche). Considering the proliferation of oculi in the early thirteenth century, however (for instance in the west front of Byland Abbey and the transepts of Lincoln Cathedral), such a reconstitution seems reasonable. Certainly the architectural context in the transepts makes this feature the most plausible for the intended scheme.

As the sum of these various deductions we can confidently visualize most of the intended design of the transepts (fig. 9). The east and west elevations of the transepts were meant to look almost as they do today except that the bay division shafts could have served as responds for quadripartite high vaults. The terminal elevation would not have been divided into bays and its triforium would undoubtedly have had a continuous arcade of narrower and slightly lower arches, probably nine in all. (The triforium arcade of the west elevation would have been correspondingly smaller in scale, with three or four arches for each bay rather than two). The clerestory would have been markedly different from the one constructed because the arch of the high vault would have severely curtailed the area available for window openings and structural articulation. In the external shell of the clerestory passage, there would probably have been a large oculus window and, because there was no relieving arch to frame the clerestory, an arcade of staggered heights in the inner shell. In the north arm, the two eastern chapels were separated by a solid wall, indicated by the scar on the present wide transverse arch (pl. 21) and on the pier between them. Their status as individual square spaces seems to have inspired the designer to crown them with octopartite vaults—that is, vaults with ridge ribs in addition to the diagonal arches—framed with wall arches on all four sides.

The south transept arm cannot be known so fully as the north because its east elevation was replaced early in the sixteenth century. However, the south and west elevations (pls. 25, 26) survive, and indicate that in general design this arm was like the north. Evidence in the eastern chapels and in the west elevation reveals a few differences which signify that the south transept was built more slowly. Despite the later rebuilding, the original walls, window embrasures, vault wall arches and respond shafts survive in the eastern chapels. The respond shafts, unlike those in the north transept chapels, are detached and cut *en délit* (pl. 29). The cluster of three such shafts between the two chapels indicates that these spaces were not separated by a wall. Moreover, the use of *en délit* shafts for the bay divisions of the west elevation places construction of that wall after the change in design. This pattern of evidence suggests that the south transept was very much less advanced than the north when construction was interrupted. The east and south walls of the chapel together with the ground story of the transept south elevation were undoubtedly raised together with the chapter house and in continuation of the south choir aisle wall. Whether or not the main east elevation was begun at the same time as that of the north transept cannot be determined. If it was not, it could possibly have received detached shafts for its bay divisions, matching the technique of the shafts on the west wall.

In the actual course of construction it appears that the east clerestory of the north arm (and perhaps also that of the south) was built when the upper story of the choir was built (pls. 3, 20). (In both areas the arches are molded in the same way, while in the terminal and west walls of the transept, the arches are plain and molded only on the upper order, pls. 22, 24). Then, while the choir was being roofed and after the transept triforium was completed, the rest of the transept clerestory was built and the roof and ceiling added. The crossing tower, however, remained unfinished above the crossing arches and was surely roofed over at that level for some time while the nave was under construction. There is no archaeological evidence on which we can deduce the intended design for this tower, but probably it would have had a blind triforium in the lower story and a clerestory with wall passage above it, a composition similar to that constructed a decade or so later.

## D. The Nave

The nave of the twelfth-century Minster[38] has been more nearly obliterated than any other part of the church (pl. 32). In the early sixteenth century, the walls were almost entirely dismantled in order to construct the present aisled nave. Twelfth-century remnants are to be found at either end of the main vessel, a fragment of a single bay at the east end and two bays at the west end (pls. 31, 33, 34). From these fragments one can immediately establish that the elevation consisted of three zones—the lower, a blank wall; the middle, a tall triforium passage; the upper, a clerestory with arcaded passage. No high vaults were intended; and one can also see that the elevation was articulated into bays of varying dimension and design.

A few years after his restoration of the church, Sir George Gilbert Scott published his proposed reconstruction of the original nave elevation (fig. 3),[39] a scheme which has been generally accepted until recent years. Scott assumed that the two west bays were the key to the reconstitution of a scheme with alternating wide and narrow bays. He explained the inconsistency of a still-narrower bay at the east end as the result of subtracting

---

[38] Most of my discussion of the nave reconstitution was previously published in articles: "On the Original Nave of Ripon Cathedral," *Journal of the British Archaeological Association*, 3rd ser., 35 (1972): 39–45, and "Postscript: On the Original Nave of Ripon Cathedral," idem, 139 (1976): 93–94. My thanks go to the editor and board of this journal for their kind permission to reprint most of this material, with only a few modifications.

[39] Scott, "Ripon Minster," 313–14.

the thickness of the wall (i.e., the crossing pier?) from the normal width of a narrow bay. This, he supposed, was balanced by a similar bay at the west end which ostensibly was removed when the west towers were constructed (fig. 1). Moreover, the arches leading from the nave into the towers in the present west bay were presumably cut after the nave was completed, in order to accommodate the added two-tower facade. However, after examination of the evidence, one can only conclude that the "thickness of the wall" could have been subtracted from no component of the nave scheme to produce the length of the east bay and that there is no evidence for modification in the west bay. Since Scott's explanation depends upon those two points, it is apparent that a doubtful reconstitution has been accepted. If a more convincing interpretation of the evidence is to be established, it must be based on a critical analysis of each of the three remaining bays. In this case, it is better to begin at the west where the bays are complete and proceed eastward where only fragments of a bay remain.

*The West Bay*

The west bay measures slightly more than 18 feet from east to west in both elevations (pls. 33–35). Its ground story consists of a tall arch, leading from the nave to the respective towers of the facade. The arch is complexly molded of many thin rolls, unlike any other portion of the twelfth-century church; and it springs from molded capitals which are similarly singular in the use of round imposts (pl. 38). The triforium story is blind and begins at a point considerably higher than the adjacent triforium unit, due to the height of the arch in the ground story. The triforium arcade consists of four pointed arches, staggered in height, beneath a round-headed relieving arch. The clerestory has a large round-headed arch backed by a window (now glazed) which opens into the tower. It is flanked by two slender pointed arches which open only into the clerestory passage.

The plausibility of the west bay as the wide bay in Scott's reconstitution scheme (fig. 3) rested implicitly upon the use of wide round arches adjacent to narrow pointed ones, which recalled the design of the choir elevation and suggested an overall consistency of design. However, examined for its own sake, this bay seems to have been designed expressly to accommodate the towers. To begin with the lower zone, the arches leading from the nave to the western towers show no sign of insertion despite the apparent anachronism of the elaborately molded arches and capitals, which suggest a later conception than the simple arches and bell capitals of the nave elevation. To be sure, irregularities in the wall masonry may have disappeared in the extensive restoration of the towers, but this restoration ostensibly did not affect the nave interior. More important, the west respond of the arch is composed entirely of shafts attached immediately to the west wall (pl. 33). Even with a new facade abutting the nave elevation, it would have been dangerous to trust a bonding of the old nave wall and the new facade masonry to carry the upper stories of a bay in which the lower story had been almost entirely removed. One would expect to find at least a stump of the original wall left to preserve a unified section of the elevation to meet the facade. Since such a remnant is missing, it is safe to assume that the arch was designed from the beginning as a feature of the west bay.

In the triforium there is again no evidence of remodeling, especially not of shortening the blind arcade to clear the lower arch (pl. 33). Rather than undermine the strength of a wall which forms one side of the tower and incur undue complications in shortening the arcade and filling it in, the builder would have been more likely to resort to cutting an ample door in the blank lower zone of the wall (which is nearly 18 feet high). Also, had this been a normal bay originally, the triforium passage would continue through it. In this bay, the triforium is not only blind but is also decorated as if it were originally intended to be so. A molded string-course runs across both the arches and the wall behind them and quatrefoil medallions are carved into both tympana and spandrels. Such details are not likely to be added or extended in a remodeling unless they relate to the new scheme. Moreover, the string-course running across the arches marks the apex of the subdividing arches in the other nave bays and seems to compensate for the interruption of an otherwise regular pattern. Finally, and most important, in the towers there is a four-part arcade on the other side of the triforium wall and, moreover, it is constructed in the later style of the west towers (pl. 36). If a triforium passage had been blocked in the west bay, the old wall would have been plain on the side facing the tower. The insertion of such an arcade in that area is highly unlikely because its insertion would have weakened the old wall structure. Evidence in the triforium, then, clearly indicates that its present form is original, making it exceptional in the nave scheme and peculiarly appropriate for the west towers alone.

The clerestory, with its unexceptional arcade and its window, does give the impression of belonging to a regular bay rather than to a tower. However, this composition is by no means implausible for a tower bay because clerestory windows opening into towers are found elsewhere in both Romanesque and Gothic practice, for instance at Chichester and Chartres Cathedrals and Llanthony Priory.

Within itself the west bay does not appear to have been modified and hence may be taken as having been designed to be integral with a pair of western towers. On the other hand, the decor and the articulation of stories have no relationship to that in the actual towers and facade. These discrepancies undoubtedly convinced Scott that the facade was an addition to the original scheme for the nave. But he apparently did not account for still another discrepancy between the interior and exterior articulation of the towers. A string-course inside the towers repeats that above the blank lower zone of the nave and continues at the same level, contrary to the articulation of both the tower exterior and the west wall interior of the nave (pls. 33, 44, 45). This correspondence with the nave elevation suggests that the towers were intended from the start but were modified in the course of construction. Since integration with the western towers is exceptional within the total nave scheme, the design for this bay was not necessarily repeated in the elevation.

At the west end of the west bay, there is a normal bay division shaft and beyond it, slightly recessed as if to continue the wall articulation into another bay, there appear to be two much smaller shafts, one above the other (pl. 37). Scott interpreted this occurrence to mean that a bay had been removed from the nave when the west towers were added. Because the bay fragment at the east end of the nave did not correspond in size to the two western bays which he supposed were standard for the nave elevation, he assumed that a similar narrow bay originally terminated the west end of the nave. He did not account for the fact, however, that the upper shaft of the two would interrupt the rationale of the elevation design. Moreover, he did not observe that this upper shaft is not a shaft at all but a projecting angle roll, returning the finished end of the wall, and anticipating a passage in the west wall of the nave. There is every reason to believe, then, that the west bay was not only designed to accommodate the towers but that it was also meant to be the terminal bay of the west arm of the church.

*The Penultimate West Bay and Its Neighbor*

The penultimate west bay remains complete, so there can be no controversy concerning its articulation (pls. 35, 39). From east to west it is 9 feet 2 inches on the south elevation and 10 feet 6 inches on the north, both measurements running from centerline to centerline of the boundary shafts. It has a blank wall beneath the tall arcaded triforium passage, which is subdivided into two arches. Hard by the west bay there is an opening to the passage in the east wall of the tower, the floor of which is four courses of stone higher than the floor in the triforium, clearly an alteration of the arrangement initially intended. There is no indication that an earlier passage was ever closed off at the east end of the west bay, and this is one location where irregularities in masonry are not likely to have been repaired. The clerestory arcade, opening into the passage behind, is composed of three narrrow pointed arches, the middle only slightly taller and wider than the flanking ones. The clerestory, too, has a door into a passage in the west wall of the tower which appears to be original.

The design of this bay raises two questions about the nave in general. The first concerns the provision for admitting light. Since the penultimate west bay is abutted on the exterior by the west wall of the tower, there was no opportunity to incorporate any windows. This circumstance complicates any effort to determine the means of lighting in the nave. The three narrow arches of the clerestory passage could scarcely accommodate windows; so light in the clerestory would have to be arranged in alternating bays, beginning with the next bay eastward. The double arches of the triforium are wide enough to frame pairs of windows in another bay of the same design; but, whatever the means, triforium windows are usually provided in addition to clerestory windows and not as substitutes for them.

The lighting problem leads to the second question, which concerns the design of the next bay to the east. Since the clerestory in the penultimate west bay could not provide window, that of the next bay certainly required a different composition. A difference in design in the middle zone is also indicated by the springing of the triforium arch into the next bay eastward, seen only on the south elevation. It is steeper than the arc of the penultimate west bay and similar to the round-headed west bay arch. But unlike the west bay arch, the curving of the arc is more gradual, indicating that it formed a pointed arch. Since it is steeper than the arch of the adjacent bay, it was also of a significantly narrower span and this represents a different design in the triforium. Because the two upper stories of the elevation differed in adjacent bays, the penultimate west bay represents one component of a scheme with alternating bay design.

## The East Bay and Its Neighbor

Only a fragment of the east bay remains (pls. 31, 40, 41). It consists of a portion of the triforium and the blank wall beneath it. In the triforium, there is a subdivided arch, similar to that in the penultimate west bay but much narrower, measuring on the south elevation 7 feet 4 inches east to west from centerline to centerline of the boundary shafts; on the north elevation, 6 feet 2 inches. Unlike the penultimate west bay, the vertical shaft on the west side of the arch terminates shortly above the arch springing in the form of a corbel suitable for supporting a detached shaft. This is the case now on the north elevation and was clearly so originally on the south. It is certain that no attached shaft on either wall ever extended to the clerestory in this location nor was the wall repaired to remove the scars of former shafts. This means that the vertical division between the east bay and its immediate neighbor was either incomplete or different from that framing the west bays. Further, on both elevations an arc identical to that of the east bay arch springs to the west. On the north elevation, just above the string-course separating the middle and lower zones, there is a small hole in the ashlar wall-facing applied during the remodeling of the nave in the early sixteenth century (pl. 41). This hole reveals the base of a colonnette placed to correspond with the subdividing member of the east bay. Hence the second arch and its subdivision repeated the composition of the east bay. These two factors combined indicate a double bay arrangement. Originally, the east bay measured between 12½ feet and 15 feet east to west with two arches in the triforium, each subdivided into two.

There is nothing left of the clerestory in the east bay on either elevation. However, evidence related to it can be obtained in the west bays (pl. 35). The decorative scheme of the penultimate west bay indicates that the arch faces of the clerestory were plain with a slight chamfer rather than the roll molding set off by hollow chamfers used in the triforium. Instead of colonnettes, the clerestory had small rectangular piers and instead of capitals, a molded string-course at the springing of the arches. The west bay window (opening into the tower), which is considerably taller than the flanking arches and those of the penultimate west bay, indicates the height of the arches provided for the clerestory windows in the rest of the nave. Since the clerestory of the east bay represents the other component in an alternating bay scheme, it would have contained windows. Although the detailing of the west bays and the height of the west bay window arch were almost certainly a part of its design, any further evidence would have to be identified elsewhere in the church.

Since the detailing of the clerestory differs markedly from the simple roll molding of the choir and transepts, its repetition in another location would be significant. This detailing occurs in the north and west interior elevations of the crossing tower which were built at the same time as the nave (pl. 30). In the lower story of these elevations there is a triforium articulated with pairs of tall, sharply-pointed arches. There is no reason that these arches should have been grouped in pairs unless the motif were a part of the comprehensive design for the nave and crossing tower. If such arches appeared also in the nave, they could have been located only in the clerestory and above the double bays of the triforium. This disposition would have the virtue of varying the height of the clerestory arches to match the west bay and of providing arches wide and tall enough to admit the light of clerestory windows behind them.

*The Twelfth-Century Nave Elevation*

The evidence provided by the fragments of the nave is sufficient to establish that the east bay had a triforium which was a double version of that in the penultimate west bay and to indicate that another variation between the wide and narrow bays could be expected in the clerestory (fig. 10). The fragment of the bay just to the east of the penultimate west bay (in the south elevation) indicates a triforium arch with an arc identical to that in the east bay. This repetition implies that the nave elevation alternated the designs of the east and penultimate west bays and that the west bay, designed to accommodate the facade towers, was not repeated (plan 2). The measurements of the whole nave and the wall fragments tend to confirm this arrangement. The total length of the nave elevations from the crossing to the east end of the west bay is 114 feet on the south and 115 feet on the north (plans 1, 2). As we have seen, no corresponding bays in the two elevations (except the west bay) have the same east to west dimension. Nevertheless, an average of the dimensions may be taken as fairly representative. The east bay fragments in their reconstituted double form average 13 feet 6 inches and the penultimate west bays average 9 feet 10 inches, measurements which can be paired five times for a total length of 116 feet 8 inches. In view of the variations in the bay dimensions,

FIG. 10. Ripon Minster, nave reconstitution according to revised scheme actually constructed.

the destroyed portions of the nave elevation could easily account for an average discrepancy of 2 feet 2 inches. In the light of this reconstitution, it becomes clear that the alternating design of the arcade should not be read as a genuine bay system but as a continuous wall, which permitted a less than precise correspondence of mural articulation between the two elevations.

The remaining problem concerns the system of lighting. The hypothetical reconstitution of pairs of tall lancet windows above the wider double bays of the triforium is highly plausible but can never be definitely proved. Nevertheless, it is difficult to imagine that the nave was lighted entirely by the five pairs of clerestory windows on each side. Although many churches with false-tribunes were lit in this way, the light was amplified in such cases by aisle windows. The lack of aisles and of windows on the ground level increased the desirability of exploiting the tall triforium to provide additional light. Ironically, while the wide bay was the plausible location of clerestory windows, the subdivision of its narrow triforium arches made the middle zone unsuitable for windows. The only practicable location for triforium windows, then, was in the narrow bays with their wider arches. Unfortunately, definite evidence is missing because it was not possible to construct windows in the penultimate west bay. The lighting scheme suggested by the plausible locations is very unorthodox because the windows in it are placed on staggered axes rather than aligned above each other (figs. 10, 15). This arrangement would seem inadmissible were it not that the system would be composed of consistent elements, with pairs of lancet windows in both stories. Each opening could be about 3 feet wide, with the triforium windows approximately double the height of those in the clerestory.

Even so, it would be difficult to accept this reconstitution were it not that similar circumstances exist in the Ripon crossing tower (pl. 30) and in related buildings. The aisleless vessel with a tall triforium lighted by pairs of lancet windows recalls the transepts of Noyon Cathedral (pls. 58). The staggered arrangement of windows resembles the aisleless west wall of the south transept of Hexham Priory, where the clerestory and triforium windows are on different axes.[40] Although the intervals between the axes at Hexham are not uniform, as they would have been at Ripon, they are consistent. Moreover, the detailing of the triforium arches on the interior there is based on that of the Ripon nave clerestory. The alternating placement of windows is not only plausible, then, but possible in the context of English medieval architecture and specifically in the architectural progeny of Ripon.

On the exterior, scars of pilaster buttresses survive behind the fragments at the east end of the nave (pl. 42) and actual buttresses survive behind the penultimate west bays (pls. 43, 44). The latter (measuring from the west tower to the east return of the buttresses 5 feet 8 inches on the south and 6 feet 9 inches on the north) are an exception to the regular system, because this narrow bay would otherwise contain windows. The irregular placement of a buttress in this location would be justified only because

---

[40] Charles Clement Hodges, *The Abbey of St. Andrew, Hexham*, ([Edinburgh], 1888) pls. 10 and 14; and date of ca.1215–1220, suggested, 27–29.

it served to reinforce the juncture of the nave and the towers of the west facade, hollowed out by wall passages (plan 2). (A similar buttress was unnecessary at the east end where the juncture of nave and transepts was reinforced by the crossing piers). The scars on the east fragments, however, are located behind the central subdivision of the double-unit arcades and so represent the standard disposition of the nave buttresses. Their width (5 feet 6 inches on the north and 5 feet on the south) is commensurate with the wall buttresses on the transepts and they were probably similar in form. From the buttresses at the west end, it is possible to determine that the exterior decoration of the nave was the same as that on the transepts, three continuous string-courses (pl. 26). This horizontal articulation was located at the sill of the triforium windows, at the springing of the triforium arches, and at the sill of the clerestory windows, approximately the same levels as in the transept but without parallel correspondence to the transept stories (fig. 16).

There is, however, in the evidence for the exterior, one structural inconsistency which indicates that the form actually constructed represented a revision of the intended scheme. That inconsistency lies in the location of pilaster buttresses on the vertical axis of bays in which the clerestory windows were ostensibly located. Yet there can be no doubt about the location of the buttresses nor can there be any substantial doubt about the location of the clerestory windows. Obviously, the elevation design was modified when construction reached the clerestory level and the buttresses were necessarily terminated at that point. This interruption did not occur in the surviving buttress at the west end (pls. 44, 47) because it covered a blind bay. In the initial design, then, both the triforium and clerestory windows would have been vertically aligned and located in the wider openings of the narrow bays (fig. 11).

The greater regularity of design implicit in an initial scheme with pairs of axially aligned triforium and clerestory windows is much closer to the general character of late twelfth-century architecture in the North of England than is the reconstitution of the actually constructed nave. Such a regularity suggests in turn that the clerestory was originally intended to be very similar in both design and decoration to the triforium. Whatever such a scheme would have gained in rational order and consistency, the variation in the bay sizes would not have prevented a certain degree of monotony. This predictable problem may well account, then, for the curious provision of corbels for detached shafts in the middle of the triforium double bays. A detached shaft rising through the clerestory would interrupt the regular articulation of stories and the rhythm of bays. Such an interruption would divide the blind double bays and thereby flank each of the lighted narrow bays with half a blind double bay.

For whatever reasons, this design was probably discarded while the nave was under construction. Within the triforium, several changes in decorative detail between the east and west ends of the nave occur which indicate an interruption. One is the change from pierced quatrefoils in the

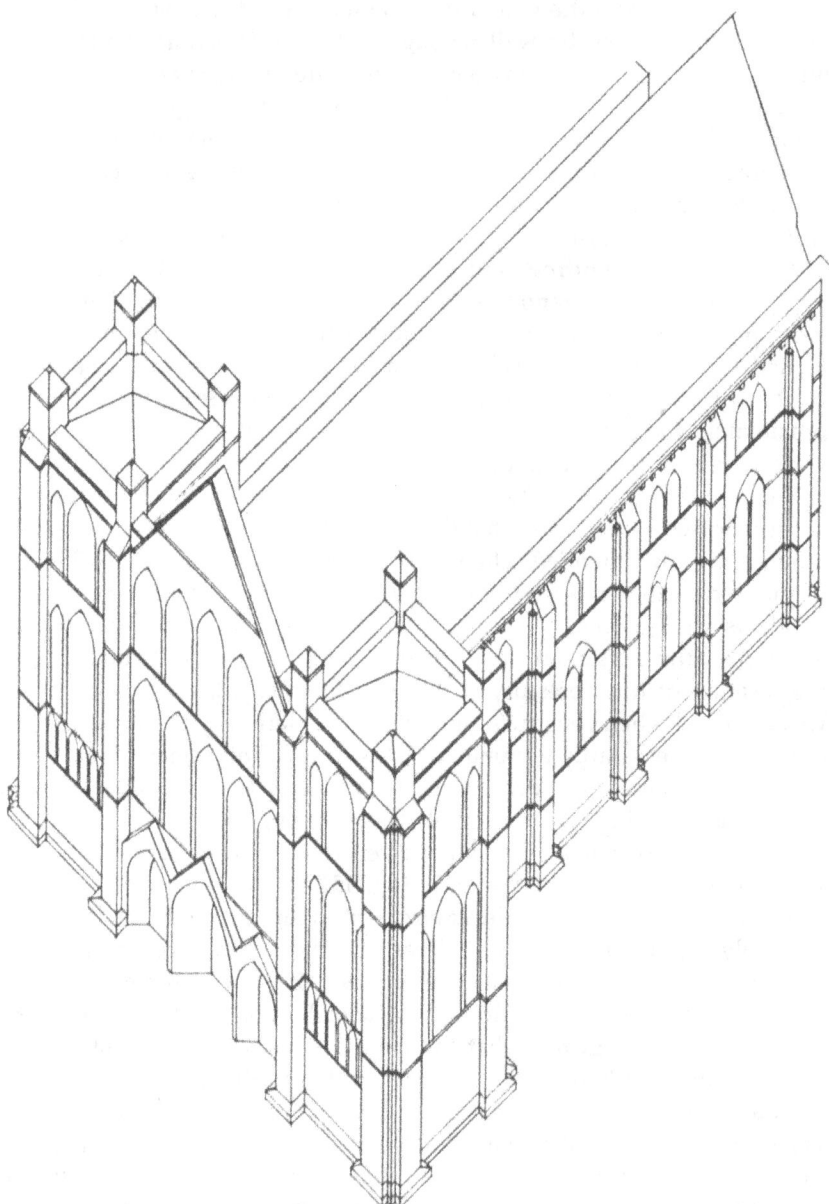

FIG. 11. Ripon Minster, reconstitution of intended nave exterior and west front.

east bay triforium to incised quatrefoils in the west bays. Others are the use of elaborate molding and round imposts in the west bay tower arches, unprecedented in the eastern portions of the church. More striking, the niche-arcade on the tower side of the triforium of the west bay (pl. 36) indicates that the west end of the nave elevation was built after a new decorative vocabulary had already been adopted in areas where it would not clash with that of the nave. Following the interruption, at some point between the two ends of the nave, the clerestory was revised and a new scheme adopted which radically altered the stylistic expression of the nave and the crossing tower. It was this new scheme which the surviving fragments of the nave permit us to reconstitute.

### E. The West Front

The west front, with its two towers flanking the nave (pl. 52), differs strikingly in scale and decor from the rest of the late twelfth-century church. In scale, the west front as a whole is very much larger, approaching twice the height of the original walls of the nave. Some of the component parts of the west front, such as windows, are both wider and taller than any in the earlier portions. In decor, everything is more elaborate: the plinth profile is taller and its molding more complex (pls. 43, 46), the buttress corners are edged with triple angle rolls, the window arches are richly molded, blind arcades are revived to flank the windows, and many moldings are embellished with nail-head or dog-tooth ornament (pls. 44, 48, 50, 52). Both in scale and in decor the differences are not so much of kind as of degree, but they are sufficient to distinguish the early and late portions of the original church so that in traditional nomenclature they are recognizable respectively as Transitional and Early English designs. From these differences Scott uncritically inferred that the west front had been added to the nave after a considerable interval and he unwittingly skewed his interpretation of the archaeological evidence in order to explain it in that way.[41] No one after him who has written about the church has reviewed the evidence with sufficient care to question his explanation.

Contrary to the assumption that the west front was a later addition to the nave is considerable evidence that the towers had been anticipated in the construction of the nave. As we have seen, a detailed examination of the nave walls indicates that the west bay has never been altered from its original form, that it was designed expressly to accommodate the west towers, and that its western edge apparently made provision for a wall passage in a terminal west wall (pl. 37). Moreover, in connection with the west bay it was noted that the ground story of the tower interiors continues the zone of blank wall from the nave together with the same type of string-course above it and at the same level (pl. 33). Even the ashlar masonry courses of the blank lower zone are consistent from the nave through the towers. More significant, on the exterior, although the plinth profile changes at the juncture of the nave wall and the east face of each tower (pl. 46), the masonry of the nave west buttresses continues without interruption into the towers. This continuity can be seen both at ground level, in the present nave aisles, and at the top of the nave buttresses, on the aisle roof (pl. 47). Had the towers not been intended when the west

---

[41] Scott, "Ripon Minster," 314, 316–317.

end of the nave was built, the discontinuity of masonry would have been virtually impossible to hide.

Although the towers were part of the original plan, the incongruity of their final form with earlier portions of the church indicates that some important modifications were made during construction. In order to discern the way in which the towers had been intended to relate to the nave, it is first necessary to investigate the sequence of construction in the actual fabric. Formal changes adopted during construction, along with masonry breaks, are keys to identifying the sequential pattern. The most conspicuous changes concern the way shafts and arch moldings were used for decoration. Detached shafts, cut *en délit* and applied singly to frame windows and to articulate blind arches (pls. 44, 48, 50) gave way to triple attached shafts laid in courses and filleted, with dog-tooth ornaments between the shafts (pl. 52). Arch moldings, already complex, were made even more elaborate with rows of nail-head ornament between the orders. The earlier shafts and moldings are found on the two lower stories of windows on the east and side faces of both towers; the later version, across all levels of windows on the west facade. A combination of the earlier detached shafts and later moldings occurs on the east and south faces of the top story of the south tower; of single shafts in courses (with fillets) and the later moldings, on the east and north faces of the north tower. Masonry breaks are indicated by uneven ashlar coursing in the first story of windows on both towers at the point where the outer western buttress meets the side face of the tower, and again, on the east face of both towers in the second story of windows between the two jambs of the windows (pl. 48). Obviously when a masonry break occurs in the middle of a window, the commitment to a certain type of decorative treatment has already been made; so the older system was necessarily retained through the second story of windows on the east face of both towers. When this carry-over occurred on the east face, it was appropriate to keep the side faces of both towers consistent with their lower stories. The west facade, on the other hand, could incorporate all modifications with a minimum of incongruity. Finally, a compromise version of this decorative pattern was appropriate on the top story of both towers.

In view of this pattern of masonry breaks and formal modifications, the sequence seems to have been as follows:

1) the blank ground story all around both towers and the west facade while the nave wall (the inner face of the towers) rose to the top of the clerestory;
2) the first story of windows of both towers through the east and side faces and the second story of windows of both towers through the inner half of the east face (fig. 15);
3) the lower window story of the whole west facade, followed immediately by the second story of windows from the east face of both towers around the whole west front;
4) the top story of both towers and the west facade gable (fig. 16).

From this sequence of construction it appears likely that an alteration in the intended scheme for the west front was decided upon and introduced between phases 2 and 3 of the sequence. Returning to additional evidence in the towers and the nave west bays, it is possible to reconstitute much of the initial design by examining each story in succession, beginning at the ground level.

As in the nave elevation, the tall blank zone of the towers must be regarded as the ground story, distinct from the lowest range of windows. Its compositional integrity with the ground story of the nave is clearly manifest not only on the interior but also on the exterior, where, despite the change of plinth profile and other details, the articulation of the ground story extends from the west nave buttress around the east and outer side faces of the tower up to the west front (pls. 44, 50). This continuity was interrupted on the west face of the towers where the window sill was raised five courses higher in the masonry and a fairly tall blind arcade was inserted underneath (pl. 52). At first, this change seems to have been occasioned by the need for more height in the west wall of the nave, probably to accommodate higher portals than were initially planned. However, the wall increment above the portals is more artificial than in the tower and probably even necessitated the addition of the awkward little gables over the door.[42] Certainly an increased height for the lower story was foreseen shortly after the nave elevation was completed because, as noted earlier, the floor of the wall passage leading from the nave triforium into the east wall of the tower was raised four courses of stone in both elevations (pls. 39, 45). The wall passage of the tower has this higher level as its standard even though it was depressed for the east and side windows in order to maintain their sill level in conformity with the earlier nave. The probable reason for the change in height is that some revision of the west front design had already been anticipated and that the increase was needed to make the ground story equal (at least on the west facade) to the one planned above it. Yet, despite these changes it is not difficult to see that the ground story of the west front was originally meant to continue the blank wall zone of the nave.

For the first story of windows above the blank zone, the intended upper and lower limits were indicated by the string-courses on the east and outer side faces of the towers (pls. 44, 50) which were continued from the nave west buttresses (pl. 43), albeit with a different decorative pattern. These limits coincide respectively with the sills of the first and second ranges of windows in the towers and they also correspond to the levels appropriate to the sill of the triforium and clerestory windows in the nave.[43]

---

[42] Engravings preserved in the British Museum illustrate the west front long before Scott's restoration, showing scars of the gables which he restored. The earlier of them, in the Prints and Drawings Room, is the "West View of Ripon Minster," drawn by W. H. Wood and engraved by F. Birnie, published 15 May 1790. The later, from the King's Topography in the Map Room, is the "South West View of the Collegiate Church of Saint Wilfrid, Ripon," by John Buckler, published 1809.

[43] Since they are placed immediately beneath the window sills, both the lower and upper string courses are four masonry courses higher than the corresponding strings on the interior.

This upper limit appears also to have been anticipated for the west wall of the nave between the towers, where a wall passage corresponding in height to the nave triforium arcade seems to have been indicated by the articulation of the west edge of the tower bay (pl. 37). Had the west facade been built as intended, the lower limit for this arcade would certainly have continued that of the triforium in the nave and towers.[44] Then the first story of windows throughout the towers and west facade was meant to correspond in height to the nave triforium (figs. 10, 11).

It was in the third stage (the second story of windows) that the most radical departure from the initial design of the west front took place. The intended upper limit of this story is strikingly indicated inside the north tower, where a corbel table juts from the nave wall just above the level of the string course over the clerestory inside the nave (pl. 49). This corbel table is like those used elsewhere on the twelfth-century church at the cornice level (pls. 14, 19) and, had the masonry above it been thickened to cover its projection, it would have been necessary to regard this feature as the cornice for a nave not designed to be flanked by towers. However, in addition to the evidence in the towers that they were planned and built with the nave is that this corbel table was left projecting, as if to receive a roof. That none of the other three walls of the tower has such a corbel table is because their design was modified before they were built. That a corbel table of this type was meant to support a roof[45] is confirmed by the use of one with almost identical format but different details to support the roof of the towers above the actual fourth stage (pl. 51). Moreover, none of the intermediate floors in the actual towers is supported by a corbel table. It is reasonable, then, to interpret this corbel table as representing not only the intended height of the third stage but also the terminal height of the towers. The same feature was also in the south tower but it has been chipped away. Nevertheless, it left a scar of the same size and at the same level, confirming the scheme originally intended of a west front in which the third stage was to be the same height as the nave clerestory.

The nature of the original design can be inferred from the dimensions already known or fixed by the nave. The interior of the square towers

---

This arrangement, normal in medieval architecture, was employed consistently on both the nave and west towers.

[44] One articulating feature of the nave exterior was not continued on the west towers: the string-course located at the springing of the triforium arches, hence also of the triforium window arches (where it undoubtedly served as an impost, as in the nave clerestory arcade). It could not be continued on the towers after the scale of the lower range of windows was altered, even if the change in decorative motifs had not excluded it from the new repertory.

[45] Another clue is in the west nave buttresses which bind the nave wall and the towers at their corner junction. Not only does the sloping termination of these buttresses coincide with the interior string-course above the clerestory arcade, indicating the roof line of the nave, but there is also no sign that the tower masonry would have continued upward beyond it. The thirteenth-century masonry which does rise from the buttress next to the tower wall clearly interrupts the intended termination of the buttress (pl. 47).

corresponds neatly to the width of the west bay (18 feet), so the two towers and the width of the nave (41 feet 6 inches) made a total internal width of 77 feet 6 inches, not counting the nave walls (plan 1). Since the walls of the nave and of the towers were designed to have internal passages and the outer tower buttresses to have stair vices, they necessarily account for more than 20 feet of additional thickness. Consequently, the total width of the facade was at least 100 feet in contrast to an external elevation of about 65 feet, counting a cornice and balustrade. Such proportions describe a version of the wide screen facades found in other English churches of the late twelfth and early thirteenth centuries, with the towers incorporated into the screen composition and probably rising no higher than the nave. The most famous example is the early thirteenth-century facade of Wells Cathedral, which is as elaborate as the Ripon west front would have been simple. Like Ripon's, the Wells facade has towers placed beyond the entire nave width. The intention of building only a screen facade may account for the rather shallow foundations which Scott reported he had found and to which he attributed the weakened state of the present towers in the nineteenth century.[46] A parallel existed in the west front of Selby (pl. 59), not far from Ripon, where the towers of the present twin-towered facade were added only in 1935 to a screen-like facade block which is also said to have had foundations insufficient to support tall towers.[47] At Ripon, the dramatic heightening of the west facade and the two towers (which formerly even had spires) can only have been intended to make a difference, that is to make a twin-towered facade out of a different type, such as the screen facade.

Ripon's intended screen facade represents a special category of the type associated primarily with English architecture, the towered screen which appears to be a facade block rather than a substantial wall. Like all varieties of screen facade this one does not purport to reflect the disposition of the structure behind it nor does it have a predetermined composition. Any insights we might gain into the details of the intended west front, then, must be inferred totally from the local context, and the structure itself. We have already seen that the three stories of the west front had been intended to reflect the height and the type of the respective three stories of the nave. Yet it is also clear that the decorative repertory had already been modified when construction began, so the actual articulation of the two stories with windows would not have exactly repeated that of the nave. Because structurally the west wall of the nave was integral with the earlier nave and tower elevations, which themselves were so closely related in articulation, this elevation almost certainly would have had a row of tall windows in the triforium story. Considering that the first story of windows in the towers was already committed when the decision to alter

---

[46] Scott, "Ripon Minster," 316–17.
[47] The Rev. J. A. P. Kent, *The Pictorial History of Selby Abbey* Pitkin "Pride of Britain" Books (London, 1968), 14, 23.

the overall composition of the west front was made, the middle story of the whole west facade was probably meant to be realized basically as it was built, albeit somewhat shorter across the west end of the nave. Because the nave was not meant to be vaulted, an oculus window in the upper story would have been inappropriate, so the second range of windows almost necessarily would have followed the first, but with a much reduced height, equal to the nave clerestory (pl. 62).

The aspect of the original design for the west front that remains to be reconstituted is the gabled termination to support the nave roof. A gable could be raised over the west wall of the nave, interrupting the continuity of the horizontal composition, or it could rise behind the west nave bays, defining the west front externally as a facade block and making possible a virtually flat roof over the west front. But since there were no tower piers to support an arch across the nave at this point, a strong gable could be constructed only over the west wall of the nave. Considering the long period of time necessary to complete both the nave and the west front, it is likely, for reasons of preservation and of utility, that the nave was roofed up to the west bays with a temporary timber gable before work on the west front had proceeded very far. The plausibility that such a procedure was followed rests upon the evidence that a much higher gable had to be built over the increased height of the west front. This evidence survives in the walls added above the clerestory in the west bays in order to make inner side faces for the heightened towers. It consists of a series of vertical indentations in the masonry of both elevations, indentations which appear to have been made to accommodate timbers for the higher roof required by the revised west facade (pl. 34). Such a higher section of roof could have been—indeed, in this case necessarily was—attached to the rest of the nave roof without benefit of a masonry gable. Yet, had the west front scheme not been revised, it is difficult to imagine how the nave roof could have been given a suitable permanent gable so that the west bays could have a flat roof. Consequently, the screen facade was almost certainly intended to have a gable over the nave west wall, very much like that at Wells Cathedral. In actuality, this screen facade (fig. 12) would have had more harmonious proportions than the present twin-towered facade (pl. 52) and such an original scheme would have made the size of the portals and windows appear normal for their respective roles in the composition of a west front.

## F. Conclusion

### The Intended Scheme for the Minster

Reconstitution of the twelfth-century structure of Ripon Minster is possible through careful analysis of the surviving fragments. Evidence within those fragments that the initial intentions of the patrons and builders were modified permits a reconstitution also of the original design for the church. Aside from the formal characteristics that can be known by looking at the fragments, the following were important aspects of the design.

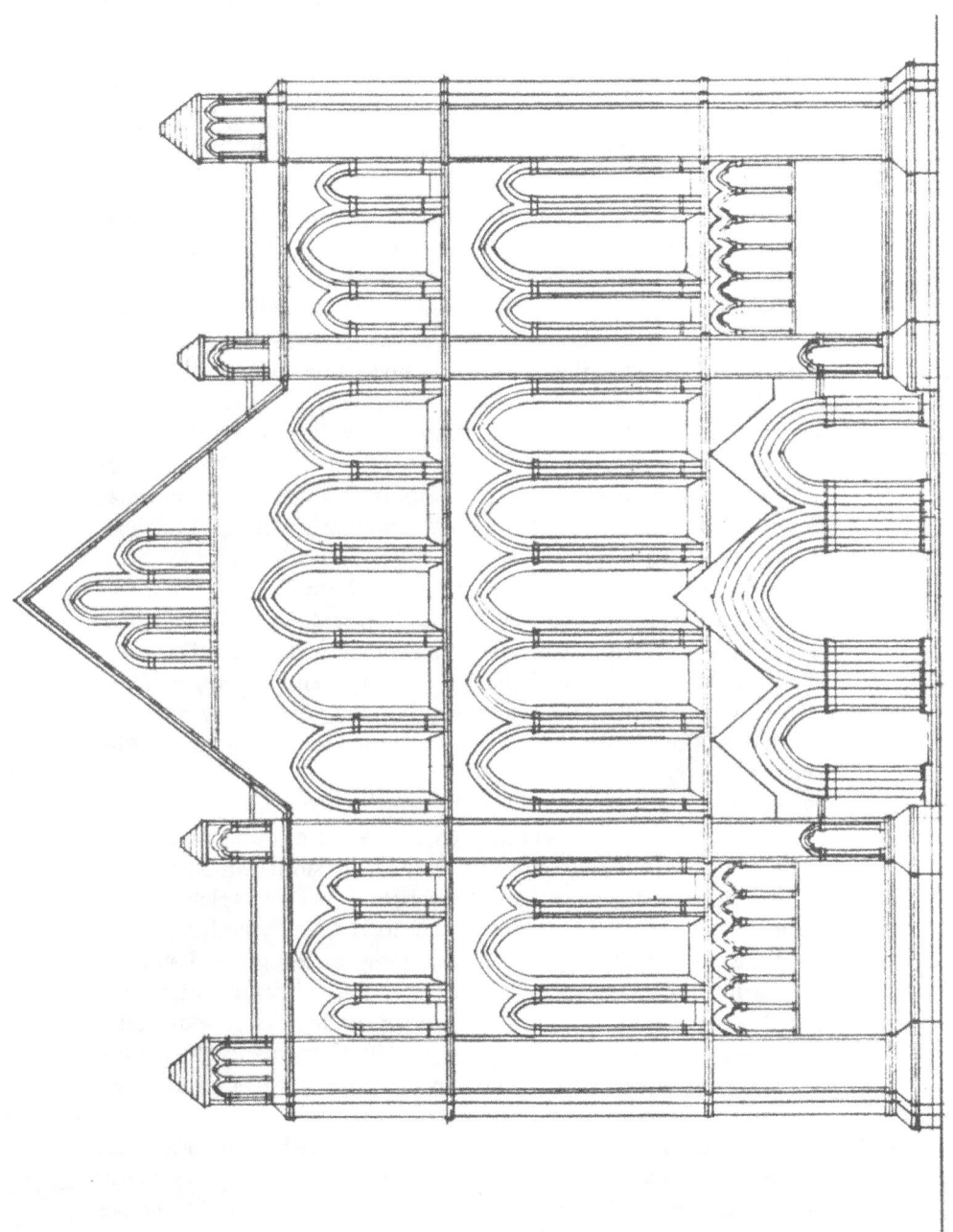

Fig. 12. Ripon Minster, west front, reconstitution of intended scheme.

1) The **choir** was six bays long, was aisled the full length and had a high, flat, east end. The three-story lateral elevation was to have been as we see it today except for the outer order of molding and shafts on the clerestory arcade. The east elevation was probably composed of three tall round-headed windows and a very large oculus which was surmounted by a relieving arch. The choir was intended to have quadripartite high vaults, undoubtedly similar in most respects to those in the aisles except that they would have been radically oblong (plans 1, 2; figs. 6, 7).
2) The **chapter house** was a two-story structure situated in the south corner between the choir and south transept. Originally, it consisted of a groin-vaulted undercroft of five and one half bays, divided into two chambers the eastern of which had an apse, and an unvaulted upper story also divided into two chambers with an eastern apse. Communicating directly with the south choir aisle, these upper chambers served as the chapter house and the vestry (plans 1, 2).
3) The **transept** arms were each three bays long with two vaulted, rectangular chapels on the east side. The east elevation resembled that of the choir except that the piers were compound rather than columnar bundles of shafts, because they framed separate openings in a wall rather than supporting a continuous arcade. The terminal elevations were intended to have three tall, round-headed windows in the lower story, a band triforium of probably nine arches, and probably an oculus window in the clerestory, framed by an arcaded passage. The west elevation would have repeated the tall windows and triforium of the terminal elevation (but divided into bays), with a clerestory like that of the east elevation. The transepts were intended to have quadripartite, high vaults (fig. 9).
4) The **crossing** was laid out on a slightly trapezoidal plan, anticipating the extra width of the aisleless nave. Its arches were round and it was intended to support a lantern tower, undoubtedly similar in basic composition to the two-story structure it ultimately received (plans 1, 2).
5) The aisleless **nave** was always intended to have a flat, wooden ceiling. Its elevations were composed of a blank zone for the ground story, a very tall triforium arcade and a clerestory. The triforium alternated blind double bays of narrow units and lighted single bays of wide units. All the units were subdivided into two (fig. 10). Presumably the clerestory would have followed the same pattern but with shorter units (fig. 11).
6) The **west front,** with two towers flanking the nave, had already been planned when the nave was laid out, probably from the very beginning of the project. The interiors of the towers and the west wall of the nave were intended to reflect the dimensions and basic forms of the nave triforium and clerestory. Open to the top on the interior, the towers were to have been no taller than the nave, forming a very wide, towered, screen facade (fig. 12).

## The Minster as it was actually constructed

The design for Ripon Minster was subjected to modification several times before the structure was completed. In actual form it was erected as follows.

1) The **choir** was constructed as intended through the triforium story. Then a decision was made not to raise high vaults, resulting in the necessity to add ornament to the clerestory arcade in order to make a rational account of the elevation articulation. The choir was completed with a flat, wooden ceiling (pl. 3, fig. 8).
2) The **chapter house** was probably completed as intended, but very much simpler in the upper story than in its late medieval form, part of which survives to the present day (plans 1, 2).
3) The **transepts** were modified in the manner of the choir when the high vaults were not built. The most striking alteration was to the design for the terminal walls, which were divided into bays. The triforium was built with fewer units on a larger scale than planned and the clerestory was totally revised to repeat the arcade of the west elevation (plans 1, 2; pls. 20, 23, 27, 28).
4) The **crossing tower** was completed after an indeterminate lapse in construction and following a significant modification of style. However, its two stages, consisting of an unlighted triforium and a clerestory, are probably similar to those originally planned (pl. 30).
5) The **nave** was modified and completed in the same building phase with the crossing tower. The revision in design was addressed to the clerestory, where the alternation of blind and lighted bays was reversed, resulting in a highly unusual composition with the windows of the two upper stories arranged with staggered axial alignment (fig. 10).
6) The towered-screen **west front** was modified, just as its intended upper story was begun, to make a twin-towered facade with tall, four-story towers flanking the nave (pl. 52).

## The Sequence of Construction

The sequence of construction in Ripon Minster began at the east end and proceeded, in a largely straightforward fashion, in phases, toward the west. There is no reason to suppose that the entire church was not laid out at once, because there are no disjunctures in the plan or breaks in construction at ground level to suggest any modification of the original spatial disposition. The phases of construction can be identified in the superstructure where they can be recognized through formal modifications and masonry breaks, even though a large portion of the building is now lost to us.

**Phase one** (fig. 13) saw the entire church laid out and the superstructure begun at the east end. The choir was constructed through the triforium story, including the roofs and vaults of the aisle. The whole ground story

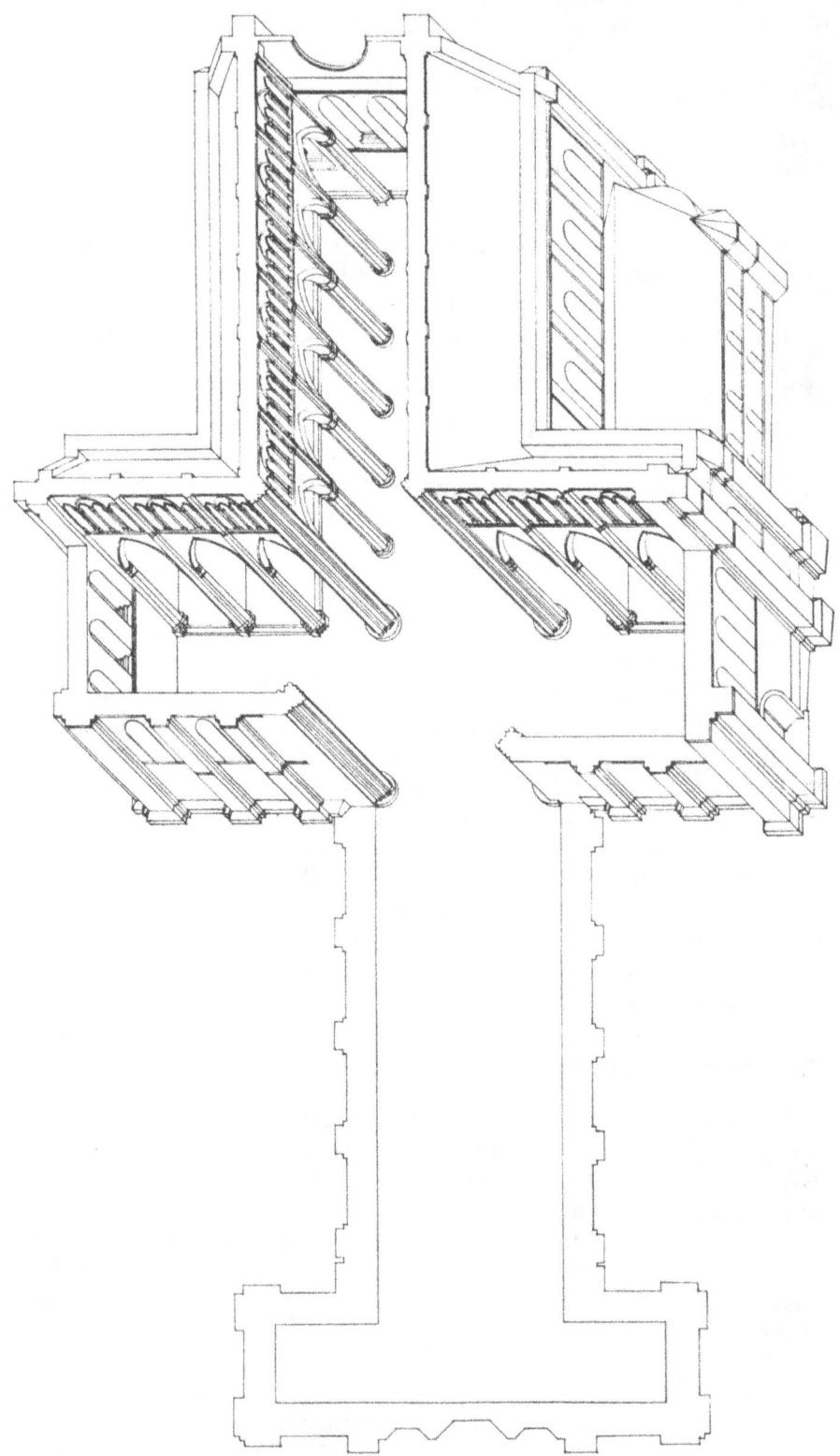

Fig. 13. Ripon Minster, extent of construction in Stage One.

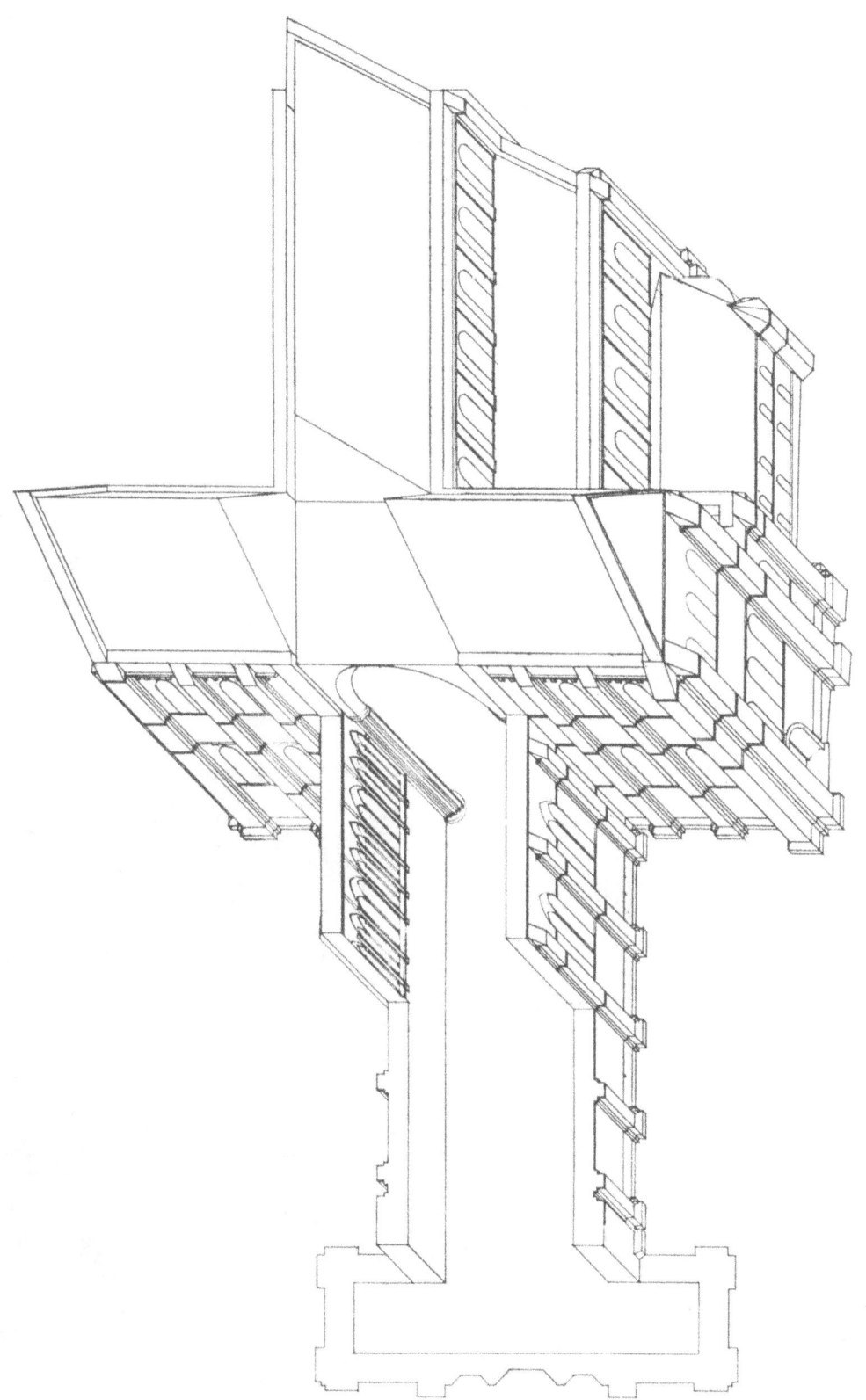

FIG. 14. Ripon Minster, extent of construction in Stage Two.

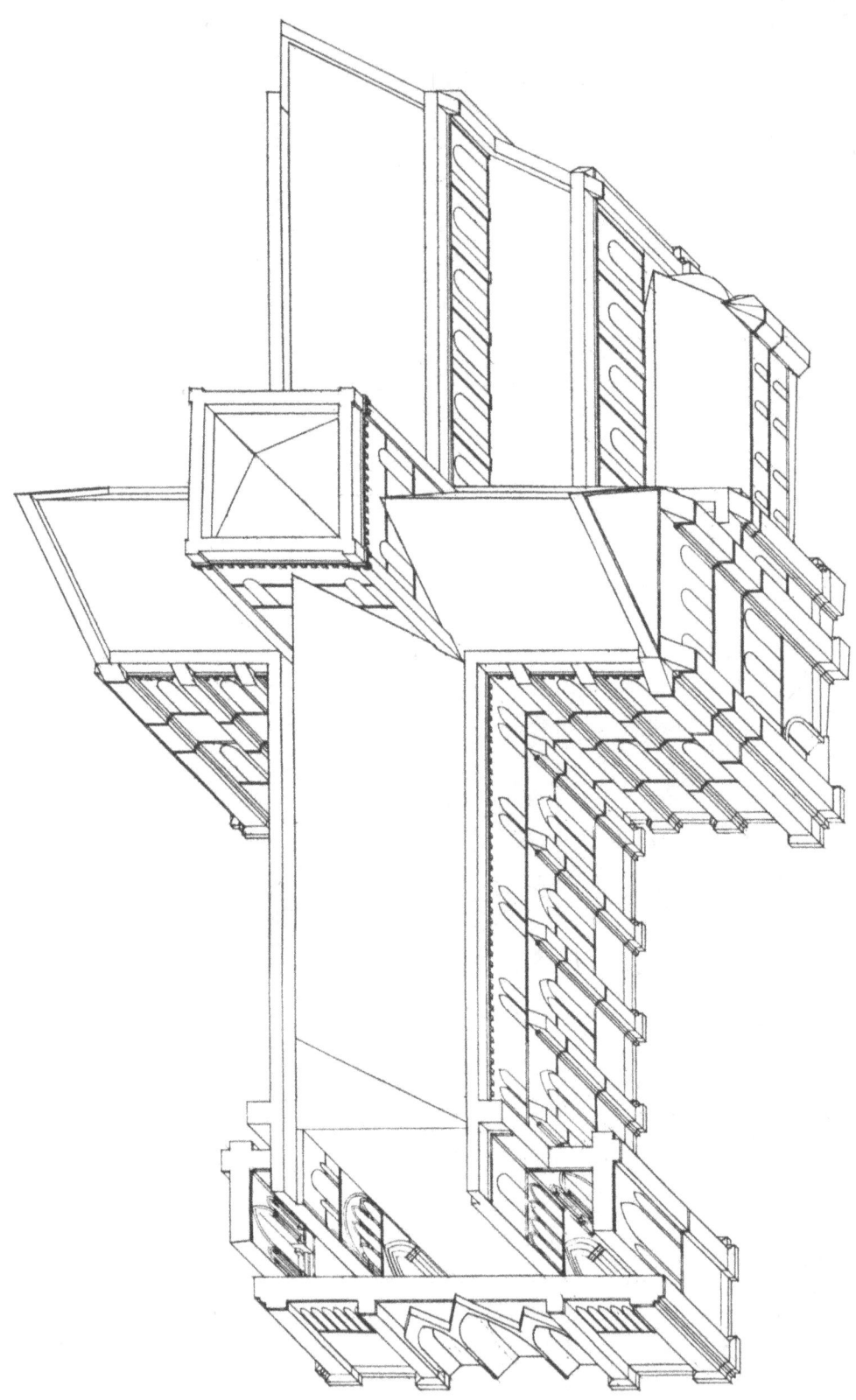

FIG. 15. Ripon Minster, extent of construction in Stage Three.

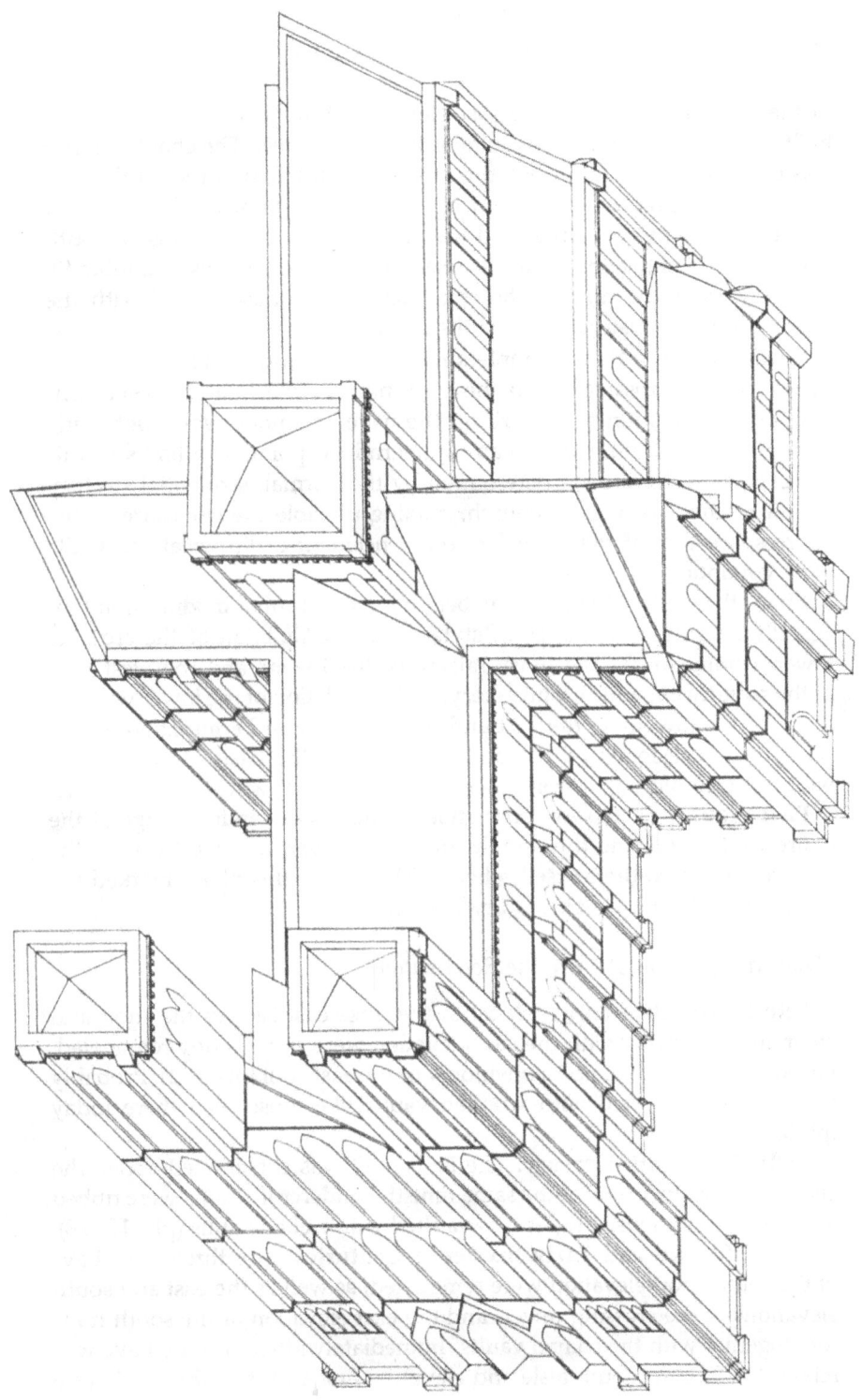

FIG. 16. Ripon Minster, as completed at the end of Stage Four.

of the north transept and the east elevation through the triforium were built, including the roof and vaults of the east chapels. The chapter house was introduced as an afterthought, during construction of the south choir aisle wall but preceding work on the south transept arm. The east wall of the south transept chapel and the ground story of the transept south wall were raised together with the chapter house which was undoubtedly roofed at the same time as the choir aisle. This phase ceased with the decision not to construct high vaults in the choir and transepts.

**Phase two** (fig. 14) saw completion of the choir and both transept arms, as well as the crossing up to the beginning of the lantern tower. Undoubtedly at this juncture work on the nave was underway, continuing through the triforium story to an undetermined point. The limits of this phase seem to have been determined by the normal, sequential strategy of construction for a great church, making possible the enclosure of the entire space east of the nave for commencement of liturgical use while work continued on the rest.

**Phase three** (fig. 15) marks the beginning of a formal modification that actually constitutes a change of style. It saw completion of the crossing tower, completion of the nave, raising of the towers and the west wall of the nave through the ground story, and completion of the lower window range of the towers on the east and outer side faces. Termination of this phase was occasioned by the decision to revise the basic design for the west front, converting it from a screen facade into a twin-towered facade.

**Phase four** (fig. 16) saw completion of the lower window range of the entire west facade and the completion of the towers and west wall of the nave according to the revised scheme. The end of this phase marked the completion of the twelfth-century church.

*Major Modifications Prior to the Reformation*

**Late Thirteenth Century.** Most of the three east bays of the choir and choir aisles, together with the east elevation were significantly remodeled, introducing the great traceried window of the east wall (pls. 1, 2). Probably the choir was vaulted with wooden vaults like those seen there today (pl. 3).

**Early Fourteenth Century.** The Lady Loft was constructed above the chapter house. Probably at the same time the undercroft vaults were ribbed and the chapter house proper was vaulted with ribbed vaults (pls. 17, 18).

**Late Fifteenth and Early Sixteenth Centuries.** The three west bays of the south choir elevation were remodeled, as well as the east and south elevations of the crossing tower, and the east elevation of the south transept together with the chapel vaults. Immediately afterward the nave was rebuilt (pl. 32), the south aisle and elevation first and then the north aisle and elevation.

# PART TWO

# HISTORICAL INTERPRETATION

## 2. THE DATES OF CONSTRUCTION

The year when Ripon was begun—the date that locates the minster's design in its historical place—is not revealed by any known document or inscription. For purposes of determining the date there are only some vague guidelines. For instance, we know that the patron, Roger of Pont l'Evêque, archbishop of York, died in 1181; hence the church was definitely begun earlier. We also know that the surviving twelfth-century fragments of the church contain many formal features that are characteristic of Cistercian architecture constructed in the North early in the last third of the century; so Ripon is easily placed between the late 1160s and 1181. But a more precise date depends upon fixing the design's chronological relationship to these buildings. This task is difficult, though, because few of the Cistercian structures are precisely dated either and even their chronological sequence is subject to debate. Accordingly, Ripon must be dated in a roundabout way, first by examining the sequence of construction among the Cistercian churches and then by establishing Ripon's position within this sequence. Such a broad excursion, however, can serve another and equally valuable purpose at the same time, that of determining the extent to which the Ripon design was derived from the Cistercian tradition.

### RIPON AND THE CISTERCIAN ARCHITECTURAL TRADITION

The association of Ripon with Cistercian architecture began when John Bilson, in the conclusion to his famous study of Cistercian architecture in England (published in 1909), cited Ripon as the medium through which the simplicity and restraint of Cistercian architecture influenced the beginning of the Gothic style in the north of England.[1] Since then, Ripon has been regarded by historians of English architecture as an off-shoot of Cistercian Gothic, an imitation of a provincial aspect of the Gothic phenomenon in France.[2] Albeit unchallenged as the earliest non-Cistercian

---

[1] John Bilson, "The Architecture of the Cistercians, with Special Reference to Some of Their Earlier Churches in England," *Archaeological Journal*, 66 (1909): 185–280, see especially 279–280.

[2] In chronological order the more important opinions are as follows: Sir Alfred Clapham, *English Romanesque Architecture after the Conquest* (Oxford, 1934), 93; Geoffrey Webb, *Architecture in Britain: The Middle Ages*, Pelican History of Art (Harmondsworth, 1956) 82–83; Nikolaus Pevsner, *Yorkshire, The West Riding*, The Buildings of England (Harmondsworth, 1959) 403; Peter Kidson, pt. 1, *A History of English Architecture*, (Harmondsworth; 1965) 70–71; Peter Fergusson, "The South Transept Elevation of Byland Abbey," *Journal of the British Archaeological Association*, 3rd ser., 38 (1975): 170–171.

example of Gothic architecture still extant in the North (and probably actually the earliest), the significance accorded to Ripon has been overshadowed by that of Canterbury and largely because of this attribution to derivative character.

To be sure, the ascription of Cistercian influence in general at Ripon— and of Cistercian Gothic influence in particular— is no idle association. An inventory of features at Ripon which are associated with Cistercian architecture in England—or which can be found nowhere else in England in a form so closely parallel—makes an impressive dossier of circumstantial evidence. These features appear variously in the church or monastic complex of the abbeys of Buildwas, Kirkstall, Roche, Byland, and Furness, and portions of the monastic complex of Fountains Abbey, all designed between ca. 1150 and ca. 1180, as well as in others, such as Dundrennan and Jervaulx Abbeys, which were definitely begun after Ripon. The formal similarities include such large-scale aspects of design as the layout of liturgical spaces and the composition of elevations and vaults, but by far the greatest number of resemblances reside in individual structural elements. All these features are located in the choir and transepts and are most conveniently identified through a systematic observation tour.

In the choir aisles, the vault responds on the aisle walls (pl. 13) are triple shaft responds, corbeled out at the window sill, leaving an unbroken expanse of wall below. Although the church at Byland has the only really parallel surviving example (pl. 65), the principle of corbeling vault responds was established as early as the nave of Fountains (1140s) and a composition of the Ripon type was implied by the much shorter corbel shaft in the nave of Kirkstall. The waterleaf capitals of these responds are virtually a signature of Cistercian architecture from the late 1150s on, appearing in various locations in some later portions of Buildwas and also at Roche, Byland (pl. 63) and Furness (pl. 69). The molded imposts with a polygonal, or semi-octagonal, plan also occurred at Buildwas (the presbytery vaults) and in various monastic buildings at Fountains and Kirkstall. On the exterior of the aisles at Ripon, waterleaf capitals are used above the shafts framing the windows. At the base of the exterior, the plinth— composed of a projecting molding and a series of superimposed chamfers beneath (pl. 19)—is parallel in type to those characteristically found on Cistercian churches, beginning with the late parts of Buildwas, and especially including those of Roche (pl. 56) and Byland.

In the lateral choir elevations, virtually all the features except the clustered bay-division shafts appear in one or more of this group of Cistercian churches. The main arcade especially bears out this kinship. The molding of the pier plinths (pl. 5) recalls the various plinths used at Byland (pl. 67), and especially those of circular plan. The molded "attic" bases (pl. 5) are by no means exclusively Cistercian, but they are similar to those used in the Kirkstall cloister, at Byland (pl. 67), and at Furness (pl. 68). The pier trunk (pl. 5), basically columnar but composed as a bundle of shafts, is of a type not only notably Cistercian but also one which seems to have evolved in the nave of Kirkstall (pl. 61) during the course of construction. The eight-shafted pier of Ripon has parallels at Roche (pl. 62), Byland (pl. 67) and Furness (pl. 68); but the particular version at Ripon, with eight round shafts, occurs specifically at Furness. The plain, inverted-bell capitals (pl. 7) had a conspicuous introduction at Roche (pl. 56) and were adopted also at Byland (pl. 64) in the upper stories. The impost profile (pl. 7), composed of a flat upper face (quirked just below its middle), poised over a large hollow and a rolled necking, has close counterparts at Furness (pl. 69), Byland (pl. 63), and the Kirkstall cloister. The profile of the main arcade soffits (pl. 4), consisting of a keeled center roll flanked by angular fillets and round angle rolls, occurs also at Byland (pl. 63) and at Furness (where the angle rolls were channeled with a hollow, pl. 69). Above the main arcade, both the triforium and the clerestory arcades (fig. 8, pl. 3) are almost exactly the same as those at Byland Abbey (fig. 17, pl. 64).

The planned scheme for high vaults in the choir and transepts (figs. 6, 9) would have employed quadripartite vaults, the same type that was already standard with the Cistercians but not yet so in French and English Gothic architecture. Such vaults had already been erected over the sanctuaries of Buildwas and Kirkstall and were constructed also over the whole church at Roche (pl. 56). Indeed, the intention at Ripon to vault the choir and transepts but not the nave recalls the earlier Cistercian custom of vaulting only the sanctuary, as at Buildwas and Kirkstall, while the springing of the vaults from the base line of the clerestory, unknown in other early Gothic churches in England, is significantly similar to Roche.

Concerning similarities of a larger scale, the proportions of the choir and transept elevations (fig. 7, pl. 20) at Ripon are remarkably like those of the surviving transept elevations at Roche (pl. 56). The proportions at Roche make the main arcade approximately equal to the two upper stories while the clerestory is about the same height as the main arcade piers (not counting plinths) and the blind triforium arcade is about the same height as the main arcade arches. Such a composition is sufficiently rare in earlier structures that the similarity between Roche and Ripon in this case implies actual filiation. Moreover, as we also saw in the reconstitution, circumstantial evidence at Ripon indicates that the east elevation was probably composed of three tall, round-headed windows surmounted by a large oculus (fig. 6). An east elevation with a large oculus has been reconstituted at Kirkstall[3] and it is possible that Roche had one also, even with three tall windows beneath it.

Finally, in the transepts, the liturgical arrangement of eastern chapels as a sequence of distinct spaces (pl. 20, plan 1) is undeniably a Cistercian feature, evident still at Fountains, Buildwas, Kirkstall (pl. 60), and Roche (pl. 56). The functional distinction between the types of piers appropriate

---

[3] William Henry St. John Hope, "Kirkstall Abbey," *Publications of the Thoresby Society*, 16(1907): 1–72.

to a continuous lateral elevation and to the entrances of separate chapels resulted in the use of columnar, shaft-bundle piers for the former and compound piers for the latter, a distinction that is expressly characteristic of Roche. Corresponding to the vertical shafts which articulate the bays of the transept east elevations, the tall shafts on the west elevations which were corbeled out at the window sill likewise reflect the arrangement at Roche, although that arrangement must be inferred from the present ruins.

These abundant similarities between Ripon and Cistercian architecture in England make specific what has long been impressionistically understood as a generality. Ripon's architectural background appears to be so heavily Cistercian that the twelfth-century minster can virtually be regarded as a direct offshoot of the Cistercian Gothic style and the conduit of that tradition to architecture in general in the North of England. In order to make clear why this impression has gained wide currency, this catalog of similarities has been presented here without distinguishing between buildings that are either definitely or possibly earlier than Ripon and those that are contemporaries and could be slightly later. In view of such heavily Cistercian associations surely no earlier scholar surveying English architecture can be blamed for having stopped at that point. However, once the development of Cistercian architecture in England has been examined, as Bilson and others after him have done, and once the beginning of the Gothic style in the North of England has been investigated, it becomes clear that the amount of expressly Cistercian influence at Ripon and the degree of its significance varies according to where Ripon fits in the relative chronology.

We must recall at the outset that Ripon appeared in Yorkshire in a generation of architecture dominated by Cistercian abbeys. Although two important non-Cistercian buildings of this period—Archbishop Roger's new choir for York Minster and the early buildings for the Abbey of St. Mary at York—are almost entirely lost to us, the fact remains that construction designed for the Cistercians was the trend-setting phenomenon. Indeed, Cistercian taste became a pervasive influence not only in Yorkshire but also throughout the North. Yet Cistercian architecture in England was never uniform in design or immune to non-Cistercian influence nor did it develop in an unbroken line of filiation. Stated more directly, Cistercian architecture, despite its characteristic simplicity, could be many different things. Indeed, as Bilson demonstrated, during the early period the Cistercian program in English abbeys was carried out largely in Anglo-Norman terms.[4] Only with Roche (among those abbeys still sufficiently extant that we can reliably visualize them) is there a definite break with the Anglo-Norman tradition. By scholarly consensus, it signals Gothic influence from northeastern France, although not the most progressive strain

---

[4] John Bilson, "The Architecture of Kirkstall Abbey Church, with Some General Remarks on the Architecture of the Cistercians," *Publications of the Thoresby Society*, 16 (1907): 123; and idem, "Cistercians", 223–224, 238–240.

in that region. After Roche there were so many deviations from French practice, despite the wholehearted adoption of a number of features derived from French Gothic precedents, that Cistercian buildings in England must be regarded as English Gothic. The aspect of Ripon that appears to be Cistercian, then, is actually related to diverse aspects of a heterogeneous tradition. Moreover, in the context of Yorkshire in the period ca.1150–ca.1180, Cistercian architecture by dint of its dominance was simply the nexus of new ideas in building, some of which would undoubtedly have turned up in new construction sponsored by anyone else. Consequently, it is necessary to know exactly where Ripon fits in the relative chronology of Cistercian architecture in order to determine the extent and nature of Cistercian influence in its design.

Although definite dates cannot be assigned to all the Cistercian churches, the relative chronology of the post-Fountains Abbey group has provoked little controversy. The church of Buildwas Abbey is known to have been begun shortly after this Savignac foundation was absorbed by the Cistercian Order in 1147.[5] Kirkstall Abbey church was begun in 1152 and completed in 1178, and its monastic buildings, such as the chapter house and cloister, were built in the last decade of this campaign.[6] Some of the monastic buildings of Fountains Abbey were constructed in those same years.[7] The estimated date of the ruins of Roche Abbey church has fluctuated more than that for any other structure in this group, that is from ca.1160 to ca.1175, but ca.1170 appears to fit best within the general English context.[8] Most scholars have regarded the abbey churches of both Byland and Furness to be later than Roche but without placing one of them before the other. It is known that the new monastic complex of Byland was occupied by the monks in 1177, but most scholars assume that the church had just been begun, only to be interrupted and then revised in design when construction was resumed a few years later.[9] Furness, which is generally thought to have been built from west to east, has

---

[5] Bilson, "Cistercians," 199.

[6] Hope, "Kirkstall Abbey," 1–72; Bilson, "Kirkstall Abbey," 73–140.

[7] William Henry St. John Hope, "Fountains Abbey," *Yorkshire Archaeological Journal*, 15 (1900) 269–402; and R. Gilyard-Beer, *Fountains Abbey, Yorkshire*, Ministry of Works Guide, (London, 1970), 4–74, *passim*.

[8] The modest literature on Roche has been surveyed by Peter Fergusson in "Roche Abbey: The Source and Date of the Eastern Remains," *Journal of the British Archaeological Association*, 3rd ser., 34, 1971: 30–42, in which he proposes for the first time a date as late as ca.1175. Earlier attributions range from an early date of ca.1160 (Kidson, *English Architecture*, 67–68) to ca.1165 (Bilson, "Cistercians," 200) and are centered on ca.1170 (Jean Bony, "French Influences on the Origins of English Gothic Architecture," *Journal of the Warburg and Courtauld Institutes*, 12, 1949: 6), the last of which is, I believe, the most accurate.

[9] In chronological order these opinions are Clapham, *English Romanesque Architecture*, 161; Peers, *Byland Abbey*, plan; T. S. R. Boase, *English Art, 1100–1216* Oxford History of English Art, (Oxford, 1953), 139; Webb, *Architecture in Britain*, 83; Pevsner, *Yorkshire, North Riding*, 94. Only Fergusson ("Byland," 168–169), places the completion of the eastern arm in the 1160s. The 1177 date is based on the Byland cartulary, preserved as B.M. Ms. Egerton 2823, and printed with other material in William Dugdale, *Monasticon Anglicanum* (London, 1825) 5: 343–354.

features that place its design around 1180.[10] Since Ripon is known to have been begun anew by Roger of Pont l'Evêque, archbishop of York from 1154 to 1181, it is clearly later than the beginning of Buildwas or Kirkstall. It is necessary, though, to determine Ripon's chronological position with respect to Roche, Furness, and Byland in order to determine the nature of its relationship to Cistercian architecture.

Roche, by nearly all accounts, was earlier than Ripon but usually its anteriority is merely asserted as a judgment rather than justified by discussion of specific comparative details. There are, as we have seen, numerous similar features of various types which can serve as points of archaeological reference. Curiously, though, only a few of them are actually chronologically telling because their differences do not denote sequential development or distinction of kind. For instance, the parallel use of shaft-bundle piers in both churches will not prove one earlier than the other because the keeled shafts of Roche (pl. 62) and the round shafts of Ripon (pl. 5) can both be traced through the entire period when shaft-bundle piers were fashionable. Likewise, the angle-roll molding which frames the window openings of the two lower stages at Roche (pl. 56) does not necessarily represent a more highly developed state than the undecorated window openings of Ripon (pl. 20). Typical of specific features that do seem to indicate a chronological relationship is the plain inverted-bell capital. At Roche, the bell capitals (pl. 56) are taller and stiffer than those at Ripon (pl. 7) suggesting that they are relatively archaic because less sensitively attuned to the association of weight and support than those of Ripon.[11] Likewise, the hollows of shaft bases and imposts are slightly deeper, slightly more curved at Ripon, suggesting a marginally later stage of development. But the most convincing difference is that the Ripon elevation is systematically articulated and embellished with shafts and arch moldings in a manner that remained the norm for all but the most purely utilitarian architecture through the next several decades. The severity of Roche, with its lower story embellished and the upper two stories unadorned, was never repeated (at least not in extant architecture) in the north of England by either Cistercian or other patrons. In the final analysis, the relative position of Roche and Ripon is decided by the obviously closer relationship of Ripon to Byland and the very much more advanced plan and elevation at Byland compared to those aspects of Roche.

Byland and Ripon, as is clear from the catalog of features shared by Ripon and Cistercian architecture, were very similar not only in numerous specific features but also in design, especially the elevation. Although

---

[10] W. H. St. John Hope, "The Abbey of St. Mary-in-Furness, Lancashire," *Transactions of the Cumberland and Westmoreland Antiquarian and Archaeological Society*, 16 (1909): 221–302; and S. C. Kaines-Smith, "Furness Abbey," *Victoria History of the Counties of England, Lancashire*, 8 (London, 1914), 287ff.

[11] See discussion of this difference in chapter 4.

Byland is now in a very ruinous state, enough survives to reconstitute the elevation and also to know that construction was interrupted after only a small amount of work had been accomplished, namely, the south nave aisle wall and the ground story of the outer wall of the south transept.[12] It is impossible to know whether or not the elevation initially intended would have been as much like that at Ripon as the one actually constructed, but the similarity of the half-pier of the main arcade (pl. 63), abutting the south transept terminal wall, to the adjacent freestanding piers suggests that both the plan and the elevation actually constructed at Byland were only slightly altered from the original scheme. Recently, Peter Fergusson has established an accurate reconstitution of the elevation actually constructed (fig. 17), showing that the arcades of the triforium and clerestory were more nearly like those at Ripon than had been previously understood.[13]

The relative chronology of Byland and Ripon, however, depends upon four quite distinct kinds of differences between their otherwise highly similar elevations (figs. 7, 17). The first of these differences emanates from the plan (fig. 18, plan 1). Byland was the first Cistercian church in England to have an aisled choir and aisled transepts rather than a plain rectangular choir and a row of separated rectangular chapels behind the transept east elevation. Consequently, the main arcade of the transept, as well as that of the choir, employed columnar rather than compound piers (although both could be articulated as a shaft-bundle, as at Ripon). While the Byland and Ripon plans are so different as to preclude relationship on that score, the enormous similarity between the two elevations makes it highly unlikely that, after Byland, Ripon would have imitated the traditional Cistercian transept chapels which Byland had rendered obsolete.

The second difference between the two churches is that Byland was designed from the start not to have clusters of bay-division shafts, hence no response for high vaults.[14] This intention is manifest in the way the two orders of the clerestory arcade (pl. 64) are arranged, with the lower order of shafts and molding recessed behind the normal wall plane and the upper order regularized to correspond with this wall plane. Because the upper order was not a substitute for wall arches of high vaults, as at

---

[12] See the stages of construction in the archaeological plan by Sir Charles Peers in his *Byland Abbey, Yorkshire*, Ministry of Works Guides, London, 1934). This break in construction has not been much discussed in print but will undoubtedly be fully treated by Peter Fergusson in his forthcoming work on Byland Abbey. The evidence of the break is easily observed and, at the relevant point in the south transept, is especially apparent in the modification of the main arcade piers. The early half-pier on the south wall stands on a low plinth of rectangular, compound composition while beneath the first free-standing pier a tall, octagonal lower plinth is provided. At the same point, in the chapel vaults, the rib profile changes to include a hollow channel in the central roll of its triple torus composition.

[13] Fergusson, "Byland Abbey," 156–160.

[14] Fergusson, "Byland Abbey," 158, 160, has shown that Byland almost certainly had a wooden barrel vault rising from the top of the walls. Fragments of the wall arch for this vault remains in the south elevation of the south transept above the level of the clerestory.

FIG. 17. Byland Abbey, south transept east elevation, reconstituted by Peter Fergusson. Reproduced with permission from *Journal of the British Archaeological Association*, 37, 1975.

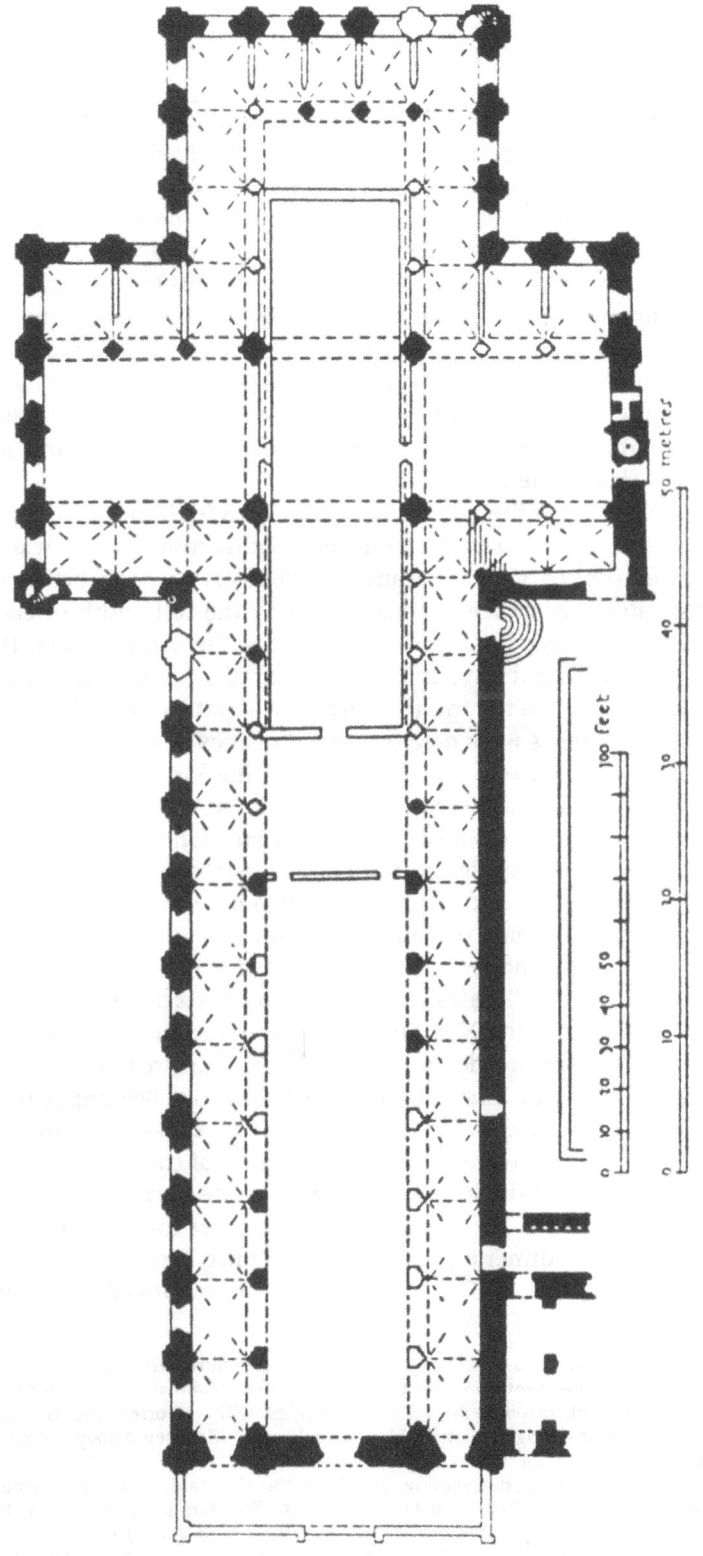

FIG. 18. Byland Abbey, plan. Reproduced with permission of Oxford University Press from Alfred Clapham, *English Romanesque Architecture after the Conquest*, Oxford, 1934.

Ripon (pl. 22), there were no projecting clerestory shafts to justify multiple responds at the bay division, reducing the quintuple clusters of Ripon to single shafts and canceling the implicit relationship of wall shafts and vault arches. Indeed, as the shaft in the east corner of the south transept (pl. 64) demonstrates, they were corbeled out halfway down the main arcade spandrels, thereby reducing the bay-division shafts to nothing more than vertical punctuation. Since this new kind of vertical articulation was widely employed in the succeeding generation of (mostly unvaulted) architecture in the north of England—for instance, Old Malton Priory and Whitby Abbey (pl. 70)—and since the Ripon articulation, with its bundles of complete shafts, was not repeated more than once,[15] the Byland arrangement was clearly the later of the two.

The third difference, in the articulation of the arcades in the two upper stories (figs. 7, 17), followed partly from the original intention at Byland not to build high ribbed vaults. Because the clerestory was to be unencumbered by vaults, its arcade needed to occupy the full width of each bay in order not to leave awkward intervals. For the same reason, the pointed side arches did not have to be lower than the round center arch. Similarly, in order to make the triforium arcade compatible with the clerestory, its blind side arches were heightened to the apex of the center arch. When this alteration occurred, the visual logic of the Ripon triforium design, composed of a four-part band arcade superimposed upon a reduced false-tribune opening, was violated. Such a modification indicates a shift of emphasis in the elevation design from articulation conceived in terms of structural composition to articulation conceived in terms of ornamental pattern, an unmistakable sign of derivative character.

The fourth difference concerns the technique used to make the clerestory passages (pls. 22, 64). Wall passages had been a conspicuous feature of English architecture since the Norman Conquest and in them the portion that separated the open arcade in each bay from that in the next had always been covered with a round-arched tunnel vault. Beginning with the generation of Ripon and Byland, however, the passages were covered with straight lintels. There were two distinct methods of constructing such a passage: in one method the impost above the arcade capitals continued across the passage to form the lintel while in the other the lintel was set above the impost. The former type had appeared once before in England, in Durham Castle in the 1160s,[16] and it was also employed, probably

---

[15] The one likely repetition was at Bardney Abbey, in Lincolnshire, where the excavated ruins revealed compound pier plinths in which radial response to diagonal ribs in high vaults seemed to be indicated. This response would be meaningless without corresponding shafts from the piers to the vault springers. See Sir Harold Brakspear, "Bardney Abbey," *Archaeological Journal*, 79 (1922): 13, 24.

[16] This wall passage occurs in the window arcade of the Constable's Hall of Durham Castle, illustrated in Webb, *Architecture in Britain*, pl. 62A. The date is most likely in the 1160s, for which see W. T. Jones "Durham Castle," *The Victoria History of the Counties of England, Durham*, vol. no. 3 (London, 1928) 78, 81–82; and H. M. Colvin, *The History of the King's Works* (London, 1963) 1: 58.

without direct filiation, in the new eastern arm of Canterbury Cathedral (pl. 57). The latter type appeared first at Ripon (pl. 22) and Byland (pl. 64) and then spread through the North. At Ripon, the lintel is underlined on the wall side of the passage by a continuous molded string-course, which repeats the profile of the imposts above the arcade capitals. At Byland, this string-course disappears and it was never used again in any of the subsequent appearances of this type of wall passage, for instance, at Lanercost (pl. 71), Jedburgh (pl. 72), Kelso, and Hexham. The string-course, then, must be regarded as an element that originally had seemed necessary to the structural rationale of this particular wall passage technique but which was subsequently judged unimportant and eliminated. From this as well as the other three differences between Ripon and Byland, one must conclude that Ripon is the earlier.

Furness figures very much less prominently than Roche and Byland in the catalog of similarities with Ripon and indeed its general design is very different. Yet the close parallel between the transept and (alternating) nave piers (with their bundles of eight round shafts, (pl. 69), their shaft-base and impost profiles, the transept chapel rib profiles, and the soffits of the main arcade (pl. 69) and their counterparts in the Ripon choir (pls. 4, 5, 6), make Furness the kind of example which seems to prove the Cistercian heritage of Ripon. Two details, however, indicate that Furness was slightly later than Byland, hence than Ripon also. The first is the use of round molded capitals and imposts on the plain columnar piers which alternate with shaft-bundle piers in the nave. Such capitals and imposts are known elsewhere in this period in the crypt of the Trinity Chapel of Canterbury Cathedral, securely dated to 1179.[17] Since Canterbury is a structure of capital architectural significance, the appearance of molded capitals there would probably have preceded their use at provincial Furness by at least a year or so.[18] Second, when the flanking tori of the main arcade soffits were channeled with a concave groove, they imitated the treatment of the central torus of the Byland south transept chapel ribs (pl. 66), which belong to its revised, actually-constructed, state. This rare detail occurs earlier in a capital structure in France, the south transept of Soissons Cathedral (pl. 76), late 1170s, where it is very much at home. Because Byland is stylistically much closer to Soissons than is Furness, and has its own direct French connections as well as indirect ones, it seems to possess this type of molding with more immediacy than does Furness. Hence Furness appears to be slightly later than both Byland and Ripon by dint of its derivative, provincial character.

---

[17] See the account of Gervase of Canterbury and accompanying interpretation in the Rev. Robert Willis, *The Architectural History of Canterbury Cathedral* (London: 1845) 51–52, and 92–93.

[18] I am indebted to Jean Bony for pointing out to me (in January, 1972) the close similarity and the likely anteriority of the Canterbury examples. Alternatively, the basic form of the Furness capitals could have been inspired directly from Bertaucourt-les-Dames, ca.1160–1170 (see discussion in chapter 4 and pl. 74), where both columnar and shaft-bundle piers were used in alternation, as at Furness.

From the comparisons, it appears to be safe to conclude that with respect to the Cistercian tradition Ripon was begun after Roche but before Byland and Furness. When the similarities from these last two churches are removed from the Ripon catalog, the apparent Cistercian influence in the minster assumes a very different character. For instance, in the lateral elevation of the choir only one literally similar decorative feature (the plain inverted-bell capital) and one virtually similar feature (the pier with a bundle of eight shafts), both from Roche, remain. In the choir aisles only the corbeled vault respond ensemble (with triple shafts, waterleaf capitals, and polygonal imposts), derived variously from Kirkstall, Buildwas, and Roche, remains. And if the quadripartite high-ribbed vaults planned for the choir and transepts are parallel to Cistercian precedents, the system of responds planned for them exists together with the same type of vaults only in a non-Cistercian context (a point to be discussed more fully in the fourth chapter), a combination which accounts also for the level at which the vaults were to spring from the elevation. The remaining similarities involve features important to the composition of the overall scheme but not fundamental to the character of its style. Among these are the precedents at Kirkstall (and Roche?) for the probable east wall of the choir with a large oculus, and, at Roche, for the proportions of the stories in the lateral choir elevations. Included also from Roche are the separated east chapels of the transept, with the consequent use of two different types of piers in the choir and transepts, and the exterior plinth profile.

The Cistercian features at Ripon, then, fall into two distinct categories, incidental stylistic details and important aspects of the overall composition. The first category involves features which a master mason might note and include as refinements in his design but which in themselves do not imbue this design with a Cistercian character (except, perhaps, in hindsight in view of subsequent Cistercian architecture). The second category involves features which do convey a distinctly Cistercian flavor of composition but which have little or nothing to do with style. In sum, Ripon bears witness to a substantial amount of influence from Cistercian architecture in England but virtually none of this influence relates to the Gothic character of Ripon's style.

This severe reduction of what can legitimately be counted as Cistercian influence at Ripon has important implications for our understanding of the twelfth-century minster and its place in the medieval architecture of England. With a fixed position relative to the chronology of English Cistercian architecture, it is possible to attribute a more nearly precise date for the design of Ripon and the beginning of its construction. With a diminished relationship to Cistercian architecture it is possible to establish the Ripon scheme, and especially its originally intended form, as stylistically much more important than it has formerly been thought to be. Before that issue can be explored in the fourth chapter, though, it is important to outline a chronology of construction for the whole church.

## The Dates of Construction

No portion of the twelfth-century minster at Ripon is precisely dated by documentary evidence. We know from the grant of Roger of Pont l'Evêque, archbishop of York, that the church was begun anew with his contribution of £1000 in "old coin."[19] Since his title as papal legate was used in the address, the date of the grant was necessarily after he was appointed to that office in 1164 or possibly somewhat later.[20] Nevertheless, no date was stated or implied, so the date of the design and the commencement of construction must be determined through archaeological comparisons. As we have seen, Ripon appears to have been begun after Roche and before Byland. While neither of these churches can be precisely dated, the year 1177 has traditionally been considered the latest likely time for the beginning of Byland. However impressionistic the association, it is one that fits all criteria for judging the remains of Byland itself and Byland's place in the context of English architecture. Equally, the approximate beginning date of 1170 for Roche has been accepted independently, based on the place of Roche in English Cistercian architecture. The design of Byland—at least that actually constructed—is based on the revised scheme for Ripon. The revision of the Ripon design can most plausibly be attributed to the necessity to provide a less expensive scheme following the death of the patron (in 1181) and the interruption at Byland cannot plausibly have been more than five years. Since Byland closely imitates Ripon and Ripon only loosely imitates Roche, it seems more likely that the date of Ripon is closer to that of Byland. A compromise date of ca.1175 for the beginning of Ripon seems to be the most likely chronological location relative to both Roche and Byland. Moreover, the attribution of a date around 1170 to Roger's new choir at York Minster,[21]

---

[19] See Appendix for the text of Roger's grant.

[20] John Browne argued that Roger did not actually come into that office until 1170 or afterward, even though Henry II had sought it for him soon after 1163. (*The History of the Metropolitan Church of Saint Peter, York*, London, 1847, 16–17). The Dictionary of National Biography, however, states unequivocally that Roger was made papal legate on 27 February 1164 (17: 109–11).

[21] Browne placed the remains of the crypt about 1170 (*York*, 16–19). Kidson (*English Architecture*, 60) implied a date soon after Roger became archbishop of York in 1154; and Webb (*Architecture in Britain*, 43) cited 1160. However, Jean Bony in "French Influences," cites 1170 as the latest likely date. Also, when establishing the chronological relationship between the York crypt piers and the similar Furness Abbey cloister vault responds, Bony presents external archaeological evidence for accepting Browne's date of ca.1170 for York. ("Origines des piles gothiques à fûts en délit," *Gedenkshrift Ernst Gall*, (Munich and Berlin, 1965) 109–11).

More recently, Eric A. Gee, publishing much of the results of excavations at York in the late 1960s and early 1970s (in "Architectural History until 1290," *A History of York Minster*, eds. G. E. Aylmer and Reginald Cant (Oxford, 1977), 121–125), placed the beginning of Roger's choir at ca.1160, with completion of the crypt by 1166, when a gift was confirmed in it, and completion of the choir itself about 1175. No justification for this date was offered in the cursory discussion but it probably hinges on the documentary mention of the crypt in connection with the gift. Archaeologically, these dates do not correspond so well with

which was still Romanesque in character, tends to confirm the appropriateness of one at least five years later for Gothic Ripon.[22] Hence the date of the design and beginning of construction of Ripon was about 1175.

The only other document that may bear upon the period of construction is the announcement in an indulgence of 1225, issued by Archbishop Walter Gray, that the relics of St. Wilfrid had been translated at Ripon on Christmas Day of 1224.[23] Such a translation does not necessarily relate to the progress of construction: the church could have been completed long before or it could still have remained unfinished. However, the chronological correspondence of archaeological evidence in the west facade to this date may well mean that the translation was regarded as an appropriate culmination of the building project. The decorative vocabulary of the later portions of the west facade includes clustered, attached shafts with rows of dogtooth ornament between them, finely molded arches with dogtooth ornament between orders, and a mixture of molded and stiff-leaf capitals with round imposts. This decoration is applied to tall lancet windows and to blind arches as well (where they are needed to complete the articulation of a wall). Both the ornament and the format are highly typical of the first four decades of the thirteenth century in England, seen separately or together in such widely disparate structures as the Tynemouth Priory choir, the Llanthony Priory west front, the Southwark Cathedral choir, the Beverley Minster choir, the St. Albans Cathedral nave, the Salisbury Cathedral Trinity Chapel, the Lincoln Cathedral great transept, the Southwell Minster choir and the Ely Cathedral retrochoir; and it is very difficult to specify a precise source for the decorative vocabulary. Nevertheless, the actual facade design as a whole is very comfortably placed in the years around 1220, so the translation may very well have been connected with completion of construction.

A span of half a century, from ca.1175 to ca.1225, is plausible for the complete construction of such a large church, especially considering the constraints imposed by economic and other difficulties during most such projects. Despite several important revisions in the overall scheme during that period, the changes succeed each other in such an orderly progression that no prolonged hiatus in the actual building process is indicated on the basis of a major stylistic disjuncture. Insofar as the archaeological evidence reveals the sequence of construction, it is difficult to specify a point when a portion of the structure could be enclosed and put to use while leaving no significant unfinished area exposed and vulnerable to damage by the elements during the interval. Without reference to historical circumstances,

---

other English buildings of the period as the beginning dates of ca.1170. Hence, while other conclusions by Gee are accepted in the next chapter, this one is not.

[22] Bony (in "Fûts en délit," 109) emphasizes the stylistic difference between the York crypt piers (1170) and others of similar composition at Canterbury (1178); and Pevsner (in *Yorkshire, The West Riding*, 403–404) notes this distinction between Archbishop Roger's buildings at York and Ripon, although he implies a greater chronological interval between their beginning dates.

[23] See Appendix for the text of the indulgence.

appearances suggest, then, that work was virtually continuous throughout the building period.

Almost nothing is known about the foundation of canons at Ripon for these decades and very little about the archbishopric of York for the period between 1181 and 1216, so one can only speculate about variations in the economic pattern of patronage. It is by no means certain that the archbishops assumed primary responsibility for the building project after Roger's initial gift. Indeed, an undated indulgence from the chapter of Ripon (usually ascribed to a time around 1224, but easily much earlier) soliciting donations toward the rebuilding of their minster,[24] suggests that the canons, and not the archbishops, were primarily responsible for raising the necessary funds. The indulgence of thirty days promulgated by Archbishop Gray on 21 January 1225, to all who should visit the shrine of St. Wilfrid at Ripon suggests only that he was involved to the extent of giving official support to a pilgrimage. If this is the case, then the probable vacancy of the see of York from 1181 to ca.1191 and the definite vacancy from 1207 to 1216[25] may not have been an important factor in the progress of construction. On the other hand, if the archbishops of York (who directed the non-capitular chapters of canons in the four Yorkshire minsters) were the principal patrons, it would be necessary to see a very discontinuous program of work. In that case, any hypothetical breaks would have to be placed either after the second phase of construction when the choir and transepts were complete, the crossing tower was yet unfinished, and the nave was just begun; or after the third phase when the nave was virtually complete and the west front was unfinished. However, within this highly uncertain situation, two dates of the building program might be regarded as plausibly fixed; that is, the first (ca.1175) and the last (ca.1225).

Regarding the first phase, the gift of Archbishop Roger undoubtedly prompted the organization of the project and the beginning of construction. The alteration of the initial scheme so that high vaults were omitted is a modification probably prompted by a sudden change in prospects for financial support. Certainly by the mid-1170s the construction of high vaults was not an undertaking from which builders and patrons might shrink, especially in midstream, on technological grounds. Moreover, nothing in the original design of Ripon suggests that the structural requirements for high vaults had not been properly foreseen and provided for. Rather, the expense of the vaults is the most likely reason they were omitted and this omission was probably prompted by the death of Archbishop Roger in 1181. The portions of the project which seem to have been accomplished at that point—the whole church laid out, the choir

---

[24] Printed in *Memorials of Ripon,* I, ed. J. T. Fowler (The Publications of the *Surtees Society,* vol. 74) (London, 1881), 98, and in *The Historians of the Church of York and Its Archbishops,* 3, ed. James Raine, Rolls Series, 71, (London, 1894), 125–126.

[25] A. Hamilton Thompson, "York: Ecclesiastical History," *The Victoria History of the Counties of England, Yorkshire,* 3 (London, 1913): 19–23.

completed up to the clerestory, the north transept half-finished, the chapter house substantially completed, and the south transept underway (fig. 13)—indicate rapid progress on an ambitiously-proportioned phase of construction. In other words, the work accomplished before the interruption implies the effort of a large, amply-funded workshop over a few years.

The fourth and last phase (assuming completion just prior to the translation of relics at the end of 1224), with its rich decorative detail and the attendant enlargement of the original scheme for the west front, appears to have been liberally supported and rapidly achieved. In all likelihood, it belongs to the reign of Archbishop Walter Gray, which began in 1216. If approximately six or seven years were devoted to the project, a workshop of moderate size would have been more than sufficient to accomplish the task.

Between the first and fourth phases, that is from 1181 to about 1217, the rest of the church was built. If construction was continuous, a very small workshop of masons and carpenters—perhaps ten in all—could have finished the choir and transept, built the nave and crossing tower, and started the west front during that period. Estimates based on masons' marks for the workshop involved in constructing the cathedral of St. Davids' in Wales during the same decades indicate approximately five masons, not counting carpenters, at any given moment for about the same number of years.[26] In such circumstances it seems likely that the Ripon choir and transepts could have been completed (fig. 14) for use sometime in the latter 1180s, especially since the only vaults left to construct were those in the south transept chapels. (Indeed, it is possible that these chapels were not initially vaulted and that this temporary expedient resulted in their not being separated in the manner of the north transept chapels). Should this have been the case, construction on the nave and west front could then await the propitious moment for a new initiative, if an interruption was unavoidable. Very possibly such an interruption was anticipated and then became unnecessary after the installation of Geoffrey Plantagenet (illegitimate half-brother of Richard I and John) as archbishop of York around 1191.[27] In any event, work continued in the nave, using largely the same repertory of forms employed in the first two phases. On the other hand, some aspects of the nave wall composition and its decorative treatment were altered while the nave rose and changes in the repertory of ornaments were also introduced in the crossing tower and the west towers, where conformity with older beginnings was not mandatory for the sake of consistency. The newer elements of this work (fig. 15) indicate a date in the early 1190s with work continuing past 1200 and possibly until the exile of Archbishop Geoffrey in 1207. Awkward as it

---

[26] E. W. Lovegrove, "The Cathedral Church of St. David's," *Archaeological Journal*, 83 (for 1926 published in 1929): 254–283.

[27] For the life of Archbishop Geoffrey, see *Dictionary of National Biography*, 7: 1018–24. See also "From 627 until the Early Thirteenth Century," by Rosalind Hill and Christopher Brooke, in *A History of York Minster*, 37–41.

may seem, the only plausible hiatus as long as a decade occurred while the west front was being erected. By coincidence, this interruption corresponds with the period, 1208–1213, when the church in England languished under the Interdict of Innocent III, a period when construction would probably have been halted. Such an interruption might account, then, for the most radical single modification in the original scheme for the church, the transformation of the west front from a screen facade into a harmonic facade (fig. 16).

To summarize the chronology of construction, Ripon Minster was designed and begun probably about 1175, under the patronage of Roger of Pont l'Eveque. Construction was briefly interrupted at Roger's death in 1181, leaving the choir, chapter house, and transepts incomplete while the rest of the church was only laid out (fig. 13). Work continued in a second phase on a much less costly scale and with a smaller workshop through most of the 1180s in order to make the choir, chapter house, transepts, and crossing usable and to close them off from the rest of the unfinished structure (fig. 14). The eastern portions of the nave were probably underway when the second phase was concluded. After no more than a short delay, the nave, crossing tower, and west front were undertaken in a third phase which presumably progressed slowly from the late 1180s until the first decade of the thirteenth century. Most of the nave may well have been roofed and closed in near the west end at the end of this work (fig. 15). Completion of the west front, comprising towers and facade, occurred after an interruption of a few years, perhaps beginning about 1217 and ending about 1224 (fig. 16). To be sure, this entire chronology is hypothetical but it is consistent with an archaeological analysis both of the surviving twelfth-century fragments of the minster and of the related buildings of its architectural milieu.

## 3. THE PATRON AND HIS PURPOSES

When Roger of Pont l'Evêque, archbishop of York, gave an enormous amount of money to the collegiate chapter at Ripon to build a new church, he—or his designated surrogate at Ripon—would not have been casual in specifying to the master mason his requirements for the new structure. Indeed, the master mason would expect the patron to set down a complete building program and he could scarcely proceed without one. Several considerations would have contributed to its formulation. First, the functions performed by the minster as a collegiate foundation, both its daily cycle of liturgical offices and its service to the laity, would have determined most aspects of its spatial organization. Second, traditions peculiar to liturgical practice in the archdiocese of York and in Ripon itself would have guided the specific shaping of this layout. Third, any new functions intended for the minster, functions which might in themselves have prompted the new construction, would have put their stamp on the formal arrangement. Finally, the motivations of the patron in initiating the new project would have been manifested in the synthesis of these three considerations, accounting for particular emphases.

The master builder, then, assumed responsibility for giving material form to this program only after the plan had been all but completely determined by the patron. Many aspects of the plan also impinged upon the structural composition as the church rose upon its foundations. Consequently, the builder had far less than a free hand in devising his design. Although it is implicit at Ripon that a building in the new Gothic style was desired, much of the design was prompted by considerations unrelated to the Gothic style. A cursory examination of the Ripon scheme reveals a number of features that deviated from the norms of Gothic architecture in its native France.

The wall, with its arcaded clerestory passage, retains the "thick-wall" structural formulation that had been traditional in England for a century. Spatially, the flat east end contrasts sharply with the French apsidal chevet with its ambulatory and radiating chapels (although this rectangular type of eastern termination was later to enjoy in France a limited vogue, most notably in the remodeled choir of Laon Cathedral, shortly after 1200). The rectangular transept chapels and the aisleless nave were equally alien to the Gothic tradition of the Ile de France. The greatest deviation from French architecture, however, was the omission of high ribbed vaults, an omission always intended in the nave and adopted during construction in the choir and transepts. In order to discover the patron's program, it is necessary to begin by identifying the features that adhere to the pre-

Gothic English tradition and by tracing their sources as precisely as is possible.

### The Wall Structure

Behind the convincingly Gothic surface of Ripon's thick walls (pl. 3) there is no special concentration of structure at the bay divisions as there was in the advanced designs of northeastern France in the 1160s and 1170s; or, to put it another way, there is no thinning of the wall between the bay divisions (pl. 10). Consequently the novel structural aspects of French Gothic architecture appear to have been lost in the transmission of the style to England, not only at Ripon but also at Canterbury. Even so, as has long been noted, at Canterbury the fact that the genuine supporting elements of the elevation, which are concentrated at the bay divisions behind the wall surface, are resting on the haunches of the aisle vaults seems to indicate a move in the direction of the French concept of skeletal structure.[1] Previously ignored in this respect, the Ripon elevation was designed to make the main arcade appear much thinner than the actual wall; in consequence, part of the thickness of the upper wall and the exterior pilaster buttresses as well rest also on the haunches of the aisle vaults. Yet these putative harbingers of a more complex structural system are misleading because subsequent Gothic structures in England did not develop in that direction. The continuous thick wall that was adopted for the next buildings in the new style [Byland (fig. 17), Chichester retrochoir, and Wells (pl. 73)], reflected the most conservative Anglo-Norman tradition of architecture with little or no vertical articulation. At Ripon and Canterbury, the anglicizing program employing only three stories, with a non-functional middle story at that, may have made the use of advanced structural concepts seem unnecessary. In their successors, the failure to give the bay-division shafts a genuine structural role probably discouraged any further concentration of structure at the bay divisions. The construction of a traditional wall structure at Ripon, then, was probably determined by the adoption of a liturgical layout that was also peculiar to English usage.

### Sources of the Spatial Composition

The Englishness of Ripon Minster, particularly of its plan (plans 1, 2) can best be appreciated by reviewing the antecedents of contemporary relatives of the various component forms; namely, the flat, east end, the transept with a row of eastern chapels, the aisleless nave, and the screen facade with hollow towers.

---

[1] Kidson (in Part One, *A History of English Architecture* (Harmondsworth, 1962), 74) explicitly signaled the quasi-French character of this structural formulation anticipated, by the Rev. Robert Willis (*The Architectural History of Canterbury Cathedral* (London, 1845), 96, and fig. 14).

The eastern termination with a straight wall across the full height of both the choir and the aisles is so typical of English Gothic architecture that the elusiveness of its origin is unexpected. The chapel of St. Cross Hospital in Winchester (ca.1160),[2] is well known as the earliest extant example in England. Yet for such a prominent aspect of the plan and massing of a church, one which cannot be divorced from the matter of liturgical requirements, St. Cross is not important enough to have been either the point of origin for the type or the model for Ripon. A much earlier precedent survives across the Channel in northern France in the church of St. Hildevert at Gournay-en-Bray (ca.1110);[3] and it probably has still earlier antecedents in less fully developed examples such as Saint-Bertin of Saint-Omer (ca.1080).[4] But this plan did not achieve great currency in France and the chief historical value of continental prototypes is that they may have influenced some of the earliest instances in England, now known only through excavation. Among these, the most important was the Anglo-Norman reconstruction of the eastern arm of Rochester Cathedral, ca.1115–1125, known as Ernulf's choir[5] (fig. 19). There may have been a small, low, rectangular axial chapel projecting beyond the high east wall, but the basic composition of the superstructure was undoubtedly of the type at issue here. The actual model for Ripon, though, was probably the reconstructed eastern arm of York Minster (fig. 20), which had been initiated by Archbishop Roger.

As at Rochester, the choir at York was raised over a full crypt. The foundation of the eastern wall, excavated along with the rest of the crypt

---

[2] C. R. Peers and Harold Brakspear, "Winchester: Hospital of St. Cross," *Victoria History of the Counties of England, Hampshire and the Isle of Wight,* 5 (London, 1912), 59–66.

[3] Louis Regnier, "Gournay-en-Bray," *Congrès Archéologique de France, Beauvais* 76 (1905): 75.

[4] Pierre Héliot, "Le chevet roman de Saint-Bertin à Saint-Omer et l'architecture franco-lotharingienne," *Revue belge d'archéologie et d'histoire de l'art* 22 (1953): 73–96; and Paul Rolland, "Un groupe belge d'églises romanes," *Revue belge d'archéologie et d'histoire de l'art* 11 (1941): 119–55.

[5] The reconstitution of this choir and its date are not without controversy. The plan was set forth by Sir William Henry St. John Hope (in "The Architectural History of the Cathedral Church and Monastery of St. Andrew at Rochester," (*Archaeologia Cantiana* 23 (1898): 204–209, and plan facing 214) and dated to the time of Bishop Gundulf, 1076–1107. The date but not the form was challenged by F. H. Fairweather (in "Gundulf's Cathedral and Priory Church, Rochester: Some Critical Remarks upon the Hitherto Accepted Plan," *Archaeological Journal* 86 (1929): 187–214) where he assigned the rectangular crypt (and choir above it) to the period immediately following a fire of 1137, albeit perhaps initiated earlier by Ernulf. Sir Alfred Clapham (in *English Romanesque Architecture after the Conquest,* (Oxford, 1934), 24, 46) assigned the elongated new choir to Ernulf, ca.1115–ca.1125, for unstated reasons. Implicit in the attribution, however, is the knowledge that Ernulf had undertaken the new choir at Canterbury, ca.1090, and that he was therefore undoubtedly an advocate of the liturgical change that prompted both rebuildings. Moreover, Ernulf did build a new chapter house, dorter, and frater at Rochester and so is a likely candidate for the choir as well. Even Hope had admitted the possibility of the Ernulf date although he ultimately opted for the earlier one (217–18). Clapham, meanwhile, doubted Hope's reconstitution but only on the ground that there were no counterparts in English architecture before the latter half of the century. Apparently he did not know the older examples in France, cited in the two previous notes.

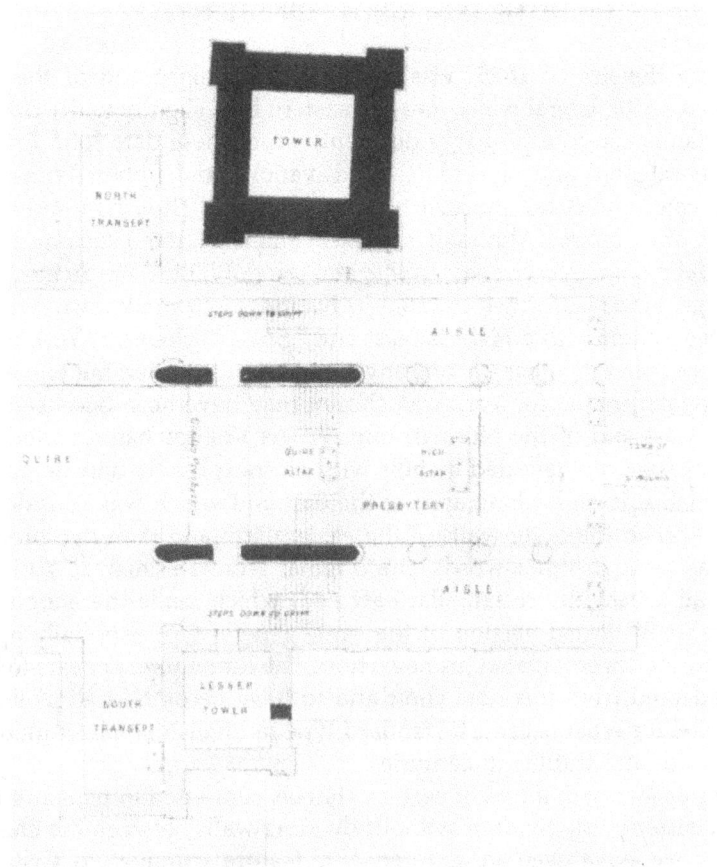

FIG. 19. Rochester Cathedral, plan of choir by St. John Hope. Reproduced from *Archaeologia Cantiana*, XXIII (1898).

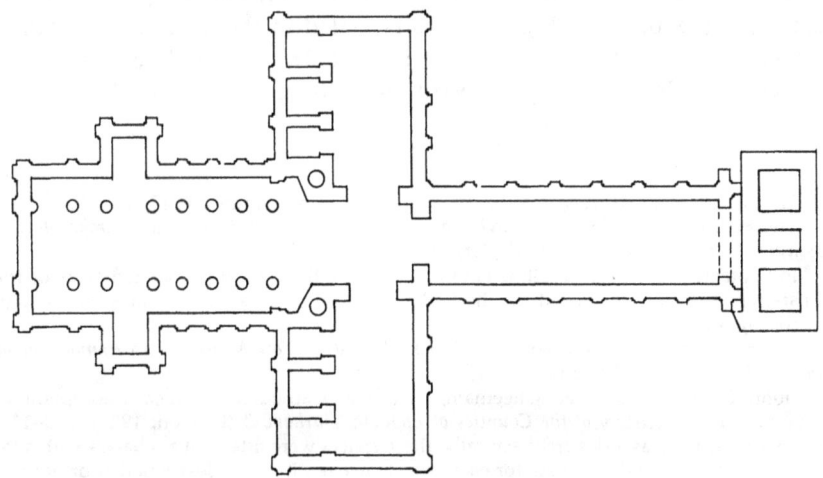

FIG. 20. York Minster, plan of the church as it stood after completion of Roger of Pont l'Evêque's choir. Adapted from various plans published by Robert Willis, Alfred Clapham, Eric Gee and Derek Phillips—not drawn to scale and not showing hypothetical access to the raised choir.

following the fire of 1829, was found to be straight and of the same thickness as the lateral walls; and the eastern bay, slightly wider than the others (and therefore probably different). From these data John Browne, who investigated and reported the excavation,[6] and Robert Willis, who reinterpreted the data,[7] thought that the crypt and choir had had a rectangular ambulatory. Although the excavations of the 1960s and early 1970s did not uncover the east wall again, Derek Phillips, the archaeologist in charge, kindly informed me that in his judgment the known evidence indicates a choir with a high flat east end.[8] Such a scheme at York resembles more than any other the one envisioned for Rochester; but one reason a rectangular model for York was chosen may have been because of the original east end of the Norman minster. As Phillips has reported,[9] the recent excavations revealed a choir with an inexplicably narrow passage along each side and a long apse at the east end which was considerably narrower than the outer walls of the eastern arm and therefore probably lower as well. In other words, the original Norman choir at York may have had a basically rectangular east end, which made the adoption of a more sophisticated version of the same general type especially appropriate when Roger initiated his new choir. The Ripon plan appears to have been adapted from this new choir and to have become in all likelihood the model for what became a standard type in English architecture of the late twelfth and thirteenth centuries.

The transept with a row of eastern chapels composed in plan and mass like an eastern aisle (with or without dividing walls between the chapels) was, as we have seen in chapter 2, a feature common to Cistercian churches, including most of the examples in England. However, before such a feature is known to have existed in Cistercian architecture, the transept with an eastern aisle had already been employed in Durham Cathedral (begun in 1093), and was repeated in the great abbey church (now cathedral) of Peterborough (begun ca.1118).[10] In modified form, with apsidal chapels projecting eastward from the eastern aisle, it appeared

---

[6] *The History of the Metropolitan Church of St. Peter, York* (London, 1847), 31–35.

[7] The Rev. Robert Willis, "The Architectural History of York Cathedral," *Archaeological Institute of Great Britain and Ireland* (York, 1846), 10–19.

[8] In September 1972, Mr. Phillips kindly guided me through the excavated areas of the minster and generously showed me the various relevant excavation drawings that he and his colleagues had prepared.

[9] "Excavations at York Minster, 1967–1973," *Friends of York Minster, 46th Annual Report* (1975), 25–27 and fig. 2 (plan).

[10] John Quekett and F. H. Cheetham, "Durham Cathedral: Detailed Description of Church," *Victoria History of the Counties of England, Durham*, 3 (London: 1928): 110–113. Although discussed as aisles architecturally, these spaces were fitted out as chapels with altar platforms, altars, and dedications for each bay. However, it is not clear whether or not this arrangement was originally intended or if screen dividers were provided

C. R. Peers, "Peterborough Minster," *Victoria History of the Counties of England, Northampton*, 2 (London: 1906): 437. These eastern aisles were used as chapels and the bays were divided by thin wooden walls in the north transept and by thin stone walls (slightly later than the original construction) in the south transept.

also at Bury St. Edmunds Abbey, most likely after 1121.[11] Such eastern aisles appear to have functioned liturgically as rows of chapels rather than as processional paths, so they could have provided the structural prototype for this feature in Cistercian churches. Yet the Cistercian formulation, with thick walls between the chapels, may have been the actual prototype that influenced the Ripon design, albeit indirectly. Once again the influence seems to have emanated from York, where recent excavations revealed considerable extension of the Norman transepts in a masonry related to Roger's new choir. However, because the aisles of Roger's choir still retained portions of the original Norman apsidal chapels, the new transepts appear to have been slightly later than the choir.[12] In that case it is difficult to determine whether or not they could be earlier than the planning of Ripon, but it is possible that they were just going up around 1175 and so provided the model for Ripon's transepts.

The aisleless nave is an element that can be recognized in the earlier ruined nave of Kirkham Priory, in Yorkshire (dated ca.1150);[13] but Kirkham was clearly a minor structure in comparison to Ripon and not a likely candidate for the model. Aisleless naves were employed in several major churches in France, for instance the cathedrals of Angoulême, Angers, and Toulouse, but always in a radically different and unrelated form,[14] so there can be no question of continental influence at Ripon. Virtually standard in Anglo-Saxon churches of all classes and very frequent in parish churches after the Conquest, the aisleless nave by 1150 was almost exclusively a feature of minor or outdated structures. One notable exception to this classification, though, and one of crucial importance for Ripon, was the Norman nave of York Minster, which had been constructed during the tenure of Thomas of Bayeaux as archbishop of York, between 1071 and 1100. Archaeological evidence to prove this configuration of the York nave was discovered in the recent excavations directed by Derek Phillips, showing that the nave had a blank lower story and above it a wall passage, probably with windows.[15] Clearly, then, York provided the model for the Ripon nave.

---

[11] A. B. Whittingham, "Bury St. Edmunds Abbey: The Plan, Design and Development of the Church and Monastic Buildings," *Archaeological Journal* 108 (1951): 170. The transepts were built in the second campaign of construction in the first two decades of the twelfth century. Unlike Durham and Peterborough, Bury St. Edmunds had apsidal chapels projecting eastward from this aisle, so the extent to which the aisle bays served also as chapels is limited to their spatial relationship with the apses.

[12] The excavations, carried out in the late 1960s and 1970s under the direction of Derek Phillips have been reported by the honorary architectural historian to the Dean and Chapter of York Minster, Eric A. Gee (in "Architectural History until 1290," *A History of York Minster*, eds. G. E. Aylmer and Reginald Cant, (Oxford, 1977) 121).

[13] Nikolaus Pevsner with John Hutchinson, *Yorkshire: York and the East Riding*, (The Buildings of England, (Harmondsworth, 1972), 298.

[14] Each of these naves was vaulted and, for that purpose, each of them was articulated into great square bays to receive their domical or ribbed vaults.

[15] "Excavations at York Minster," 24–25 and fig. 2 (plan); see also Willis, *York Cathedral*, 5–6; Browne, *York*, 12–14; and Gee, in *York Minster*, 115–17, 118.

The intended screen facade, with its two square towers projecting beyond the width of the nave, is even rarer than the box nave. The closest extant analogues are the facade of Wells Cathedral begun in the 1220s, in which the west bay of the aisles intervenes between the nave and the towers;[16] the facade of Augustinian Llanthony Priory (Monmouthshire), begun ca.1200, in which the towers stand at the end of the aisles (and may possibly have had an additional story, which would disqualify the west front as a screen type);[17] and the facade of Benedictine Selby Abbey (pl. 59), probably built shortly before 1200, in which the towers relate to the nave like those of a harmonic facade except that they were never taller than the nave until the twentieth century[18] (nor probably intended to be so). None of these examples relates spatially to the nave in the same way or in the manner of the Ripon facade. Moreover, they are all later than Ripon so none could have served as the prototype. The origin of the Ripon facade seems once again to have been in York Minster.[19] In the excavations of the 1970s, a foundation was uncovered near the present west front which indicates the existence of a prior facade, composed of two large square towers placed close together but nevertheless projecting beyond the width of the box nave. Connected by a passage about 15 feet wide, these towers were probably too close together to represent a harmonic facade. Hence, it is likely that the facade was of the screen type, similar to that envisioned at Ripon, although the paucity of evidence prevents a conclusive reconstitution. The date of this facade is attributed to a period between 1089, when William Rufus granted the land it stood on to the minster, and the early thirteenth century. The most likely explanation is that the facade was built immediately after the grant was made, ca.1090, during the reign of Archbishop Thomas and the next most likely is that it comprised part of the project of Archbishop Roger, when the choir was rebuilt (ca.1170). The intended purpose or symbolic meaning of this facade would be virtually impossible to decipher, since its form can be only vaguely discerned; but if the assumption of a screen type is correct, this western block had no known Continental counterparts and was probably an English invention. It appears, then, that the Ripon facade was based on that of York, along with the spatial scheme of the church.

The main features of the Ripon plan were not only expressly English but also markedly different from their counterparts in French Gothic practice: they necessarily resulted in significant deviations from the spatial effects normally achieved in French churches. It is entirely possible that

---

[16] Nikolaus Pevsner (in *North Somerset and Bristol*, The Buildings of England (Harmondsworth, 1958), 27 and 285–88) set the date at ca.1230; but in her forthcoming study on the Wells facade, Carolyn Malone has been able to demonstrate that it was begun nearly a decade earlier.

[17] O. E. Craster, *Llanthony Priory, Monmouthshire*, Ministry of Works Guides (London: 1963), 5, 15–16, plate IV and plan.

[18] The Rev. J. A. P. Kent, *The Pictorial History of Selby Abbey*, (London, Pitkin's "Pride of Britain" Series, (London, ca.1968), 14, 24.

[19] Gee, in *York Minster*, 125–27.

these features, particularly the aisleless nave, were responsible also for the retention of the traditional English structural system, with its double-shell clerestory. Hence, the differences between Ripon and its French relatives may have been largely due to the deliberate retention of English forms which were peculiarly appropriate to the requirements for this church. The highly individual character of the design probably denotes a specific liturgical program.

## The Patron and His Purposes

At Ripon, the plan of the new minster with its rectangular east end, its transept with eastern chapels, its aisleless nave, and its west front with towers projecting beyond the nave, reflected in updated form the most conspicuous features of the probable plan of York Minster as it stood in Roger's time. Such a virtual replication is highly singular, partly because the structure at York it imitated juxtaposed portions that had been designed as much as a century apart and hence were formally inconsistent, and partly because the scheme at York presented a remarkably atypical model. Under these circumstances the decision to impose upon Ripon Minster the image of York cannot be regarded as a matter of course or taken for granted. Indeed, it undoubtedly determined the symbolic identity of the building program, which fulfilled the liturgical purposes of the new structure. These aspects of the project cannot have been left to the discretion of the designer but surely represent the desires of the patron. In the case of Ripon, as we know, the patron was not the chapter of canons but the archbishop of York, Roger of Pont l'Evêque, 1154–1181.

The undated grant of money from Roger, stating that he had begun the church anew,[20] leaves little doubt that he was the initiating patron. Moreover, the amount of money he gave (£1000 in "old coin") apparently was truly munificent.[21] If not enough to build the entire church, it was clearly sufficient to support the project for several years while the chapter of Ripon could organize support both from its own revenues and from the donations of the laity. The grant, however, does not tell us why Roger chose to rebuild Ripon Minster or what purpose he had in doing so. While definite answers may never be forthcoming, particular circumstances from Roger's own life and his experience as archbishop of York suggest reasons and motives for this project which seem to be corroborated by evidence in later documents and in the building itself.

---

[20] See Appendix for the Latin text. For the grant see Darnborough Ms. IV, in *Memorials of Ripon*, 1 The Publications of the *Surtees Society*, vol. 74 (London, 1881), 97.

[21] Willis, *York Cathedral*, Note A, 54–57, speculated on the annual expenditures for fourteenth-century construction at Westminster, Ely, and York which ranged from £235 to £627. Given the inflationary economic trend since the late twelfth century and the express mention in Roger's grant that the gift was in old coinage (almost certainly meant to be a notation of positive import), the £1,000 was probably sufficient for about five or six years. Undated indulgences and grants of land collected in the Darnborough MS suggest that the chapter eventually had to raise funds to complete the building, *Memorials of Ripon* 1: 98–104.

Before considering biographical motives, though, it is appropriate to examine the ecclesiastical context in which the minster was begun. As a college of secular canons, the Ripon chapter had no formally constituted head and was directly responsible to the archbishop of York. Such a foundation within the archdiocese of York was designated a minster, of which there were four—at York, Ripon, Beverley, and Southwell.[22] Southwell had been rebuilt upon the initiative of Archbishop Thomas II (1108–1114)[23] and was probably completed just before Roger came to office in 1154. Roger, as we have seen, had already begun a new eastern arm at York, ca.1170, which presumably had been completed when he was buried in it in 1181.[24] Documents about Beverley are vague concerning the minster fabric in the twelfth century but some scholars have inferred that it had been rebuilt after the Conquest.[25] The rebuilding of Ripon, then, could well have marked simply the completion of a long-standing program to provide each of the four minsters with a suitable and reasonably modern structure.[26] On the other hand, the lack of any definite motive for rebuilding only the choir and transepts at York dilutes the case for this interpretation, especially since nearly every important church in England was rebuilt, for a variety of reasons, between the Conquest and the end of the twelfth century. Even the definite rebuilding of Beverley in the early thirteenth century,[27] viewed as the fourth such project among the minsters, cannot sustain the theory without documentary confirmation. Thus another line of investigation appears to be appropriate in order to explain the Ripon plan.

In every respect, as we shall see, Ripon seems to have had a special relationship to York and to Archbishop Roger which set it apart from the other two minsters. Much of this relationship may be explained by certain factors in the life of Roger of Pont l'Evêque and the history of his associations with Thomas à Becket and the cathedral of Canterbury.[28] Both Roger and Thomas had been educated in the cathedral school at Canter-

---

[22] J. T. Fowler, ed., *Memorials of Ripon* 3: The Publications of the *Surtees Society*, 81 (London, 1886), viii–xix.

[23] A. Hamilton Thompson, "Southwell Minster," *Transactions of the Thoroton Society* 15, (1912): 15–62.

[24] Browne, *York*, 19.

[25] John Bilson, "Beverley Minster," *The Antiquary* 27 (1893): 23, and idem., *Architectural Review* 3 (1897): 197ff. The basis for believing that such a church existed is the presence of apparently reused stones with Norman chevron ornament in the Gothic nave triforium. See also Pevsner, *York and the East Riding*, 169; K. A. Macmahon, (*The Pictorial History of Beverley Minster*, Pitkin's "Pride of Britain" Series, (London, ca. 1960), 4) admits the possibility of a twelfth-century nave, but is skeptical in view of the lack of additional evidence.

[26] This theory was kindly suggested to me by Dr. Kit Galbraith of Birkbeck College, University of London, in March 1977.

[27] Charles Hiatt, *Beverley Minster*, Bell's Cathedral Series, (London, 1898), 33–34 and *passim.*; Pevsner, *York and the East Riding*, 169–74.

[28] The most precise accounts of the lives of Roger and Thomas are those (based on surviving medieval documents) in the *Dictionary of National Biography*, 17: 109–111; and 19: 645–652. Additional interesting material concerning the relationship of Roger and Thomas is found in David Knowles, *The Episcopal Colleagues of Archbishop Thomas Becket* (Cambridge: 1951).

bury where the ambitious Roger developed so deep a jealousy of Thomas that it was to feed a life-long enmity. Roger was the elder by several years but no sooner did he gain each preferment in his career than Thomas would receive one equal or superior to it. During the early 1140s, when they were both in the service of Theobald, archbishop of Canterbury, Roger secured Thomas's dismissal from the Canterbury establishment more than once, but Thomas always returned. In 1148 Roger became archdeacon of Canterbury and soon thereafter may also have been appointed provost of Beverley Minster, a post normally granted for service to the crown.[29] Theobald advanced Roger's candidacy to the archbishopric of York and consecrated him in Westminster Abbey on 10 October 1154, whereupon Thomas immediately succeeded him as archdeacon of Canterbury. Early the next year, when Henry II came to the throne, Roger was comfortably superior to his rival on the always-sensitive occasion of the coronation.

Then the tables turned. Following the coronation Thomas began to enjoy the king's special attention and favor. First he was made provost of Beverley in addition to his office at Canterbury, thus following closely upon the heels of Roger in one and perhaps in both posts. Almost immediately afterward Thomas was appointed chancellor of England. This rise to great prominence had the virtue of putting both men in largely non-competing spheres of activity. The balance was broken, however, when Henry II prevailed upon Thomas to accept the archbishopric of Canterbury in 1162. Roger claimed the right to consecrate Thomas and could have gained thereby some satisfaction in being the instrument necessary to install his rival in the superior office. Unhappily for Roger his claim was rejected, although his injured pride was placated a few weeks later by receipt of papal permission to carry his archiepiscopal cross in the province of Canterbury (a gesture close to proclamation of metropolitan equality) and the right to crown kings. Thomas protested, probably with justification, and made his opposition to these two concessions stick. Then, within a matter of months, the famous issue arose concerning the prosecution of criminous clerics. While Roger was actually the first to oppose the king on this matter, Henry had won him over by 1163. Thomas denounced Roger for what he regarded as a betrayal, whereupon Roger whole-heartedly became the king's ally. From this point, with Thomas clearly in the superior position, the enmity between the two archbishops became open and bitter.

There followed an acrimonious display of rivalry. As a reward for his support, Henry had asked Pope Alexander III to appoint Roger papal legate. The office was conferred early in 1164. At this point Roger was in position to deal with Thomas as a virtual equal. However, in 1166, Thomas persuaded the pope to withdraw from Roger the permission to

---

[29] Arthur Francis Leach, ed., *Memorials of Beverley Minster: The Chapter Acts Book*, The Publications of the Surtees Society, 108, (London, 1903), viiff.

crown kings on the ground that it was illegal. In the next year Roger obtained an explicit exception for the immediate purpose of crowning the young Henry before his father's death. At this juncture Roger was somewhat ahead in the battle for primacy and there was a standoff for the next three years while Thomas was in exile abroad. It seems very likely that it was in this period just prior to 1170 that Roger initiated the rebuilding of the choir at York.

Six aspects of Roger's new eastern arm of York (fig. 20)[30] that can still be discerned from its remains suggest that he conceived the choir to serve symbolically as an analogue to the sumptuous Anglo-Norman choir of Canterbury[31] (fig. 21), hence a sanctuary appropriate for the cathedral of a primate. First, the choir was seven bays long, longer than any earlier choir in England except that of Canterbury[32] (and, inexplicably, that of the abbey of Bury Saint Edmunds).[33] Second, this choir was flanked by eastern transeptal projections, perhaps hollow towers. Whether or not they communicated with the high vessel of the choir as transepts cannot be definitely determined by the surviving evidence. Third, a crypt extended beneath almost all the eastern arm, including the eastern transeptal projections. Fourth, the floor of the choir was built at a substantially higher level than the nave and main transepts and it was probably reached by two sets of steps in the crossing as well as tall staircases at the west end of the choir aisles. Similarly, the crypt was only partially underground and was ostensibly reached by low staircases within the piers of the eastern crossing arch.[34] (Incidentally, no other major crypt had been built in the north of England.) Fifth, the remains of the massive piers in the crypt, scored with incised designs like those on the piers of Durham Cathedral, suggest that the decor of the choir was basically Romanesque and that it was richly decorated in a manner similar to that reported of the Canterbury choir prior to the fire of 1174. Sixth, the new eastern arm was added to the nave and transepts of a church that had been rebuilt in the generation immediately following the Norman Conquest. The York and Canterbury choirs, then, were remarkably similar in highly particular ways.

---

[30] For a description of the remains and probable form of the eastern arm, see Willis, *York Cathedral*, 8–19; and Gee, *York Minster*, 121–25.

[31] This motive for rebuilding the York choir was first suggested by Willis (*York Cathedral*, 14–15) and was accepted by Kidson (*English Architecture*, 70).

[32] For a description of the remains and probable form of the Anglo-Norman choir of Canterbury, see Willis, *Canterbury Cathedral*, 41–48.

[33] Only slightly shorter than the eastern arms of Canterbury and York, the Bury St. Edmunds choir had five straight bays and an apse with ambulatory. However, part of this length may not have been originally intended because the western bay was added in the second campaign to correspond with the transept eastern aisle. See Whittingham, "Bury St. Edmunds," 170, 173–74.

[34] The problem of access has been discussed only by Willis (*York Cathedral*, 17). He based the hypothetical steps in the crossing on those of Canterbury and those at the west end of the choir aisles on his reading of the archaeological evidence for crypt entrances within the eastern crossing piers.

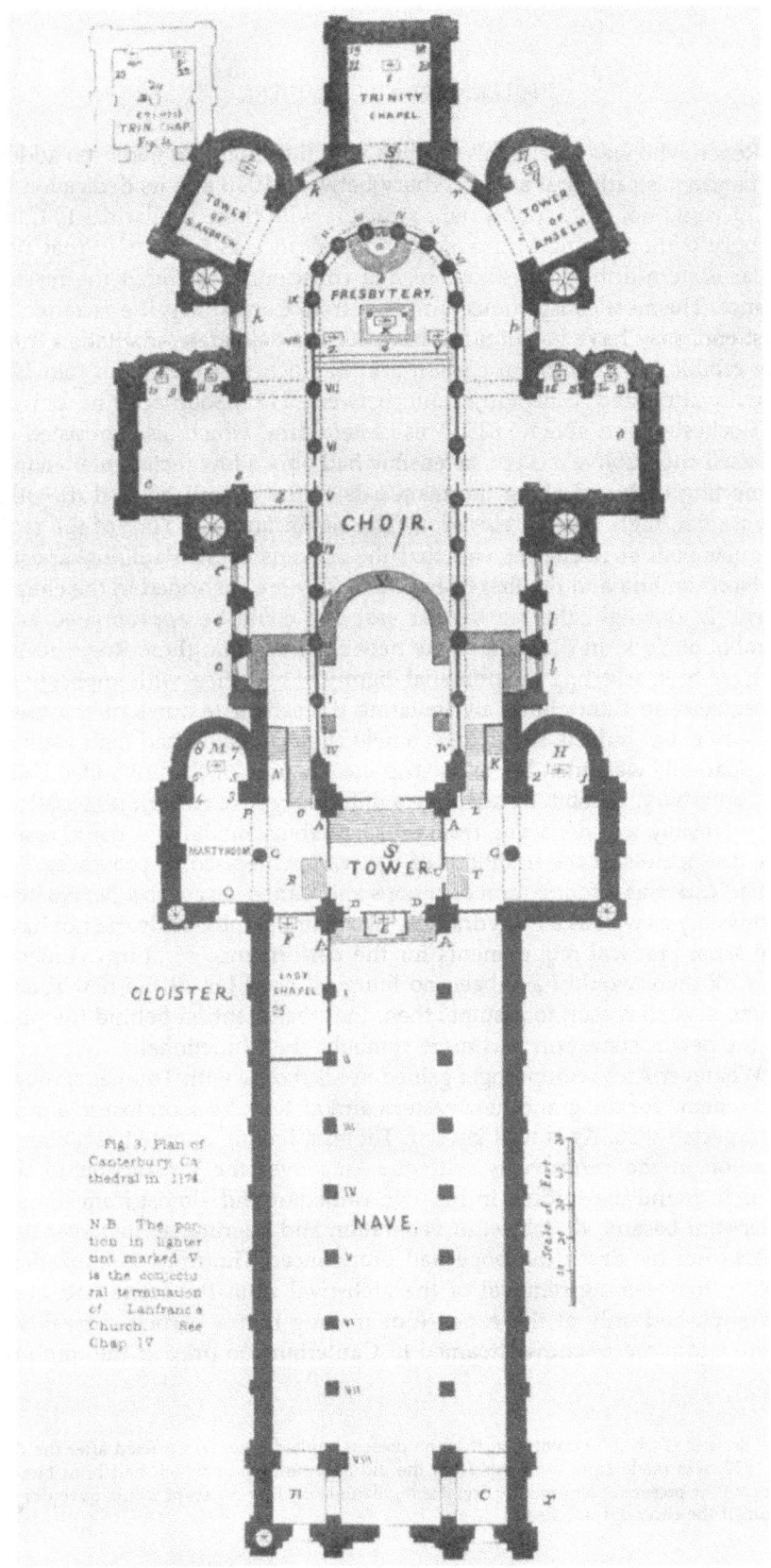

FIG. 21. Canterbury Cathedral, plan of Romanesque choir. Reproduced from the Rev. Robert Willis, *The Architectural History of Canterbury Cathedral*, London, 1845.

Roger, who was thoroughly familiar with the choir that had been added to Lanfranc's cathedral at Canterbury between 1090 and its dedication in 1130, could not have sponsored a structure with these similarities to Canterbury without being aware of their significance as features in that singular eastern arm and without having consciously intended the resemblance. The most conspicuous difference from Canterbury, the rectangular east end, may have been (as we have seen) a deliberate adaptation from the rebuilt Anglo-Norman eastern arm of Rochester Cathedral (fig. 19), usually attributed to Bishop Ernulf, between 1115, soon after he arrived at Rochester, and about 1125. This eastern arm, which also consisted of a raised choir above a crypt, ostensibly had only a low rectangular chapel projecting eastward along the main axis of the church beyond the otherwise flat, high, eastern elevation. The significance for York of the rectangular plan at Rochester was that the remains of St. Paulinus, apostle to Northumbria and the first bishop of York were enshrined in the chapel there. In this light the rectangular east end could be appropriated as a symbol of York. In the plan of the new choir at York, then, Roger seems to have been asserting the primatial dignity of his office, with implications of equality to Canterbury, by imitating the salient features of the Canterbury choir. Indeed, since Roger's new choir probably had high vaults[35] it apparently was intended to outstrip the splendor of the unvaulted choir at Canterbury. Second, by adapting a different type of eastern termination, he ostensibly was departing from the Canterbury model in order to assert the distinctness of the traditions of the two archiepiscopal provinces. Because York was a foundation of canons and Canterbury was a Benedictine monastery as well as a cathedral, the two churches obviously did not have the same practical requirements for the performance of liturgy. Indeed, at York there would have been no liturgical need for all the new space. There is good reason to assume, then, that the intention behind the plan of the new eastern arm was more symbolic than functional.

Whatever Archbishop Roger gained in his rivalry with Thomas through the scheme for the grand new eastern arm at York he soon lost in a most unexpected way. As is well known, Thomas, having adopted an extreme position in the controversy with the king over the jurisdiction of the church, found martyrdom in his own cathedral and almost immediately afterward became the object of veneration and pilgrimage. Just over two years after his death the pope had pronounced Thomas's canonization. Hence the seeming removal of the arch-rival from the scene had been accomplished only at the expense of making him a perpetual rival. As more and more pilgrims streamed to Canterbury to pray at the tomb of

---

[35] Browne (*York*, 275) points out that the present vaulted crypt constructed after the fire of 1829, was made from remnants from the old crypt and choir which had been buried beneath the present choir until the fire. It is highly unlikely that the crypt would have ribbed vaults if the choir did not also.

Thomas, the great eastern arm of that cathedral happened to burn in 1174. This catastrophe resulted in the rebuilding of the choir in the Gothic style, providing also a splendid new chapel to house the shrine of St. Thomas. There were few ways in which Roger could counter this eclipse of his own prestige by Thomas and of his remodeled York Minster by the new Canterbury choir. The recourse most likely to be effective was to sponsor a rival pilgrimage to the tomb of another saint. Roger's immediate predecessor as archbishop of York, William, had already been venerated as a saint[36] but he was not glamorous enough to vie with Thomas for the veneration of the faithful. The same was true also of St. John of Beverley, an early bishop of Hexham and then of York (died 721), who was venerated as a saint at Beverley from the eleventh century on.[37] In the whole of the archdiocese of York only two "resident" saints could be regarded in the same league with Thomas. Of these, the famous St. Cuthbert was already splendidly enshrined at Durham Cathedral.[38] The other, and the one readily available for Roger's purposes, was St. Wilfrid at Ripon.

There were several reasons why this late seventh-century saint could have been regarded as a suitable choice to fulfill such a purpose. Bede had recorded in his *History of the English Church and People* that Wilfrid was the first bishop of English blood,[39] hence one who could be appropriately promoted as a national symbol of the church. Although Bede was mistaken about this assertion, he would certainly have been regarded as an authoritative source in the twelfth century. Moreover, Wilfrid was known to have been the victorious advocate of obedience to the Roman church at the Synod of Whitby in 664,[40] thus also an appropriate symbol of orthodoxy. Eadmer of Canterbury, writing in the early twelfth century and knowing that Wilfrid had been bishop in the north of England, assumed that he was the ecclesiastical ruler of York but without explicitly using the term "archbishop."[41] Having grown up in the milieu of Can-

---

[36] Willis, *York Cathedral*, 50–53.

[37] For the life of St. John of Beverley see Bede, *A History of the English Church and People* (V. 2–6), Leo Shirley-Price, trans. and ed. (Harmondsworth, 1955), 266–274; *Dictionary of National Biography*, 10: 872–873: Translated at Beverley soon after he was canonized in 1037, he was apparently very quietly venerated until a retranslation of 1197 was made to a costly shrine, perhaps to instigate a pilgrimage.

[38] John Bilson, "On the Recent Discoveries at the East End of the Cathedral Church at Durham," *Archaeological Journal* 53 (1896), 4, 15. This disposition of Cuthbert's remains was documented by William of Malmesbury, *De Gestis Regum Anglorum*, (V. 145), William Stubbs ed. Rolls Series, 2, (London, 1889), 517.

[39] Bede, *History* (IV. 2), Shirley-Price, ed., 201.

[40] Bede, *History* (III. 25), Shirley-Price, ed., 184–188.

[41] Eadmer used the title *pontificis Eboricensum* when referring to St. Wilfrid while he used the explicit title *archiepiscopus* when he referred to any archbishop of Canterbury. The Latin text is cited, with English translation, by Willis in *Canterbury Cathedral*, 5, 10. Eadmer probably did not intend to slight the dignity of Wilfrid but to observe the delicate distinction between the metropolitanates of York and Canterbury. Willis, incidentally, always translates these references to Wilfrid with the term "archbishop."

terbury, Roger probably also thought of Wilfrid as an archbishop of York even though the seventh-century account by Eddius Stephanus does not associate him with that office except briefly as bishop of Ripon and York.[42] Although Roger may well have known of that earlier history when he began the new choir at York he probably would not have regarded the lack of coordination between the two sources as mutually exclusive in this regard, so Wilfrid could readily have been accepted as a symbol of the archbishopric of York. Finally, throughout his long ecclesiastical career, Wilfrid was three times displaced from his episcopal dignity, at least once and probably twice because of the intervention of the archbishop of Canterbury, from whose actions he appealed to the pope. Roger might well have regarded him as a symbol of the traditional struggle of the archbishops of York with the archbishops of Canterbury over matters of rank and authority.[43] St. Wilfrid, then, could signify a number of important matters—the ancient dignity of the see of York, the first English-born bishop-saint, the prominence of York in England's Roman orthodoxy, and the vindication of York in its struggles with Canterbury—all of them close to Roger's own concerns. St. Wilfrid was therefore also sufficiently important to serve as the chief attraction for a pilgrimage. Eadmer of Canterbury had written that, soon after his death in 709, Wilfrid's aura of sanctity had inspired a popular pilgrimage to Ripon.[44] Hence Roger could easily have made a pious claim that he wished only to see that pilgrimage revived and St. Wilfrid receive his due from the faithful.

However apt the choice of St. Wilfrid might have been to serve the venal purposes imputed above to the patron-archbishop, this explanation of Roger's motives in rebuilding Ripon Minster can be accepted only in conjunction with evidence that he did attempt to establish a pilgrimage. Unfortunately, no document survives from his own time to substantiate explicitly this interpretation. On the other hand, Archbishop Gray, on 21 January 1225, less than a month after he had translated the body of St. Wilfrid to its resting place in the new minster at Ripon, proclaimed an indulgence of thirty days to all who should visit the tomb of St. Wilfrid and there sincerely confess their sins. Although indulgences were frequently issued by ecclesiastical authorities to raise money for church con-

---

[42] Although Wilfrid's incumbency in the bishopric of York and Ripon was short in duration, the association was widely and vividly recorded in connection with his repair of York Minster. The accounts, in *Memorials of Ripon*, I, are from Eddius (*Vita Wilfridi*, XVI, 8), Eadmer (*Vita Wilfridi*, XVIII, 11), and William of Malmesbury (*Gesta Pontificum Anglorum*, 321), as well as the tenth-century poem of Fridegoda of Canterbury, (*Vita S. Wilfridi*, 437–80). Roger certainly knew the first two and may well have known all of them.

[43] Most of the archbishops of York since the Conquest had had similar difficulties with their archbishops of Canterbury; see accounts of their lives in the *Dictionary of National Biography*, s.v., Thomas of Bayeux, 1071–1100 (19: 640–43); Thomas II, 1108–1114 (19: 643–45); Thurstan, 1114–1140 (19: 832–37); William, 1140–1154 (21: 173–76).

[44] *Vita Wilfridi* (LIV), *Memorials of Ripon* 1: 20–21.

struction, such instruments include the exhortation to contribute.[45] In this document there is no mention of money and the emphasis upon visitation clearly implies that the purpose of the indulgence is to attract pilgrims.[46] Indeed, the translation itself may have been similarly motivated. Albeit performed by a successor to Roger and long after Roger began the new church, it is difficult to imagine that the translation was anything other than consonant with Roger's purposes.

### Glimpses of the Liturgical Program

The unusual plan at Ripon (plan 1) suggests that it was designed to accommodate a special liturgical program required by the patron. If construction of the new church was motivated by the desire to establish a cult of St. Wilfrid, as circumstantial evidence indicates, provision for the cult would almost necessarily have been one of the conspicuous components of the scheme. Although the intended site of the tomb or shrine was not recorded, its location might be deduced and help to explain the liturgical program.

One would almost automatically assume that Wilfrid was enshrined at or near the high altar. In the original church, constructed by Wilfrid, the saint had been laid to rest, according to Bede, on the south side of the high altar,[47] so it would have been reasonable to locate him similarly in the new minster. Even among the possible architectural antecedents for the liturgical layout of Ripon, for instance, Rochester Cathedral (a structure which, as we have seen, may have been the source of inspiration for the flat east end at York Minster) the shrine of St. Paulinus was located in the low axial chapel behind the high altar.[48] In a parallel situation in the archdiocese of York, the shrine of St. Cuthbert at Durham Cathedral had been installed in the apse behind the high altar in 1104.[49] As for Wilfrid himself, the relics of this saint at Canterbury Cathedral had always been near the east end, either at or near the high altar, or, as in the new Gothic choir, in the axial chapel (the corona).[50] Finally, regarding the location of Wilfrid's remains in the new Ripon Minster, two documents of the very late Middle Ages refer respectively to the shrine as being located in the choir or to the north of the high altar.[51] Yet these circumstantial testimonies cannot suffice to explain the original arrangement at Ripon.

---

[45] Examples of two such indulgences issued to support construction at Ripon, one undated and the other from 1258, are printed in *Memorials of Ripon* 1: 98, 113.

[46] See Appendix for the Latin text, cited from *Memorials of Ripon*, 1: 49–50.

[47] Bede, *History* (V. 19), Shirley-Price, ed., 307.

[48] See note 4.

[49] See note 38.

[50] Willis, *Canterbury Cathedral*, for citations from Eadmer (15–16, 16–17), Gervase (46, 56), and the list of relics in Cotton Ms. Galba E. IV (122).

[51] The former is a fabric roll from 1354–1355, in *Memorials of Ripon* 3: 95; see also Fowler's preface, xx. The latter is from John Leland's description of Ripon Minster, written 1538, in *Memorials of Ripon* 1: 87.

The assumption that the relics of St. Wilfrid were located in the choir is challenged by indirect evidence implicit in the indulgence promulgated by Archbishop Gray.[52] Referring to the translation at Christmas, 1224, the indulgence states that Archbishop Gray had found the body of St. Wilfrid whole. This report implies exhumation from a burial older than living memory; indeed, its reference to the translation by St. Oswald (in the late tenth century) suggests that Wilfrid was being translated for the first time since that earlier occasion. The new translation resulted in enshrining the body and the head separately, at unspecified locations. This action, occurring almost fifty years after the new minster was begun, was as likely a revision as a consummation of the original intention. If the body had already been in the choir it is less likely that the head would have been removed to create a second relic than if the burial was originally located outside the choir. Consequently, there is a reasonable case for supposing that St. Wilfrid's body had initially been located elsewhere in the new minster and very possibly intended by Archbishop Roger to remain there.

If we consider the apparent dependence of the Ripon plan upon that of York, especially as regards the aisleless nave, it may be significant that York probably provided a precedent for a saint's burial outside the choir. It is most likely that Roger's predecessor as archbishop, St. William of York, who had been popularly venerated since his death in 1153, was buried near the east end of the nave, on the north side of the altar.[53] Although it was chosen before he was venerated (indeed, he was officially canonized only in 1226), the site of his tomb immediately became the center of a minor cult. Hence in Roger's time the nave could be regarded as a suitable location for a saint's burial. Moreover, the translation of St. William's remains to the York choir in 1283 represents a situation which may impute specific significance to the remodeling of the Ripon choir a few years later, namely, that the cult center was transferred at that time to the choir. At any rate there was in Roger's time a sensitively placed precedent for locating a saint's tomb outside the choir.

The preservation of the presumed crypt of Wilfrid's seventh-century church (plan 1) and provision for entry into it from the crossing (behind the nave altar) of the new minster imply that a special importance was attached to it and for a special purpose. After all, this crypt represents the unique instance before the thirteenth century of incorporating a portion of an Anglo-Saxon church as a permanent feature of a new church in post-Conquest England.[54] J. T. Micklethwaite, the principal scholar of the

---

[52] See Appendix for the Latin text, in *Memorials of Ripon* 1: 49–50. Eadmer of Canterbury, by contrast, had recorded that the body of St. Wilfrid had been removed from Ripon to Canterbury by Archbishop Odo (about 950) and enshrined in the "great altar" of his Saxon cathedral, for which see Willis, *Canterbury Cathedral*, 10, 28.

[53] Willis, *York Cathedral*, 50–53.

[54] About 1215–1220, Hexham Priory was rebuilt over the crypt which St. Wilfrid had constructed with this church there. The principal study of Hexham remains the monograph of Charles Clement Hodges, *The Abbey of St. Andrew, Hexham* ([Edinburgh], 1888).

Ripon crypt, concluded from his study of the available documents and the archaeological evidence that, upon his death, St. Wilfrid had initially been buried in the crypt (at the original west end of the south chamber) and remained there until a new entry into the crypt was made at that location sometime in the thirteenth century or later.[55] Although the translation of 1224 probably signals the removal of the body from that tomb to a more prominent place—perhaps to the main chamber of the crypt, perhaps to an altar above the crypt in the crossing, or possibly even to the choir—it is likely that the liturgical program of the new church had been deliberately calculated to place the crossing rather than the choir over the crypt. In such an event it is most likely that Roger's intention had been to leave St. Wilfrid undisturbed in his grave and that the saint's removal to a shrine in 1224 was instigated by the much-belated removal in 1220 of St. Thomas à Becket from his grave in the Canterbury crypt to the chapel built in his honor behind the high altar.[56] This hypothesis must be tested, however, against the archaeological evidence available to explain the location of the new church relative to the old crypt.

Following careful analysis of the crypt and of all documents and previous studies related to it, as well as all of the similar evidence and evaluation pertaining to the parallel but slightly later crypt at Hexham Priory, Micklethwaite, and Hallett both concluded that the crypt had not only belonged to St. Wilfrid's church but also that its layout implied a structure oriented toward the west rather than the east.[57] Reflecting on this conclusion, Hallett[58] inferred that the (putative) church which replaced that of St. Wilfrid—one ostensibly built by St. Oswald ca.972–992—was oriented to the east, hence that the crypt marked the western extremity of the first church and the eastern extremity of the second. By implication, Roger's church had been laid out to the east of this second church so that its choir could be completed and used for services before the old church was torn down. Such an explanation reflects routine practice in twelfth-century England and serves to justify the present location of the crypt beneath the crossing. However, there is one major problem attendant upon this reasoning: at no point have remains of an intermediate church been discovered on the site.[59] Moreover, documentary evidence for such

---

[55] "On the Crypts at Hexham and Ripon," *Archaeological Journal* 39 (1882): 347–54; and idem., "Something About Saxon Church Building," *Archaeological Journal* 53 (1896): 344. The modification of the crypt provided a new entry from the east end of the nave, against the south wall, through the south chamber of the crypt. The date of this modification has been reckoned from the use of thirteenth-century tombstones at two places in the overhead masonry of the new entry passage. It is unlikely that tombstones would be reused in this manner until they were quite old, hence the earliest feasible date for the modification is probably the end of the thirteenth century, when the choir was being remodeled.

[56] Willis, *Canterbury Cathedral*, 62.

[57] "Crypts," 351–54; and Cecil Hallett, *The Cathedral Church of Ripon*, Bell's Cathedral Series (London, 1909), 71–78.

[58] Hallett, *Ripon*, 78.

[59] Recent excavations made in the eastern portions of the nave (where the stone flagging was replaced) and in the crossing (where the north entry into the crypt was opened) revealed

a structure does not specify reuse of the actual site of St. Wilfrid's church. Consequently, since no new structure is known to have been erected there prior to Roger's church, the location of the crossing over the crypt appears to have been deliberate and implies that the crypt was meant to play a special role in the liturgical program and to do so outside the choir.

No new program for the crypt was either more likely or appropriate than that of a pilgrimage cult around the resting place of St. Wilfrid. Yet it is by no means certain and cannot be proven unless unexpected evidence should yet come to light. Nevertheless, the thirteenth-century alterations to the crypt, which provided a south entrance from the nave,[60] suggest that the original function was being enhanced or at least modified and the most plausible explanation for such a change is that the pilgrimage cult was already located in the crypt or above it in the crossing, from which the crypt was entered. This explanation seems to be affirmed by the fact that the one recorded altar location, the altar of St. Wilfrid, was in the crypt.[61] Thus the placement of the new crossing directly over the crypt implies that the transepts were meant to be the focal points of the pilgrimage cult. (Indeed, it may be significant that Ripon was dedicated to St. Peter as well as to St. Wilfrid since the pilgrimage cult in Old St. Peter's in Rome was focused on a crypt located beneath the transept).

Another aspect of the layout which indicates that the transepts were the loci of the pilgrimage cult is that each of the arms has an elaborate door in its terminal elevation. Curiously, these doors are both placed off-center, almost adjacent to the west wall of the transepts, perhaps to avoid conflict with services in the chapels along the eastern elevation. Even so, these transept portals, always a rare feature in England, were the second known pair of corresponding transept portals in English architecture prior to the thirteenth century.[62] Certainly traffic circulation through the tran-

---

no definite evidence of any church built between Wilfrid's and the present one. A portion of stone foundation or wall was found on the north side of the crossing, where it can be seen beneath a trap door in the paving, but neither the configuration nor the masonry technique will permit it to be interpreted as part of such a church. A large round stone, flat on top and bottom was found in the crossing area and has been exhibited in the west end of the north nave aisle with a label identifying it as possibly a pier base for Oswald's tenth-century church. Such an attribution, however, violates everything known about the likely plan and scale of English architecture before the Conquest (or after, as regards form). If there was an intermediate church, then, it was probably located on another site. Doubts have been entertained that the church attributed to Oswald was actually erected at Worcester or York, more likely the former; see *Memorials of Ripon* 1: 42n, with reference to Eadmer's *Vita S. Oswaldi*.

[60] See note 55.

[61] When this altar was mentioned in the records of the Court of High Commission at York, 12 February 1567–1568, it was regarded as old (*Memorials of Ripon* 3: 346–47).

[62] There was one earlier example of corresponding transept doors in the monastic cathedral of Norwich, begun ca.1096. These portals, however, were neither monumental in form nor accessible to anyone outside the monastic community. See the plan of the entire complex by A. B. Whittingham, 1938, published in *Archaeological Journal* 106 (1949), opposite p. 86.

septs was the major consideration behind this feature and provision for traffic is usually associated with pilgrimages.[63]

The only other evidence that might shed light on the liturgical program of the minster is that indicating the location of altars at various points in the church. In most cases this evidence consists of aumbries (recesses in the masonry of the wall to hold the eucharistic vessels) and piscinae (drains in similar recesses which carry away the water of sacred ablutions) adjacent to the site of an altar. Readily identifiable evidence for altars appears in the following places: at the east end of the choir aisles and against the east wall of the choir, in each of the four transept chapels, at the east end of the nave, in each of the west towers (at ground level), and in the apse of the chapter house. In addition, the high altar is known by tradition to have been located one bay west of the east elevation, permitting a processional path behind it.[64] And there could have been an altar in the crossing over the crypt, but its existence is purely conjectural. There were, then, 13 or 14 altars in all, 12 or 13 of them inside the church proper.[65] This list of altar locations, in conjunction with peculiar aspects of this plan, contributes to a telling pattern of circumstances that can be sketchily interpreted.

The plan of Ripon (plan 1), with its resemblances to York (fig. 20), was not just symbolic of York but also functionally akin to it. Both were minsters with a chapter of canons who ministered to a large lay congregation and who maintained a daily schedule of liturgical offices appropriate respectively to a church of extra-parochial or archiepiscopal dignity. As revealed by excavations in recent years, the York Minster that Roger inherited when he became archbishop was a large cruciform church with aisleless transepts and nave and a choir either literally or virtually aisleless. In other words, it was a gigantic version of a simple parish church (considerably more than 300 feet long). The choir[66] was somewhat longer than was usual in Norman churches, so that it could have accommodated a fair number of worshippers; but the (probable) lack of normal aisles suggests that it would have been used primarily for the chapter offices and that

---

[63] Abbot Suger at Saint-Denis justified the rebuilding of the choir of that abbey church on the grounds that an ambulatory was needed to accommodate the traffic of pilgrims; *Libellus alter de consecratione sancti dionysii*, Erwin Panofsky, ed. and trans., *Abbot Suger on the Abbey Church of St.-Denis and Its Art Treasures* (Princeton, 1946), 86–89. Also, on the continent the Romanesque churches that are expressly associated as typical of the pilgrimage roads to Santiago have conspicuous transept portals. Notable examples are Saint-Sernin in Toulouse and Santiago Cathedral.

[64] Fowler, *Memorials of Ripon* 3: xx.

[65] I am happily indebted to Arnold Klukas who made a special point of identifying these features when he assisted me with photographing and measuring Ripon Cathedral in March 1977. He had then just completed research for his dissertation "Altaria Superioria," in which he was concerned with interpretation of liturgical arrangements, and so was more qualified than almost any other scholar to make an accurate identification of these features.

[66] Phillips, "Excavations," fig. 2 (plan).

the nave, accordingly, would have been the principal location for worship by the laity. When Roger built his new choir at York largely in imitation of the monastic choir at Canterbury, he was probably introducing a more elaborate observance of chapter offices rather than revising the arrangements for the traditional liturgy of the minster. Hence in building Ripon substantially in imitation of York, but deleting those features which might be regarded as symbolic of archiepiscopal dignity, he probably intended the choir to serve mainly the chapter offices[67] and the altars in the choir and chapels to accommodate the canons in their individual daily masses. Significantly, the number of these altars (excluding the high altar) corresponds to the number of canons—seven—who probably comprised the normal chapter constituency (plan 1).[68] The nave would serve large-scale parochial purposes and especially large congregations of pilgrims, most notably those on the feasts of St. Wilfrid (on October 12, the date of his death, and on April 24, the date of the translation of his relics by St. Oswald, in 979).[69] The arms of the transepts, with their respective entrances, could accommodate the necessary traffic of pilgrims to the tomb of St. Wilfrid, relieving the regular cycle of services in the choir or those in the nave from unnecessary intrusion. And the three-part auxiliary structure on the south side of the eastern arm adequately served the non-liturgical requirements of the chapter of canons. In sum, these various needs differ just enough from the common denominator of liturgical requirements in other large churches to signify a distinctive building program. They also correspond to the specific circumstances that made Ripon Minster singular in its patronage and purpose.

The use of traditional English features in the plan of the minster possibly inhibited the Ripon Master from developing a technically innovative structure or applying the more advanced structural ideas from his past experiences. To be sure, under the surface this building is scarcely different from some Anglo-Norman Romanesque churches. Yet, in view of this degree of conservative influence by the patron, the application of the Gothic style of the design that articulates the structure becomes all the more significant, for it suggests that the style had a meaning, beyond a new fashion in building, which pertains to its purpose. Namely, the use of the Gothic style at Ripon may have been related to its presumed function as a shrine for St. Wilfrid.

As Steven Wander has observed, there appears to have been an association in the twelfth century between the Gothic style and the shrine

---

[67] It is difficult to know whether the present solid stone screen (ca. 1500) at the west end of the choir replaced another of the same type or introduced a new usage, but Francis Bond (in *The Chancel of English Churches*, London, 1916, 101) has pointed out that in churches with solid screens the laity were expected not to worship at the high altar.

[68] Fowler, *Memorials of Ripon* 3: x.

[69] In addition, the birth of St. Wilfrid was celebrated in the parish of Ripon on the Sunday after Lammas Day (*Memorials of Ripon*, 1: 35n., and 50).

of saints. Not only was the style invented while building a new choir to house the shrine of St. Denis, but also in both France and England a considerable number of shrine-choirs were built as additions to Romanesque churches without any definite plan to rebuild the rest of the church. Obviously, if no undamaged church stood on the site—as at Ripon—the entire structure would be built in the Gothic style, but partial rebuildings were most likely to be addressed only to the shrine area. Characteristically such new construction housed the shrine of an apostolic saint (that is, first, or one of the first, to bring Christianity to a given region).[70] St. Wilfrid qualified in that respect even though St. Thomas at Canterbury did not. It is possible, then, that Roger's intention as much as current taste was influential in determining the style in which the new minster was built. Either way, both in the layout of the plan and in the style of the superstructure of his new church, we can probably see evidence of his controlling hand. Thus, we come to recognize the central role played by the patron in the creation of medieval architecture.

---

[70] Stephan Wander, "Westminster Abbey: A Case Study in the Meaning of Architecture," Ph.D. dissertation, Stanford University, 1974 (Ann Arbor Microfilms, 1975), 70–133; and idem., "Westminster Abbey and the Apostolic Churches of Northern France: A Contribution towards an Iconography of Medieval Architecture," *Studies in Iconography* 4 (1978): 3–22.

# 4. A SEARCH FOR THE ORIGIN OF THE RIPON MASTER

The task of the master builder at Ripon was to provide a useful and stable structure for the patron's program and to embellish it in a suitable manner. While the designer was probably eager to demonstrate his facility in working in the new Gothic mode—and the patron may even have chosen him for this ability—both he and his patron would have understood the style to be the means whereby the predetermined program was appropriately expressed, that is, that style was subordinate to theme. It was up to the builder, though, to devise an embellishment appropriate to the program and, in this instance, to determine how the Gothic style was to be applied. Undoubtedly the patron was consulted and gave his approval, but the main contribution of the builder was to endow the patron's program with its stylistic component. Put more concretely, if the patron specified the plan and massing of the scheme, it was the builder who designed the elevations and vaults.

The builder's design would not have been conceived *ex nihilo*, without reference to past experience. Except in rare instances, every feature of a design would be borrowed or adapted from a similar concept in earlier structures that the builder had worked on or examined. To understand the design in terms of its artistic context, then, requires tracing by means of archaeological comparison the source of each feature. Through this procedure we come to understand that the specific combination of features from different buildings implies certain aesthetic intentions and preferences. Moreover, the geographic pattern of the sources and their chronological arrangement tell us a good deal about the Ripon Master himself, namely, his professional background and architectural experience. Toward this end, we should begin by observing how the Gothic style was employed at Ripon so we can have a conscious appreciation of the scheme we wish to investigate.

The most salient visual aspect of the Ripon interior (pls. 3, 20; fig. 7) is the pattern composed of shafts and arch-moldings that defines its design. All these articulating features are relatively thin, conveying the impression that they are sculpturally rounded lines. In this respect, the subdivision of the main arcade piers as a bundle of shafts and the multiplication of the bay-division shafts—provided as responds for the arches of high vaults—contribute to the consistency of the overall linear quality. The composition of shafts and moldings grows out of logical relationships in which all articulations of the structure are represented as molded arches supported by corresponding shafts. This system of arches and shafts is sometimes employed to create an illusion of structural consistency between dissimilar areas, such as the triforium and clerestory. In both of these upper stories an arcade composed of a round-headed arch flanked by lower and narrower pointed arches provides the basic frame, either for a hole in the wall in the triforium or for an open wall passage in the clerestory. Moreover, throughout the elevation the quantity and disposition of the shafts and arch-moldings are severely restrained, curtailing the expression of layered plasticity in the wall and making it appear to be a thin, flat surface, much thinner than it actually is.

The system of shafts and moldings remains expressly distinct from the flat surface of the wall. The distinctness is technically manifest in three ways. First, the arch moldings are always set off from the flat wall masonry by a concave hollow, deep enough to create a shadow along the edge of the molding. Second, the basically columnar main arcade piers do not partake of the wall (unlike compound piers); instead, the wall is set upon them. Third, when shafts are applied to the wall, even in masonry courses, they are applied directly and not to a pilaster so that they do not partake of the wall as an embellishment of plastic layering but are superimposed upon its planar surface. This distinctness holds true even of the compound piers in the transepts where only the core of the pier actually belongs to the wall. Because of this quality, the system of shafts and moldings articulates the wall into units of pattern rather than units of structure, unlike Anglo-Norman architecture. Indeed, the use of columnar piers rather than compound piers emphasizes the continuity of the wall fabric set upon them, an expression amplified at Ripon by the corbeling of the vault respond shafts at the window-sill level in the choir aisles so that the continuity of the aisle wall is also manifest. The total effect of the articulating members is the imposition of a plastic, linear order of architecture upon a flat, planar order.

This effect constitutes that aspect of the formal expressiveness of the Ripon design which we identify as Gothic. It is precisely this Gothic nature of the elevation articulation that cannot be explained either as an evolutionary outgrowth of English Romanesque architecture or of Cistercian architecture in England, although examples of the latter were to manifest these qualities soon after Ripon was begun. The source of inspiration must then be sought in the context where such qualities had already been developed, the early Gothic architecture of the Ile de France. In order to make this investigation of sources a rigorous one, each component of the elevation design—that of the choir primarily—will be treated separately and in sequence, beginning with the main arcade and proceeding through the upper stories to the overall articulation and the intended vaults. In this discussion the stylistic nuances of each component will be explored more specifically than in the general characterization above.

## A. The Main Arcade and the Vaults of the Aisles and Chapels

### The Piers

The main arcade piers of the choir (pls. 4, 5) are fundamentally columnar in type, by virtue of being completely self-contained beneath the arches and vaults they support and of conforming to a basically circular circumference. The trunks of these piers are composed of a bundle of eight round shafts, with larger shafts facing the cardinal compass directions and smaller shafts in the diagonal positions. This columnar shaft-bundle stands on a circular plinth composed of two layers, the upper slightly smaller than the lower. Each shaft has an attic base and a plain inverted-bell capital surmounted by a rectangular, molded impost. The bases, capitals, and imposts are compound forms, each carved from a single block.

The use of the shaft-bundle pier in the Ripon choir introduced an unprecedented refinement to this type of highly-articulated elevation design. While a simple columnar pier shaft shares the basic form of the wall shafts and arcade colonnettes which are incorporated in the upper stories, receiving the same effects of light and shadow that endow these smaller members with the quality of plastic lines, the discrepancy of scale disrupts the apprehension of their structural kinship and formal consistency. The shaft-bundle pier not only solved this problem but it also avoided the compromising integration of the pier with the wall structure that a compound pier, similarly articulated, would have introduced. Further, the articulation of the trunk provided virtual responds to the various arches and bay-division shafts which the pier supports, even to the extent of varying their thickness according to the relative importance of the members. While the shaft-bundle pier historically had played no such role, other than to correspond on occasion to the various orders of a main arcade, the formal meaning of its composition was modified by the act of adopting it for an elevation with sophisticated vertical articulation.[1]

In addition to these subtleties, the inverted-bell capitals (pl. 3) introduced another refinement and one unexpected in medieval architecture.

---

[1] Before Ripon, and in many instances afterward, the shaft-bundle pier appeared in churches of various designs which had neither vertical wall articulation nor high vaults and in which the number of orders in the main arcades was arbitrary and the only rib vaults associated with these piers were in aisles. Peter Fergusson (in "The Late Twelfth-Century Rebuilding at Dundrennan Abbey, *Antiquaries Journal* 53 (1973): 237–38; and in "The South Transept Elevation of Byland Abbey," *Journal of the British Archaeological Association*, 3rd ser., 38 (1975): 162–64) sees a direct connection in English Cistercian architecture between the number of shafts in a pier and the number of responds needed. He particularly sees a connection between the development of the shaft-bundle pier and the introduction of the ribbed vault in aisles. However, in a wider context, while there usually is some correspondence between the number of shafts on the pier and the number of orders in the main arcade, there is frequently no formal relationship between the profile of the arch orders and the pier shafts. More often than not, there is no relationship between vaulting arches and the pier shafts. Most important, this type of pier first flourished in architectural traditions where the logical response of shafts to arches was of minor importance. Even when the shaft-bundle pier was combined with a cluster of vertical bay-division shafts at Ripon, as we shall see later in detail, the point was less one of literal response than of textural consistency.

Noticeably shorter than the capitals of the same type at Roche (pl. 56), the curvature of their profile is also much more pronounced. That this curvature was meant to be regarded as significant is implied by the fact that the profiles of the main arcade capitals are more radically curved than the profiles of capitals of the same height at the top of the clusters of bay-division shafts. Accordingly, these profiles appear to have been adjusted to express the transition between weight and support, a weight which would be far greater in the ground story than at the springing of the intended high vaults. Certainly the kind of organic expressiveness we attribute to Doric architecture could not be claimed for Gothic, hence not for Ripon, but the subtlety with which every feature of the Ripon pier is formulated (as we shall see) and with which the pier is coordinated with the rest of the elevation clearly testifies to a degree of deliberation in planning that would be extraordinary even in High Gothic design.

The sources of the main arcade piers are not to be found in England. In order to know that, however, it is necessary to make a substantial digression to disprove their association with Cistercian architecture and especially that of England. Although no English Cistercian church produced an exact precedent for the Ripon piers, the shaft-bundle type was so common in England during the last three decades of the twelfth century that it is difficult to dissociate this feature from its English context. The shaft-bundle pier is distinct from an apparently similar type, the lobed pier, in that each of its articulated components is more than half a circle, usually about three-quarters. Curiously, the two types exist together in the nave of Kirkstall (pl. 61), the lobed in the eastern bays and the shaft-bundle in the later, western bays.[2] For this reason, the shaft-bundle pier in English Cistercian architecture might be taken to be the result of an evolutionary development initiated at Kirkstall itself, especially since Kirkstall appears to have easily the earliest shaft-bundle piers in England. Certainly, after Kirkstall, this type of pier, in one or another of its various manifestations, appeared in most of the new church construction in the North of England.

The filiations of shaft-bundle piers are extremely difficult to trace.[3] In their normal forms, these piers usually have eight or twelve shafts, either

---

[2] For a discussion of these two types of piers, see Fergusson, "Byland," 161–63; for the development of shaft-bundle piers at Kirkstall, see John Bilson, "The Architecture of Kirkstall Abbey Church, with Some General Remarks on the Architecture of the Cistercians," *The Publications of the Thoresby Society* 16 (1907): 124–25.

[3] For purposes of analyzing the development of the shaft-bundle pier, all elements of the piers of each of the following twelfth-century churches were correlated formally and chronologically: Cistercian abbeys—Kirkstall, Fountains (monastic complex), Roche, Byland, Furness, Jervaulx, and Dundrennan; Benedictine abbeys—Selby nave and Bardney; Augustinian abbeys and priories—Jedburgh nave and Cartmel choir; other—Ripon choir, Old Malton nave, Arbroath Abbey. Thirteenth-century examples, such as Rievaulx choir and transepts, Hexham, Whitby, Southwark, Lincoln, Southwell choir, and Beverley were also taken into consideration. French examples were also included, especially Bertaucourt-les-Dames and Dommartin, and numerous other churches which are recorded in Eugène Lefevre-Pontalis, *L'Architecture religieuse dans l'ancien diocèse de Soissons* (Paris, 1894), 2 vols. *passim*; and Camille Enlart, *Manuel d'archéologie française* (Paris, 1925) 1: 349–51.

all the same size or varied in thickness according to a hierarchical scheme of relative importance. The shafts may be round or keeled and either uniform in type or used in combinations. These piers stand on plinths that can have highly various shapes and heights. The plan of the plinth may be one simple shape—square, octagonal, or circular—underneath the entire bundle of shafts or it may have a compound composition that provides an articulated element, either rectangular or lobed, for each shaft. In some cases, one type of plinth is superimposed upon another. The plinth may jut only a few inches above the floor or rise to any height up to about two feet. Also, the plinth profile may be plain, simply chamfered, or molded in varying degrees of complexity. The capitals, after Kirkstall, may be of the inverted-bell type, the water-leaf type (in one of its several forms), or, from around 1200 on, of the molded type. Finally, any given church may employ more than one type, either to provide variety in the design or as the result of modifications introduced in subsequent stages of construction. So far as I know, no shaft-bundle pier was ever fully reproduced, with all its formal characteristics intact, in another building. Moreover, the chronological spread of each of the characteristics overlaps to such an extent that these variations cannot be assigned a sequential order of development. It appears, then, that the shaft-bundle pier was always regarded as a formula which was susceptible to wide variation according to taste.

Yet another complication must be accounted for in this analysis. The use of shaft-bundle piers was by no means confined to the Cistercians but was known also among the Augustinians and the Benedictines, not to mention the secular canons of Ripon. In this light it would appear that the shaft-bundle pier, despite its early appearance and fairly frequent use in France as well as England, was so much a part of the English architectural tradition by the late twelfth century that if its presence at Ripon cannot be attributed expressly to a Cistercian source then it must nevertheless be to an English one. Certainly the report by Harold Brakspear on the ruins of Bardney Abbey, an ancient Benedictine house in Lincolnshire, rebuilt in the twelfth century and modified in the thirteenth,[4] would seem to indicate the availability of a non-Cistercian antecedent or contemporary of the Ripon piers. Because Brakspear judged it to have been vaulted throughout, Bardney could readily be attributed to the decade when Roche was under construction and Ripon was being planned,[5] that is, before high vaulting was generally abandoned in the North from ca. 1180 to ca. 1200.

The portion of Bardney that could be regarded as early enough to be a model for Ripon is the south transept, which ostensibly had a range of

---

[4] Brakspear, "Bardney Abbey," *Archaeological Journal* 79 (1922): 1–92, especially 22–25.

[5] Brakspear, "Bardney Abbey," 13, 24. Because the plinths of the shaft-bundle piers in the south transept had canted elements flanking the shafts beneath the wall axis, Brakspear interpreted them to indicate responds for diagonal ribs in high vaults. Fergusson ("Byland," 164, n. 2) places these piers in the 1170s.

separated, square eastern chapels much like those of the Cistercians and of Ripon. Curiously for such a transept, these piers were of the columnar type (hence unaffected by the dividing walls of the chapels, which might have been a later addition). The pier trunks were composed of twelve round shafts and had a compound plinth, superimposed upon another, in which four elements were canted diagonally as if to indicate that their shafts were responds for the ribs of high vaults. Corresponding evidence for full-length shaft responds on the west wall of the transept seems to confirm the relationship of the shafts to vaulting. The reported profile of the shaft bases is sufficiently close to that at Ripon, both in its attic type and the depth of its curvature, to raise no problems for an early date. Capitals found on that portion of the site confirm the use of a version of the water-leaf variety,[6] the general type that occurs in the earliest portions of Ripon, namely, the choir aisles.

This evidence provided by the ruins of Bardney does not permit, however, a very discriminating comparison with Ripon for the purpose of establishing the anteriority of one over the other. Nevertheless, three features might be taken as chronologically significant within a broader architectural context. First, the use of columnar shaft-bundle piers with a range of transept east chapels suggests that the transept design was derived from the Cistercian tradition but at a time when such chapels were no longer conceived as separate spaces, beginning with Byland and Furness. Second, the diagonally-canted elements in the upper plinth have no counterparts among twelfth-century English churches until the appearance of the canted vault responds in the late portions of Roche and the early portions of Byland; indeed, the refined complexity of these plinths suggests that they came after the various experiments in plinth design at Byland.[7] Third, if Bardney had high vaults with canted responds in the piers it probably also had multiple bay-division shafts, the only church besides Ripon in which this feature seems to have occurred in combination with shaft-bundle piers. Because on two counts the Bardney transept appears to have been influenced by the work at Byland, itself slightly later than Ripon, its multiple bay-division shafts could reasonably be attributed to an imitation of those at Ripon. Hence the Bardney transept, probably designed in the early 1180s, cannot reasonably be regarded as the source for the Ripon choir piers.

In the final analysis the shaft-bundle piers of Ripon seem to have only two reasonably secure antecedents in England, Kirkstall and Roche. No

---

[6] Brakspear, "Bardney Abbey," 22–25 and fig. 4.
[7] At Byland there were no diagonally-canted plinth elements but the vault responds in the aisles of the transepts and choir had imposts with side units canted to receive the diagonal ribs. In England, within the architectural tradition that employed shaft-bundle piers, the treatment of imposts first involved compositions of frontal elements (e.g. Kirkstall), followed by polygonal elements (e.g. Roche choir and transept chapels, Ripon choir aisles), before compound compositions with canted elements appeared (e.g. Roche transept high vaults, Byland transept and choir aisles). The corresponding (upper) plinths of the piers at Byland all have compound frontal elements.

one who has studied Roche has supposed that its piers (pl. 62) were based on those of Kirkstall (pl. 61), which, after all, have a hexagonal rather than a circular girth and so are not even pure examples of the type. The source of the Roche piers has been attributed instead to prototypes in Picardy.[8] The Ripon piers, then, might have had a similar source. It is probably significant that Cistercian churches in England before the second campaign at Byland had either square or compound-cruciform plinths supporting their shaft-bundle piers. Ripon, on the other hand, has circular plinths, a form always rare and definitely not found in any earlier English building. For such an early example of shaft-bundle piers in England the influence of a specific prototype is far more likely than in later instances.

The existence in Picardy of a definite precedent for the Ripon piers, with a cluster of eight round shafts on a round plinth, is too significant to be ignored as a candidate for the actual Ripon prototypes. To be sure, these piers, located in the nave of the parish church of Bertaucourt-les-Dames (pl. 74), near Amiens, and dated before 1160,[9] are not exactly like those of Ripon. Between the circular plinth and the shaft bases is an inconspicuous compound plinth, composed of radially-disposed squares. At Ripon, the corresponding member is the upper layer of the circular plinth. The Bertaucourt shafts are not rounded to quite the same extent as those at Ripon and the shafts facing the cardinal compass directions are not thicker than those in the diagonal positions, as they are at Ripon. Also, the inverted-bell capitals of Bertaucourt are decorated with foliage and the impost is slightly taller, relative to the capital. However, each element of the pier ensemble—plinth, bases, shafts, capitals, and imposts—is of the same type as at Ripon. Given this extraordinary degree of similarity between the piers of the two churches, and the lack of it between Ripon and the relevant examples in England, the resemblance suggests a direct relationship. Considering the options available for imitation in the Ile de France and even in the northeastern sector, it is unlikely that the designer of Ripon would have selected expressly the piers of Bertaucourt for a model unless they could serve a purpose no others could fulfill. That this might have been the case can be determined only after identification of the prototypes for all of the other features in his design. However, it is equally plausible that the Bertaucourt piers had been imitated from a much more prominent example, now lost, which was the actual model for Ripon. In any event, the Ripon piers were almost certainly based on a prototype in France rather than one in England.

---

[8] Jean Bony, "French Influences on the Origins of English Gothic Architecture," *Journal of the Warburg and Courtauld Institutes* 12 (1949): 6; and Peter Fergusson, "Roche Abbey: the Source and Date of the Eastern Remains," *Journal of the British Archaeological Association*, 3rd ser. 34: (1971), 30–42.

[9] François Deshoulières, "Bertaucourt-les-Dames," *Congrès archéologiques de France, Amiens* 99 (1936): 127–128; and Camille Enlart, *Monuments religieux de l'architecture romane et de transition dans la région picarde* (Paris, 1895), 75.

## The Arches of the Main Arcade and Vaults

The arches of the main arcade (pls. 3, 4) are as distinctive as the piers in their details. They consist of a single order with an elaborate layer of molding applied to the soffit. The angle roll that outlines each arch is flanked by concave hollows so wide and deep that the arch molding reads as a virtually distinct member in the wall composition. The soffit molding, as we saw in the discussion of Cistercian influence, consists of a keeled roll flanked by angular fillets and round rolls. Together these features create the impression of a new concept of wall formulation, appearing in England for the first time with the Gothic style. The wall seems to be much thinner, in part because it is relatively thinner than in earlier construction and in part because the arcade is articulated in only one order and embellished with thin, linear moldings. This treatment of articulation and decoration results in a new emphasis upon the surface of the wall as a flat plane of reference, rejecting the earlier tradition of walls articulated in several layers to create a sculptural structure. Against the flatness of the wall, the arch moldings and shafts contrast to make a composition of plastic lines, unlike Romanesque elevations where these ornaments simply enhance the plasticity of the wall.

The arches of the aisle vaults (pl. 12) are molded with a degree of elaboration that is generally more typical of the English twelfth-century tradition than of the French. Yet the molding is of a lightness and fineness of detail unknown in England before the 1170s. The diagonal ribs of the vaults present a profile that emphasizes the linearity of the vault articulation. A simplified version of the main arcade soffits, this profile is composed of a keeled roll flanked by round rolls, omitting the angle fillets between the rolls. The transverse arches have a less delicate profile composed of one large keeled roll flanked by hollow chamfers. A smaller version of the same profile was adapted for the wall arches also. Discounting some irregularities, the masonry of the vault severies is laid in courses running perpendicular to the four boundary arches of each bay—the method identified earlier in our own era as the "French method."[10]

Like the piers, the arches and vaults also have an ambiguous relationship to Cistercian architecture in England and early Gothic in France. Yet, as we saw in the previous chapter, to determine the chronological position of Ripon in its English context is to remove all of the pertinent examples

---

[10] The difference between the "French" and "English" methods of laying the webbing masonry of vault severies, already recognized in the nineteenth century by archeologues such as Viollet-le-Duc, was understood to represent a real difference in national traditions of construction even though both types of vaulting could be found on both sides of the channel. Emphasized in the early twentieth century, when interest in vaulting was at its apogee, it was explained in detail by English writers such as Francis Bond, in *An Introduction to English Church Architecture from the Eleventh to the Sixteenth Century* (London, 1913) 1: 322–327, and Thomas Graham Jackson, *Gothic Architecture in France, England, and Italy* (Cambridge, 1915) 1: 212–214.

as possible prototypes for these features. The prototype, then, must be sought in France.

The prototypes are both general and specific in nature. Among the general prototypes are the basically thin and flat wall treatment, with the arch articulated in one order, and the arch molding set off by wide, deep concavities. Virtually all early Gothic churches of ambitious scale and advanced stylistic character in France that were begun after 1160 share these traits. Scattered throughout the northeast of the Ile de France and especially concentrated in the Soissonnais are the application of an elaborate soffit molding to the main arcade arches and the practice of molding vault arches, as well as soffits, with clusters of rolls, both round and keeled, in varying combinations. In French Early Gothic architecture, the Soissonnais appears to have been the true home of this type of arch molding by virtue of both chronological anteriority and density of occurrence.[11] Some of the closest parallels to Ripon are to be found in a variety of small churches that typically are dated in the third quarter of the twelfth century. The profile of the main arcade soffit molding is found in the small priory at Bellefontaine (pl. 75), dated approximately 1150.[12] The rib profile of the Bellefontaine high vaults is very similar to that of the aisle vaults at Ripon but it differs by retaining the angle fillets of the soffit profile between the three rolls. An exact parallel to the Ripon profile is found in the small parish church of Crézancy (ca. 1130); and, mounted on a more emphatic dosseret and set off by hollow chamfers, it also appears at Nouvron-Vingré and Coulonges.[13] A profile like that of the Ripon transverse arches occurred in a somewhat primitive version on the transverse arches of the aisle vaults in the parish church of Béthizy-Saint-Pierre (before 1150) and in a fashion exactly like Ripon on both the transverse and wall arches of the apse in the parish church at Veuilly-la-Poterie (ca. 1175).[14]

In the Ripon transepts the arch moldings of the main arcade (pl. 20) and of the chapel vaults (pl. 21) differ only slightly from those of the choir and the aisle vaults. The soffit profile has the same general composition as that in the choir; but its center roll is rounded rather than keeled, a minor variation. The rib profile is the same as that in the choir aisles. Since the chapels in the north transept were separated by a wall, there were no transverse arches. However, these vaults mark the introduction of the ridge rib, a single round roll, which was coordinated with wall arches of the same profile on all four sides of the vault. While England had already produced a Romanesque vault with ridge ribs in the treasury

---

[11] Bony, "French Influences," 6. For examples see Lefevre-Pontalis, *L'Ancien diocèse de Soissons, passim.*

[12] Lefevre-Pontalis, *L'Ancien diocèse de Soissons*, 2: 4–8, pl. XIX; and Fergusson, "Roche Abbey," 37, n. 1.

[13] Lefevre-Pontalis, *L'Ancien diocèse de Soissons*, 2: 44–46 and pl. XXIV, fig. 6; 72–74 and pl. XXXIV; and 136–39 and pl. LVI, respectively.

[14] Lefevre-Pontalis, *L'Ancien diocèse de Soissons*, 2: 18–22, pl. XXIII; and 217–20, pl. XCII, respectively.

of Canterbury Cathedral (ca. 1160),[15] the use of this feature at Ripon seems to have been inspired by an early Gothic example in Picardy which employed ridge members of the same single-torus profile, that is, the west bay vault of the nave at Airaines (shortly after 1140),[16] where there is an equivalent disproportion between the thickness of the diagonal ribs and the ridge ribs.

These widely scattered examples cannot be taken to represent the actual prototypes for the Ripon arch moldings, gathered selectively by the designer as he traveled from church to church. Rather they represent close analogues drawn from the general practice of a region, a practice with which the Ripon designer ostensibly had a first-hand knowledge. The example of Bellefontaine helps to explain why the designer may have chosen to imitate this tradition. It combines molded arch soffits and vault arches of similar profile with the use of shaft-bundle piers. (Indeed, the pier is of the type composed of eight round shafts, albeit here a half-pier attached to the wall, and the capital and impost are also the same types as those used at Ripon). The general effect that the Ripon Master sought to borrow is that of textural consistency, in which the articulating features of the main arcade, even of the whole elevation, are composed of multiples of small units harmoniously related in scale.

## B. The Upper Stories

### The Triforium

The triforium of the lateral choir elevations (pl. 11) and the transept east elevations (pl. 20) consists of a round-arched opening in the middle portion of the bay, an opening which is subdivided into two pointed arches and flanked by blind pointed arches of the same height and virtually the same width as those beneath the round arch. The blind arches and the round arch are articulated in the same plane, while the subdividing arches are set in a recessed plane. Even so, the four pointed arches create a regular band-type triforium arcade across the width of each bay. The spandrel above the subdividing arches is pierced by a quatrefoil opening. Although the single, subdivided opening which stands the full height of the story is reminiscent of the middle story of the galleried churches so characteristic of English Romanesque architecture, this version with the opening only in the center of the bay is not related to that tradition or to its formal successor, the false-tribune. Indeed, every aspect of this triforium composition is new to English architecture; and, in its totality, it is unprecedented elsewhere. Its components were derived from diverse sources for the purpose of creating a design which harmonized very subtly with the rest of the elevation, as we shall see.

---

[15] For its context, see Bony, "French Influences," 5. See also, John Bilson, "The Norman School and the Beginnings of Gothic Architecture, Two Octopartite Vaults: Montivilliers and Canterbury," *Archaeological Journal* 74 (1917): 1–35.

[16] Marcel Aubert, "Airaines," *Congrès archéologique de France, Amiens* 99 (1936): 463.

Before the sources for the design can be identified, it is necessary to determine whether the composition of open and blind arches represents an established tradition in triforium articulation or a new combination of two different triforium types. Tracing the prototypes for the design of the reconstituted elevation of Byland, Peter Fergusson cited examples of "open and closed arcading" as precedents for the triforium.[17] As we saw in the previous chapter, the Byland triforium (fig. 17) made the flanking, blind pointed arches as tall as the rounded center arch; for that composition the attribution of the Byland triforium to such a tradition seems completely reasonable. However, the Byland triforium is a modification of the Ripon design[18] and at Ripon the relationship of the four pointed arches had been carefully established to express an even band across the width of the bay. It appears, then, more likely that the composition at Ripon was intended to superimpose a band triforium upon a triforium with a subdivided arch in the center of the bay. The combination of the two had the virtue of maintaining the vertical axis of the bay while achieving horizontal continuity along the elevation. In this light, in 1175 the inspiration for the band triforium effect could have come from Noyon (pl. 58) or Laon (pl. 77) cathedrals or, more aptly for a three-story elevation, from the newly designed abbey of Saint-Vincent in Laon.[19] The subdivided open arch has its most apposite precedent in the nave of the Picard collegiate church of Lillers (pl. 81), ca. 1145.[20]

The articulation of the triforium opening with a round-headed arch enclosing two pointed arches was almost certainly not an automatic result of combining the two triforium types. At the beginning of this century, the twelfth-century use of both kinds of arch together was interpreted as a lack of stylistic resolution, signifying an evolutionary transition from

---

[17] Fergusson, "Byland," 166–67.

[18] Peter Fergusson's reconstitution of the Byland elevation (see his "Byland," 156–60, and fig. 2) is an invaluable correction of the unsatisfactory one by Edmund Sharpe (*Architectural Parallels*, (London, 1848) pl. 19) which had been uncritically accepted and repeated for more than 125 years. Curiously, Scott's reconstitution of the Ripon choir elevation was apparently based in part on the Byland illustration (see Scott, "Ripon Minster," 349) rather than on observation of the actual building for it erroneously makes the flanking blind arches of the triforium arcade as tall as the central one. This error, too, has been repeated uncritically until the present time. However, when Fergusson's Byland elevation and the actual Ripon elevation are compared there can be no doubt that the former is derived from the latter.

[19] Saint-Vincent was probably being planned in 1174 or shortly thereafter, just before the Ripon Master designed the new minster. For Saint-Vincent, see Elie Lambert, "L'Ancienne abbaye de Saint-Vincent de Laon," *Académie des Inscriptions et belleslettres, comptes rendue des séances de l'année 1939*, 124–38.

[20] Pierre Héliot, "Lillers," *Congrès archéologique de France, Amiens* 99 (1936) 580 (for the nave); 582–83 (for the choir). See also Bony, "French Influences," 2; n. 5, for a date of ca.1135–1140. The choir triforium contrasts interestingly with that of the nave because it is a band triforium, undivided into bays, with an alternation of open and blind arch units. In a sense, the two types of triforium at Lillers are combined at Ripon in an elegant and stylishly updated version. Another example of a church with a subdivided triforium opening only in the middle of the bay is the nave of Saint-Etienne in Beauvais (ca. 1155) but Lillers is a much more likely source for Ripon.

Romanesque to Gothic style.²¹ This apparent anachronism, however, had the dual virtues of reflecting the clerestory arcade (itself influenced by the retention of round-headed arches for windows) and of providing a foil for the row of pointed arches. Regardless of the sensitivity with which it was adapted for this purpose, the enclosure of two pointed arches with a round arch was a motif that belonged expressly to early Gothic architecture in the northeast and east of France. It was employed in the church tower at Daméry (ca. 1160),²² (fig. 22), and also in the choir of the abbey church at Vézelay (ca. 1185).²³ It undoubtedly appeared in other churches between those dates, especially in the northeast, but, as is well known, the architecture of this period in this region has been heavily victimized by destruction.²⁴ That the motif was widely fashionable, especially in the 1170s, is indicated by its simultaneous adoption (albeit in double units) for the choir of Canterbury Cathedral and, during the rest of the century, by its frequent imitation from Ripon and Canterbury in numerous other churches in England.²⁵

The pierced spandrel (in this case, by a quatrefoil) marks one of the earliest instances of this feature in England and among the earliest anywhere. The one surviving English example that is definitely anterior to that at Ripon is the gallery arcade of Peterborough Cathedral (designed ca. 1118).²⁶ At Peterborough, the pierced spandrels are cut either by a single circle or by a lozenge-shaped group of four circles, all of which are circumscribed by a frame. Pierced spandrels were also employed, but without a frame, in the exterior clerestory passage of the Noyon Cathedral transepts. Located in the straight bays, the pierced motif was a trefoil rather than a quatrefoil (pl. 80). Although it is uncertain whether or not

---

[21] Typical characterizations of the mixture of arch types as transitional are those of George Gilbert Scott, "The Transition from the Romanesque to the Pointed Style in England," *Archaeological Journal* 32 (1875): 364–67; and Edward S. Prior, in *A History of Gothic Art in England* (London, 1900), 83–86. Hallet (*Ripon Cathedral*, 101) made no judgment when he used the term "transitional," but it is clear that he had in mind definitions of style in which the consistent use of pointed arches is essential to the purity of Gothic character.

[22] Lefevre-Pontalis, *L'Ancien diocèse de Soissons*, 2: 151–54, pl. 65.

[23] Francis Salet, *La Madeleine de Vézelay* (Melun, 1948), 72–73, 82–83.

[24] The most likely center of this motif was in the group of destroyed cathedrals in the northeast of France: Arras (1160–1200), Cambrai (1148–67) and Valenciennes (begun ca. 1171). The basis for this assertion is that the motif appears at both Canterbury and Vézelay, at each of which influence from one or more of these churches has been detected; see Bony, "French Influences," 9, for Canterbury, and Robert Branner, *Burgundian Gothic Architecture* (London, 1960), 30–34. See also Pierre Héliot's quotation from Jean Bony in "Les oeuvres capitales du gothique francais primitif et l'influence de l'architecture anglaise," *Wallraf-Richartz Jahrbuch* 20 (1958): 98.

[25] Instances stemming from Ripon and its influence are Byland, Old Malton, Lanercost, Tynemouth choir, Jedburgh nave, Hexham, and Whitby; from Canterbury, they are Chichester retrochoir and York transept.

[26] Pierced spandrels occur only in the two easternmost, straight bays of the choir, in the north elevation. They are, however, original and their use is too deliberate to have been regarded as insignificant. See C. R. Peers, "Peterborough Minster," *Victoria History of the Counties of England, Northamptonshire*, vol. 2 (London, 1906), 435.

Fig. 22. Daméry Church, tower arcade, reproduced from E. Lefevre-Pontalis, *L'Architecture religieuse dans l'ancien diocèse de Soissons* (Paris, 1894).

this portion of Noyon had been built before 1175,[27] pierced trefoils also appear there in the spandrels of the nave gallery, so this was probably a feature that figured in the design proposal and hence was likely planned at an earlier date when it could have been known before Ripon was designed. At Noyon and Ripon, the omission of a frame enhances the significance of piercing the spandrel because the lack of explicit limits for the hole diminished the integrity of the spandrel membrane. This innovation did not lead directly to the transformation of the subdividing arches into a tracery pattern, as would happen in the next century, but already it does visually detach the pair of pointed arches from the round arch framing them, thereby increasing the formal relationship of all four pointed arches in the triforium composition as a whole. It appears, then, that every aspect of this composition, from structural outline to decorative details, was calculated to make the middle story enhance both vertical and horizontal continuity in the elevation, to make it the instrument of harmony in the overall design.

---

[27] For the dates of the transepts and nave of Noyon, see Charles Seymour, Jr., *Notre-Dame of Noyon in the Twelfth Century* (New Haven, 1939), 55–62, recently republished in French as *La cathédrale Notre-Dame de Noyon au XIIe siècle* (Droz and Geneva, 1975), 37–42.

## The Clerestory

The clerestory (pl. 3) follows the century-old English practice (which, by 1175, had become a national tradition) of constructing the upper story with a passage in the thickness of the wall, with windows piercing the outer shell and an open arcade articulating the inner shell. The triple-arch rhythm of the arcade was also traditional. The design of this arcade resulted from the adaptation of the traditional format to the formal vocabulary of the new style. The round center arch was dictated primarily by the retention of round-headed windows, but the combination of this round arch and the pointed flanking arches was adopted to harmonize with the triforium arcade. The only inconsistency with the triforium is the doubling of the freestanding colonnettes in the arcade. This expedient was necessary in order to maintain the same scale for colonnettes in the two upper stories and, at the same time, to make the clerestory arcade physically and visually stable.

The one truly new aspect of the clerestory is the technique employed to construct the wall passage. As we saw in the last chapter, the novelty of this technique consisted generally of connecting the arcade supports and the outer wall with a flat lintel rather than springing an arch across the void. But specifically the novelty lay in the way the lintel was connected to the arcade and the wall and it is this method which leads to the prototypes. Unlike the new work at Canterbury (pl. 57), the lintel in the Ripon passage (pl. 22) was laid on top of the arcade impost rather than being an extension of the impost itself. This feature, previously unknown in England, first appeared (in a context relevant to the origins of the Ripon design) in the transepts of Noyon Cathedral (ca. 1170) in the arcaded passageway of the tall, third-story triforium (pl. 58). At Ripon, the junction of the lintel and the wall was underlined by a string-course which repeated both the height and the profile of the arcade impost. In other words, both ends of the lintel were supported by similar elements. The supporting string-course was a feature of the terminal-wall passageway of the transepts in Laon Cathedral (ca. 1170) (pl. 79).[28] At Laon, this feature was inserted in the wall at the level of the arcade capitals, so it did not provide the same kind of formal consistency that it did at Ripon. The combination of the techniques from Noyon and Laon produced the most logically refined formulation for a wall passageway that had been devised. At Canterbury, where the Laon technique has been detected,[29] and at Byland,

---

[28] Most writers have avoided assigning a date to the Laon transept. I am indebted to William Clark for sharing with me the detailed chronology of construction from his forthcoming monograph on Laon Cathedral, based on meticulous archaeological observations which he made in conjunction with Richard King. Lacking documents for a precise date, Clark tends to favor dating with a five-year leeway, citing ca.1170/1175 for the terminal walls of the transepts.

[29] Bony, "French Influences," 11.

where the Ripon formulation was first imitated (pl. 64) the supporting string-course was omitted and, to my knowledge, it never appeared again. At Ripon, however, this feature of the passage design survived throughout the various modifications of the general scheme until the last, after 1200, when it was discontinued for the west wall of the nave and the top story of the crossing tower.

*The Bay-Division Shafts and the Intended High Vaults*

The three stories of the choir elevation are visually united by clusters of bay-division shafts that rise from the imposts of the main arcade piers to the base of the clerestory, where they anticipated receiving the arches of high vaults. The shafts (pl. 3) are formulated as if they were detached and cut *en délit;* that is, they are mounted on the wall without an intervening pilaster. Consistent with the illusion of detached, *en délit* shafts, the outer shafts of each cluster even overlap the lower courses of the molding of the main arcade arches. However, the shafts were actually laid in ashlar courses corresponding to the courses of the wall and their masonry is integral with that of the wall. The clusters are composed of five shafts each, intended to serve as direct responds to the transverse, diagonal, and wall arches of high vaults. Each shaft has its own square plinth, elaborated on the front with a small bracket that extends forward to receive the oversailing segment of the attic base on which the shaft stands. The shafts are ringed just above the halfway point by the string-course at the base of the triforium. The capitals and imposts are articulated to correspond to the number of shafts, but each of these two members is cut from a single stone that covers all five shafts. The capitals and imposts of the three central shafts are set frontally, even though two of them were intended to receive diagonal ribs. Those of the outer shafts, rounded as if to receive diagonal ribs, were intended instead to receive the wall arches. Yet, apart from response to arches, these round outer capitals and imposts serve the function of providing a smooth, visual transition across the bay-division shafts from one bay to the next. This smooth transition is all the more effective because the impost covering the capitals continues along the wall as the string-course at the base of the clerestory. The clusters of shafts clearly indicate that the intended high vaults would have been quadripartite vaults with a full complement of arches and that these arches would have been sprung from the base of the clerestory.

The source of inspiration for nearly all aspects of the bay-division shafts and for the basic aspects of the intended high vaults can be traced unambiguously to a single structure, the cathedral of Laon, begun about 1160. More particularly, the source is in the transepts of this great church (pl. 77), which were among the first major structures articulated with a regular system of single bays covered with quadripartite vaults (pl. 78), displacing the previous standard in Gothic architecture of a double bay system covered with sexpartite vaults. The essential issue of the filiation here, however, resides primarily in the circumstance that in an elevation supported by columnar piers, vertical articulation which was intended to provide response to vaulting arches had to be formulated as a cluster of shafts rising from the top of the main arcade piers. When quadripartite high vaults with wall arches were anticipated, the number of shafts in the cluster had to be five. The Laon transepts were the only structures where exactly that situation had existed prior to Ripon. The number of shafts and the inclusion of wall arches in the intended vaulting scheme, itself the first fully-formulated instance in England,[30] clarifies the identification of Laon rather than English Cistercian architecture as the prototype for the Ripon quadripartite vaults. The use of square plinths and attic bases for the shafts, the ringing of shafts with a string-course, the cutting of multiple capitals and imposts from single blocks, and the identification of the imposts with a string-course, are all details which the Laon and Ripon bay-division shafts hold in common.

Some aspects of the shaft and vault ensemble are not exclusive to Laon in early French Gothic architecture but they are sufficiently typical of Laon that their adoption at Ripon in the company of closely associated features must be recognized as probably derivative from Laon. One of these is the springing of vaults from the base of the clerestory, which was also done in the choir of Noyon Cathedral but not in the transepts and nave. At Laon this usage was consistent (pl. 78). Another such feature is the rounding off of the outer pair of capitals and imposts, while the others are square and frontally disposed. In the Laon choir, where the clusters of shafts alternate between three and five members, the outer shafts—which in each case receive the wall arches (as at Ripon)—have a ring around them equivalent to an impost but they have no capital (pl. 55). Thus a rounded shape was introduced on either side of the capital and impost cluster. This feature had already been used in the same situation in the Noyon choir, but, in view of the other attributions, Laon is the more likely source. Finally, in the light of the number and type of influences from Laon, similarities of more general currency can probably be safely attributed to this specific source. These are the manner of embellishing arches with a simple, roll molding set off by a relatively wide and deep, concave hollow and the manner of treating the wall as a thin, flat plane of reference (pl. 77). While the pointed arch had reached England long before,[31] its consistent use in a design could not yet be taken for granted. In the final

---

[30] Because the chapel of St. Cross Hospital, Winchester, was begun ca. 1160 its quadripartite vaults might be considered rivals of Ripon for anteriority since they were completed ca. 1175, after modification of the original design; for discussion, see Bony, "French Influences," 5. It should be noted, however, that although the St. Cross vaults include modest wall arches (in contrast to elaborately embellished diagonal and transverse arches) and the responds basically comprise five shafts, there is no rational correspondence between all the arches and the shafts.

[31] In 1128, with the coming of the Cistercians to found Waverley Abbey and shortly afterward, Tintern Abbey, the high vaults of Durham Cathedral introduced the pointed arch into non-Cistercian English architecture about the same time. See Bony, "French Influences," 2–3.

analysis, these general and specific features of the Ripon choir (and, to a large extent, its transepts and nave) that make it Gothic are to be found earlier in a basically parallel usage in the transepts of Laon Cathedral, which were probably the most advanced example of the Gothic style under construction when Ripon was designed.

## C. Other Features of the Choir, Transepts, and Nave

### Oculus Windows

Likewise indefinite, but in the opposite manner, are the sources of features presumed to have existed at Ripon or in specific prototypes, but which cannot be verified in both locations. Among the conjectural features is the oculus or rose window. Although the hypothetical use of an oculus in the east elevation at Ripon may have been inspired by Kirkstall or some other closely related Cistercian example, the sympathy of the Ripon Master for such a feature in the transepts or in the choir, or both, may well have been inspired by the great oculus windows of the transept terminal elevations of Laon Cathedral.

### Elevation Proportions

Among the unverifiable prototypes is the source for the proportions of the three stories of the Ripon choir and transepts. Although the elevations of Roche, particularly the transepts, may have been the actual model, it is possible that they both had a common model in France. As others have suggested, Roche seems to be remarkably Picard in character.[32] Moreover, they have noted, the frequent use of shaft-bundle piers in Picardy in the years around 1160 indicates that such piers may have been a feature of the old cathedral of Amiens, dedicated in 1152.[33] It is difficult to ignore the coincidence that the vertical proportions of the stories shared by Roche and Ripon are the same as those of the much later High Gothic cathedral of Amiens. Quite possibly, these proportions reflect a tradition in Amiens, stemming from the old cathedral. If so, then Amiens is an even more likely source for the proportions of the Ripon elevation, in view of the other sources, than is Roche.

### Nave Triforium

Unlike the original scheme for the choir and transepts, the Ripon nave design has little in common with French Gothic architecture, either in its aisleless plan or its intentionally unvaulted superstructure (fig. 10). Even the use of a tall triforium was not primarily related to matters of style. However, the manner in which the tall triforium (pls. 39, 41) was made is a matter of style. Although the formal means can be found in the most

---

[32] See note 8.
[33] Fergusson, "Byland," 164.

nearly analogous situations in the eastern portions of the church, the example for such a triforium was provided by the same portion of the Noyon Cathedral transepts (pl. 58) that had furnished part of the technique for building the Ripon wall passages. Assuming that the reconstruction of the nave triforium with paired lancet windows in every other bay is correct, the Noyon transepts again offer a prototype in its use of tall, paired windows.

*Inventions of the Ripon Master*

In the course of composing his design the Ripon Master had to deal with some situations that had not been anticipated in the models he imitated or adapted. These situations forced him to modify the design of the prototypes or to invent forms that would serve his purposes. One of the most important of the modifications was made necessary by the combination of the Laon bay-division shafts (pl. 77) and the shaft-bundle piers of the sort found at Bertaucourt-les-Dames (pl. 74). while the shaft-bundle piers made a highly satisfactory complement both in form and scale to the clusters of bay-division shafts, the construction of the piers in ashlar courses meant that the use of *en délit* shafts in the upper zone would introduce an unfortunate contrast of texture exactly where consistency was needed. It was desirable, then, to construct the shaft clusters in courses also (pl. 3, fig. 7). Accordingly, it is unlikely that he had recourse to a specific prototype as a source of inspiration, even though a precedent did exist in the choir bay-division shafts of Notre-Dame in Paris, designed ca. 1163. Although the Ripon Master apparently intended no transformation of structural conception when he made this change, it is interesting to note that he anticipated by two decades one of the significant innovations of the master of Chartres Cathedral.

Besides this modification, a genuine invention was occasioned by the lack of coordination between the plinth necessary for the bay-division shafts and, beneath it, the impost of the shaft-bundle pier. Unlike the tall, widely-flared capitals on the columnar Laon piers (pl. 77), the capitals on the Ripon piers (pl. 7) were short and much less widely-flared because they were articulated as a cluster of eight small capitals, corresponding with the slender shafts. Consequently, the Ripon impost block did not project as far as that at Laon and there was insufficient room on it to accommodate the plinths of the bay-division shafts. It was necessary, then, to provide more support surface to receive the oversailing segment of the shaft bases. This provision took the form of the little molded brackets which were added to the center and outermost plinths of each five-shaft cluster. To my knowledge the only other church in which a similar situation occurred was the contemporary eastern arm of Canterbury Cathedral, where the tall foliate capitals on the columnar piers were not flared sufficiently to accommodate the plinths of the triple detached shafts. However, these two examples appear to be independent formulations.

One other adaptation, located in the transept east elevation, was made necessary by the piers between the chapel entrances. These piers (pl. 20) had a core that was part of the actual walls, but for the sake of consistency with the choir they were articulated with shafts that have no pilaster backing. The closest equivalent to the articulation of the choir piers that was feasible was an application of three shafts to each of the three unencumbered sides of the square pier core, with the center shaft of each triplet thicker than the flanking ones and slightly projecting. The resultant triple bay-division shaft-cluster on the elevation (which omitted response for wall arches) has several French counterparts, but none combining both the lack of a pilaster backing for the shafts and the lack of angular canting for the diagonal rib responds. It is plausible that formulation of this feature did not require a prototype but was inherent in the elements already employed in the choir elevation. The rest of the transept design can be readily envisioned as a consistent adaptation of formal devices in the choir to circumstances dictated by the liturgical layout.

### D. The Ripon Master

Regarded as a group, the specific French Gothic influences that can be discerned in the choir and other portions of Ripon Minster have a coherent geographical provenance. They appear to be centered in Laon with some significant contributions from nearby Noyon and from the equally proximate neighborhood of Soissons. The remainder of the influences seem to come from the vicinity of Amiens and from locations between Amiens and Calais. With this pattern it is possible to reconstruct in its broad outlines the earlier career of the Ripon Master and to explain how he came to compose the Ripon elevation design as he did.

Through whatever process he rose professionally to become a workshop master, he probably had his earliest experience in the Soissonnais, in which regional tradition his taste for delicately scaled articulation was formed. Before he was called to Yorkshire he had apparently been engaged in the construction of the Laon Cathedral transepts, his intimate knowledge of which indicates that he was probably a highly responsible assistant master. Having speculated on the design of Laon and the unsolved problems he ostensibly perceived in it, he took special note of certain features in recent and current construction projects located nearby and along his route from Laon via Amiens to the English Channel. Either in the course of traveling to the North of England or at the behest of his archiepiscopal patron there, he seems to have inspected the work in progress at Roche and the finished church at Kirkstall and so had freshly in mind all the examples he would need to draw upon in order to realize the stylistic aspects of his architectural vision. Whether the Ripon Master was native to France or to England cannot be determined. In the light of the contemporary project at Canterbury, where the portion with an English flavor is known to be the work of a Frenchman and where the portion with a more nearly French design is known to be the work of an Englishman, the distinction may not make a difference. Whatever his origins, his initial scheme for the choir elevation and vaults was at least as French as any part of Canterbury.

Such a hypothetical scenario may describe with some degree of accuracy how the Ripon Master came to know certain buildings that seem to figure in his formulation of the Ripon design. Yet it falls short of explaining how his design came to embody a degree of logical cogency virtually unparalleled in Early Gothic architecture. Taking the very advanced design of Laon Cathedral as a point of departure, the Ripon Master appears to have pursued every logical flaw he could perceive in its composition. With the exception of the reduced number of stories (which was more a matter of liturgical program than of stylistic vision), and hence also the reduced height, the Ripon choir elevation (fig. 7) is that of the Laon transepts (pl. 77) refined by features from other churches which fulfilled the master's aesthetic desire for visual logic. As we have seen in the discussion of individual features of the elevation, each element of the design was calculated to produce a rational relationship of parts to each other and to the whole, to maintain a consistency of articulation in both texture and scale, and to establish an unprecedented degree of harmony between the vertical relationship of stories and the horizontal continuity of bays. The Ripon Master appears to have selected those elements that are derived from churches other than Laon for the express purpose of fulfilling these aims.

In their intended form, the choir and transepts of Ripon Minster (figs. 6, 9) represent a major achievement in Early Gothic design, but one that has been obscured to us by modification and destruction. Had these eastern portions of the church been erected in France according to their original design—and, to be sure, with a French approach to structure as well as decorative articulation—they would not only have been completely at home but would also have represented the most advanced level of the Gothic style up to that time. Even so, the beginning of the construction of Ripon about 1175 constituted an event of considerable importance for the development of English architecture, and, along with the beginning of Canterbury in 1175, it marked one of the initial instances of the international dissemination of the style.

# 5. THE ENGLISH CONCEPT OF THE GOTHIC STYLE

The date of ca. 1175 for the beginning of Ripon Minster is significant because it makes Ripon an immediate contemporary of the first Gothic building in England, the choir of Canterbury Cathedral, as well as the earliest truly Gothic building in the northern region. The massive infusion of direct influence from the most advanced French Gothic architecture on its design makes Ripon a close stylistic relative of Canterbury as well as a seminal example of the new style in England. Its presumed function as the site of a pilgrimage to St. Wilfrid, putatively in competition with the Canterbury pilgrimage of St. Thomas, implies that Ripon was an intended rival of Canterbury as well as yet another example of a Gothic structure built to enshrine a saint. Chronologically, stylistically, and functionally, then, Ripon is parallel to Canterbury and so can be appropriately compared to it for all purposes in which their similarities and differences would enhance our understanding of the earliest Gothic architecture in England, keeping in mind of course that Canterbury is much the more important of the two buildings. Such a comparative discussion must be made on the basis of the intended design of Ripon (at least that portion of it which can be known beyond reasonable doubt) rather than on the scheme actually constructed because Ripon's greater importance for the history of architectural style resides in the former.

When the vaulted version of the Ripon choir design (pl. 3, fig. 6), and the actual Canterbury choir (pl. 82) are considered together, it is abundantly clear that while they have much in common they also have so many differences that neither could have been modeled after the other. On the one hand, their comparability is enhanced by the fact that each church possesses an elevation composed of three similar stories: each has a tall main arcade set on columnar piers; each has a nonfunctional middle story, articulated on the wall as a triforium but constructed as a false gallery; and each has a clerestory wall passage. Hence their superstructures belong to the same architectural family. Moreover, in addition to other features of more general import, each of these churches employs in the triforium the rather unusual motif of round-headed arches embracing pairs of pointed arches, a sign of stylistic kinship. On the other hand, their plans differ radically and their elevations also have many dissimilarities. The columnar main arcade piers, the triforium arcades, the clerestory arcades, the bay-division shafts, and the types of high ribbed vaults all are markedly different. The approach to decoration is also very different, as can be noted in the treatment of capitals, in the materials employed for shafts and string-courses, and in the molding profiles of both wall and vault arches. Clearly each of these choirs was designed independently of the other but within the stylistic limits of one particular generation of the Gothic tradition.

We have already seen that the stylistic aspects of the Ripon design were based on prototypes in the Early Gothic architecture of the Ile de France; that is, from examples dated between ca. 1150 and ca. 1175. For Canterbury, on the other hand, Jean Bony concisely identified three decades ago the French Gothic sources of the Canterbury eastern arm.[1] As at Ripon, most of the prototypes were located in the advanced architecture of northeastern France in the 1160s and 1170s, although there were significant contributions from the area of Paris also. Excepting the motif of the round arch embracing two pointed arches, the origin of which cannot be exactly identified, none of the individual instances of French influence coincides in the two English churches. Thus, while cut from the same type of cloth, Ripon and Canterbury were fashioned as quite different expressions of the same style: the simplicity of Ripon reflects the most classical version of Early Gothic; the sumptuousness of Canterbury, the most ornate. Both of these designs are distinctly and equally Gothic and at the same time, they both share the same kind of divergence from French practice. Although their surface details, the articulating features, are up-to-date and French, their actual structure is neither fully thinner nor consistently concentrated at the bay divisions in the French manner. Indeed, as has long been recognized, the thick continuous upper walls are still basically Romanesque in the manner of one version of the Anglo-Norman tradition.[2] De-

---

[1] "French Influences on the Origins of English Gothic Architecture," *Journal of the Warburg and Courtauld Institutes* 12 (1949): 7–11. The specific influences at Canterbury are listed as follows: from *Sens*, the general elevation composition in which double-bays are covered by sexpartite vaults; from *Saint-Denis*, the continuous wall set on columnar piers; from *Notre-Dame* in Paris, the combination of columnar piers and sexpartite vaults; from *Amblény* and the *Soissonnais* in general, elaborate arch moldings and dogtooth ornament (also from Picardy); from *Châlons-sur-Marne*, ribbed-vault bosses in the south aisle; from *Dhuigel* (Aisne), dogtooth ornament in vault ribs; from *Noyon, Laon, Valenciennes,* and *Saint-Rémi in Reims,* detached shafts for vertical articulation; from *Laon, Bagneux, Notre-Dame in Paris, Cambrai* and *Soissons*, detached shafts on main arcade piers; from *Saint-Rémi in Reims*, foliate capitals, the use of twin columnar piers, and groups of windows which fill the ambulatory walls; from *Bertaucourt-les-Dames*, near Amiens, molded capitals and round imposts; and from *Laon*, the passage in the ambulatory wall and the band triforium.

Peter Kidson (in Part One, *A History of English Architecture*, (Harmondsworth, 1962), 72–75) commented on the general French aspects of Canterbury but added no specific prototypes.

[2] Anglo-Norman architecture had one strain in which the arches of three stories were conceptually cut from an otherwise continuous wall fabric that had little or no vertical articulation. Surviving examples are Chichester Cathedral (ca. 1090); St. Bartholomew's Priory, Smithfield, London (1123); and the nave of Southwell Minster (ca. 1140). It is reasonably certain that the Romanesque predecessor of the Canterbury choir, designed about 1090, also had this type of structure although it had no genuine middle story; see the Rev. Robert Willis, *The Architectural History of Canterbury Cathedral*, (London, 1845), 42–43, for the account by Gervase and 74–75, for Willis' interpretation, represented in fig. 15.

spite their differences, then, Ripon and Canterbury stand together, related by their special kind of contrast to the Gothic architecture of France.

In the nineteenth and the early twentieth century this structural divergence was regarded as evidence of a still incomplete absorption of the Gothic style, representing a period of transition from the Romanesque to the Gothic.[3] The retention of some round-headed arches in the midst of pointed ones was considered the signet of this transition. However, the first maturity of English Gothic architecture—the full-blown Early English of Lincoln (pl. 86) and Salisbury—never demonstrated the fulfillment of the expected structural transition; indeed, the matter of which changes should have occurred in the transition was quietly dropped in discussions of these slightly later buildings whose Gothic credentials were not questioned. More recently, the divergence of Canterbury has been attributed to the compromises required of William of Sens in the retention of the Romanesque crypt and outer walls for the Gothic choir, the consequence of which was a faulty understanding by English builders of the essential nature of the French Gothic style.[4] Since William of Sens was incontestably a French builder, this explanation has seemed plausible, even though his successor, William the Englishman, albeit working against fewer such constraints, achieved a more convincing expression of the French manner.[5] However, the clarifications of the intended form, the beginning date, and the stylistic provenance of Ripon widen the base of data for this analysis and help to shift the burden of the argument to other grounds.

Although we cannot know for a certainty the national origin of the Ripon Master, we can be confident from his use of current French features[6] that he was equally as conversant in French Gothic architecture as William of Sens. Unlike William, he seems to have had to make no compromising adjustments to earlier structures on the site, although his patron appears to have imposed on the project a program no less insular in character.[7] Yet to suppose that William and the Ripon Master acquiesced to demands which necessarily introduced alien qualities into their work—be they pre-Gothic, non-Gothic, or anti-Gothic qualities—is to assume that they were artists whose respective visions of a purer style both, by coincidence, fell victim to the compromising demands of philistine patrons. We cannot plausibly imagine that the monastic community at Canterbury or Arch-

---

It is important, however, to recall that some Anglo-Norman architecture was more truly skeletal in conception than was the first generation of French Gothic architecture. Examples are the East Anglian cathedrals of Ely (ca. 1084) and Norwich (ca. 1096). Peterborough Abbey (ca. 1118) and, in the south, Romsey Abbey (ca. 1120).

[3] For Ripon the most important assessments are those of Sir George Gilbert Scott, in "Ripon Minster," *Archaeological Journal* 31 (1874): 309–18; and in "The Transition from the Romanesque to the Pointed Style in England," 32 (1875): 347–368.

[4] Bony, "French Influences," 14–15, and Kidson, *English Architecture*, 74–75.

[5] John Newman ("Introduction," *North East and East Kent*, The Buildings of England, ed. Nikolaus Pevsner (Harmondsworth, 1968), 43–44, 179–81) enlarges upon this point, originally raised by Bony in "French Influences," 11.

[6] See chap. 4, above, for full discussion.

[7] See chap. 3, above, for full discussion.

bishop Roger at Ripon were insensitive to the aesthetic implications of the designs proposed by their builders. Indeed, as Gervase tells us, the Canterbury monks agreed to let William of Sens alter the original scope of the project in order to have "the work as good as he promised."[8] And what little we know of Roger suggests that he was too well connected with the cultural mainstream, too discriminating in his architectural patronage, and too conscientious in his struggle for equal status with Canterbury to be guilty of imposing provincial ignorance and vulgarity on his builder.[9] In both projects the patrons were undoubtedly desirous of getting the best work possible and were capable of making informed decisions to secure it. In other words, both of the building masters were surely free to incorporate those aspects of the Gothic style which they regarded as indispensable. Hence they were not hampered in this respect by the practical compromises they accepted.

In view of their common, structural divergence from the French Gothic tradition, what constitutes the stylistic character which these two English churches share with that tradition? Certainly this character does not reside in an assemblage of particular features imitated from French Gothic churches. Rather, the special quality of the Gothic style is chiefly conveyed by the manner in which these features are assembled. As we saw when tracing French infuence at Ripon, these features can be reduced to certain kinds of shafts and arch moldings, but their Gothic quality emanates from the way they are made, how they are related to each other and to the flat, unarticulated areas of the wall. To be sure, the pointed arch is also fundamental to the projection of this quality, but the use of a few round-headed arches does not seriously compromise the effect. The common denominator of the Gothic style was a series of techniques for visually isolating the articulating features from the mass of the wall and vault masonry and for relating them to each other.

What, exactly, were these techniques and how were they employed? Piers and shafts were to be defined as plastic lines distinct from the wall masonry and in contrast to it so that they could appear to have a vertical thrust. The most obvious way to achieve that end was to cut the shafts *en délit* in long vertical segments so that the grain of the stone as well as its form contrasted with the flat wall.[10] A similar effect could be achieved with piers and attached shafts laid in normal ashlar courses if the shafts were more than half round and were applied without a pilaster backing. Molded arches were also to be defined as plastic lines distinct from the wall masonry so that they could appear to describe a curved trajectory. So long as the roll molding on the angles of the arches was more than half round and so long as the concave hollows, which set the angle roll off from the flat wall surface and arch soffit, were at least half round, this

---

[8] Willis, *Canterbury*, 36. For the complete Latin text see William Stubbs, ed. *The Historical Works of Gervase of Canterbury*. Rolls Series, Vol. 73 (London, 1879), 1: 3-28.

[9] See chap. 3, above, for details and references.

[10] See chap. 1, n. 17 above, for an explanation of this technique.

effect would be achieved regardless of how few or how many orders the arch had and whether or not it had a molded soffit. The trajectory defined by the arch moldings acquired the effect of leaping upward when it was applied to a pointed arch.[11] When shafts were added as responds to molded arches the combined elements created a unit which conveyed the illusion of an organic relationship endowed with dynamic vitality. This combination was equally effective in the articulation of bays, high vaults, and decorative arcades. The change from diagonal to vertical tooling of ashlar blocks in the third quarter of the twelfth century and the application of extremely thin layers of mortar made it possible to create a smooth, flat wall which appeared to be a continuous surface, thereby enhancing its value as a foil for the shafts and arch moldings. Coordinated with a rational cogency, or even applied with only an approximate formal relationship but in profusion, these shafts and moldings could create the effect of a dynamic order of architecture, an insubstantial network of plastic lines, superimposed upon an inert order, composed of flat walls.

The designers of Canterbury and Ripon appear to have understood the visual implications of these techniques and to have perceived the Gothic style to be a manner of building—expressed as a mode of decoration—and not as a structural ideal. Together their contrasting visions represent the extreme limits of the English perception of the Gothic style in the 1170s, visions that profoundly influenced the subsequent course of its development over the next half-century. The design of each of these churches informs our understanding of the other. Without the addition of Ripon to the body of evidence provided by Canterbury, there would be no basis for characterizing the deviations of the latter from French practice in terms of principle. Moreover, if an enhanced appreciation of the importance of Ripon is useful in interpreting the significance of Canterbury for the beginnings of the Gothic style in England, it can be equally useful in interpreting the well-known eyewitness description of Canterbury written by the monk Gervase. Characterizing the new work on the

---

[11] An exception which appears to try the validity of this analysis is the Romanesque transept of Peterborough Abbey (now Cathedral). In this transept every arch is outlined by an angle roll set off by concave hollows. And the arch-respond and bay-division shafts, though laid in courses and attached to the ashlar wall masonry, are more than half round and applied without an intermediary pilaster. Technically, then, these features should be regarded as Gothic, if such are truly the essential elements of the Gothic style. Formally, though, they do not convey a Gothic expressiveness. It is in just such a situation that we see the necessity of the pointed arch for the expression of organic vitality in the arch moldings. Moreover, the use of bay-division shafts as nothing more than vertical articulation (because there are no high vaults) also robs them of the same quality; hence, the rational relationship of shafts to arches must also be acknowledged as indispensible to Gothic expressiveness. In the final analysis, Peterborough lacks the features that follow shafts and arch moldings in importance but which are nevertheless necessary to the Gothic style. Even so, must Peterborough be regarded as the prototype *manqué* for the Gothic style? Although the choir was begun ca. 1118 the actual construction of the transepts has been assigned to the 1150s (see C. R. Peers, "Peterborough Minster," *The Victoria History of the Counties of England, Northampton* 2 (London, 1906) 437), so its use of features associated with the Gothic style is not precocious but *retardataire*.

whole as "of a different fashion" and "more noble" than its Romanesque predecessor,[12] he clearly was sensitive to its conveying a different aesthetic effect, an effect which he regarded as superior to that of the fondly-remembered, older choir. Yet Gervase is regarded as unenlightening on matters of style, even though he set out a list of contrasts between the old and new choirs:

> It has been above stated, that after the fire nearly all the old portions of the choir were destroyed and changed into somewhat new and of a more noble fashion. The differences between the two works may now be enumerated. The pillars of the old and new work are alike in form and thickness but different in length. For the new pillars were elongated by almost twelve feet. In the old capitals the work was plain, in the new ones exquisite in sculpture. There the circuit of the choir had twenty-two pillars, here are twenty-eight. There the arches and everything else was plain, or sculptured with an axe and not with a chisel. But here almost throughout is appropriate sculpture. No marble columns were there, but here are innumerable ones. There, in the circuit around the choir, the vaults were plain, but here they are arch-ribbed and have keystones. There a wall set upon pillars divided the crosses from the choir, but here the crosses are separated from the choir by no such partition, and converge together in one keystone, which is placed in the middle of the great vault which rests on the four principal pillars. There, there was a ceiling of wood decorated with excellent painting, but here is a vault beautifully constructed of stone and light tufa. There, was a single triforium, but here are two in the choir and a third in the aisle of the church. All which will be better understood from inspection than by any description.
>
> This must be made known, however, that the new work is higher than the old by so much as the upper windows of the body of the choir, as well as of its aisles, are raised above the marble tabling. [There follows a lengthy explanation, omitted here for the sake of brevity, for reducing the width of the eastward choir extension in order to retain two old tower-chapels.] . . . This much was said that the differences between the old and new work might be made manifest.[13]

The extent to which his stylistic perceptions may be deduced depends upon the extent to which his list of distinctions can be correlated with specific architectural practices that are indicative of the English understanding of the Gothic style. Some of Gervase's distinctions concern structural differences that are only tangential to matters of style; they refer to aspects of the building that enhance Gothic effects but which, as described, are not exclusive to Gothic architecture. For example, he observes that the "pillars" (piers) of the new choir are like the old ones in form but are much taller, by which he could be referring to the quality of verticality, usually associated with the Gothic style. He approaches this point from another direction near the end of the list of contrasts, remarking that the new structure is taller than the old by the amount of the respective cleresto-

---

[12] Willis, *Canterbury*, 36 and 58, respectively.
[13] The English translation of this passage is quoted from Willis, *Canterbury*, 58–61. The Latin text of the *Chronica Gervassii* is transcribed by Stubbs in *Historical Works of Gervase*, 1: 27–38. See Appendix II for the Latin text.

ries in the choir and aisles. Also, reporting the increased number of "pillars" in the new eastern arm, piers which represented its extension further eastward, and the modification of the transept arms to make them join the main vessel of the choir in a proper crossing, Gervase could be referring to a quality of spaciousness which Abbot Suger had described as "the beauty of length and width" in his new choir at Saint-Denis.[14] He raises the issue of space again at the end of the list of contrasts, where he explains in detail the reasons for contracting the width of the choir in order to accommodate its eastward extension beyond the old tower chapels. Indeed, his reference to high vaults in contrast to a flat wooden ceiling could be associated either with the concept of spaciousness or with a feature associated primarily with the Gothic style. Finally, his interest in the increased number of "triforia," be they the clerestory wall passage of the choir and aisle elevations or the open arcades of the middle story, could be interpreted as an appreciation for the diaphanous quality of structure sometimes regarded as quintessentially Gothic.[15] Overall, though, it would be risky to assume that Gervase means anything other than that the new eastern arm was higher, longer, and structurally more complex than its predecessor. Certainly none of these differences can be regarded as the result of a new manner of building.

Gervase's other distinctions between the Romanesque and Gothic choirs concern specific features that, by virtue of either direct or oblique reference to the relevant techniques, signify those features which convey the quality of organic vitality peculiar to Gothic expressiveness. When he contrasts the plainness of the old capitals to the refined (*subtilis*) sculpture of the new ones, Gervase is not just contrasting simplicity and ornateness: a comparison of surviving Romanesque capitals in the aisles (pl. 83) and Gothic capitals in the main arcade (pl. 84) reveals a telling stylistic difference between the inert blockiness of Romanesque cubic capitals and the organic vitality of Gothic foliate capitals. Consequently, we have a concrete demonstration that when Gervase uses the adjective *subtilis* to describe the sculptural technique, he is not only referring to the highest level of artistic skill but also a purposive use of its stylistic effects.[16] He reinforces this meaning when he contrasts the plainness of the older (main arcade) arches and "everything else" to the decoration of the corresponding features of the new choir.

---

[14] "Libellus alter de consecratione ecclesiae sancti Dionysii," ed. trans. Erwin Panofsky, *Abbot Suger on the Abbey of St.-Denis and Its Art Treasures* (Princeton, 1946), 100, 101.

[15] The theory of diaphanous quality originated with Hans Jantzen, *High Gothic, The Classic Cathedrals of Chartres, Reims, Amiens,* trans. James Palmes (Letchworth, 1962), 73–80.

[16] The term *subtilis* denoted much more than "subtle." While it referred to fineness and excellence of execution on the most direct level of meaning, less directly it also referred to ingenuity of conception. (Earlier in his account of Canterbury, Gervase had described William of Sens as *artifex subtilissimus*). On both levels the term was associated with a high degree of artifice which could mean any stylistic formulation that required a highly deliberative conception. See Edgar de Bruyne, *Etudes d'esthétique médiévale* (Bruges, 1946) 2: 84–85.

First he points out that the difference was made possible by a change in the tools employed, when the axe was replaced by the chisel. Then he elaborates the meaning of this difference by referring to the arch moldings and, immediately afterward, to the other decorative features as having been "sculpted" (using this term in the same sense that he did in applying it to the capitals). He seems to be referring thereby to something much more significant than the mere addition of embellishment. A comparison of unmolded Romanesque arches surviving in other structures (pl. 81) to the Gothic Canterbury arches (pl. 82), with their delicate angle rolls, flanked by concave hollows, outlining each order of every arch and their meticulous dogtooth or billet embellishment bordering most arches, shows that Gervase's observation has touched both technically and formally on an aspect of the structure that is central to its Gothic expressiveness. He next addresses his attention to vertical members, substituting the more general term "column" for his accustomed word "pillar" and doing so presumably for the purpose of referring to the many detached shafts as well as the piers. Noting that they are made of marble, he implies his awareness that they are physically independent of the ashlar masonry and that they are different in hue and texture from the wall, hence that they provide a marked contrast to the flat portions of the elevation. Observing that they are innumerable, he thus suggests that luxurious material was employed unsparingly and also that the piers and shafts are very prominent in the design. Immediately afterward, he points out that in the old choir the aisle vaults were plain while the new aisles have arcuated vaults. Here, of course, he is contrasting groined vaults to ribbed vaults. But, having already referred to high ribbed vaults in contrast to a flat wooden ceiling, his point here seems to be that the change in vaulting technique provided textural articulation of stylistic import distinct from concerns for improved engineering.

Thus the direct and indirect references to technique with regard to the capitals, the arches, the piers and shafts, and the vault ribs, but to no other features, suggest that Gervase understood its relationship to their formulation to be of primary importance in creating the "different fashion" which made the eastern arm "more noble" than its predecessor. Indeed, these observations seem to comprise his definition of the style which we now designate as Gothic. When, after noting all the other features, he reports the increased number of triforia; he then remarks that the building will be better understood from a personal viewing than from his description. He undoubtedly means this statement to be construed as comprehensive, but his having contrived to save the remark about triforia for last implies that he is aware that the visual effectiveness of the decorative system is enhanced by the emphasis on the shafts and arch moldings afforded by these passages, and hence that the importance of the decorative order would be immediately understood by the viewer during a visit to the church.

However conveniently this textual interpretation of Gervase's perception of the Gothic style may tally with a formal analysis of the first Gothic churches in England, we must question whether or not the composition of his description is compatible with it. The skeptic will note that both of the categories of distinctions discussed above are actually intermingled in his discussion of contrasts. Consequently, the analysis of Gervase's perceptions could be challenged either on the ground that all these observations relate to his notion of the Gothic style, so that one category is not more important than the other, or on the ground that the mixture precludes our assigning the significance of style definition to any of his observations. However, two factors seem to indicate that neither challenge is prejudicial to my argument. The first is that the mingling of the observations is not arbitrary but based on an orderly viewing sequence from the floor upward and, within a given zone, from west to east (following the sequence of the project). It begins with the main arcade piers and capitals of the choir and continues, sequentially, with the piers of the eastern chapel, the main arcade arches, the wall shafts, the aisle vaults, the changes in the wall structure at the eastern crossing, the high vaults, and the triforia. An explanation of the contraction of the choir width toward the east is appended as an afterthought. Only the high vaults were included out of sequence, ostensibly because Gervase wanted to mention them in connection with the crossing. Hence his analytical remarks were organized to follow a visual tour. While he did not segregate his quantitative and qualitative contrasts, he undoubtedly expected that his reader could distinguish between them. The second supporting factor is that all these comparative observations stand together at the end of his narrative account of the construction sequence, and clearly are meant to be interpreted on a different level as analytical rather than descriptive remarks. Surely, then, the qualitative observations are intended to refer to his perception of style. Thus to the extent that they can be correlated to actual examples of architecture, it is reasonable to regard Gervase's remarks as representative of his understanding of the Gothic style.

Obviously Gervase was concerned solely with Canterbury in his description and undoubtedly he never saw the new minster at Ripon or knew anything very definite about it. Yet the shared similarities of these two churches to French Gothic architecture as well as their differences from it show that the masters who designed them perceived in the same way the essential aspects of the Gothic style and this perception seems to be reflected also in Gervase's account of Canterbury. Since Gervase was English and William of Sens was French, national origin does not appear to have been an important factor in determining this perception. Ripon, then, makes it possible to interpret both Canterbury and Gervase's account more fully and to explain more plausibly why English Gothic architecture was so different from French Gothic. This explanation in turn may make possible a clearer understanding of some of the complexities in the development of French Gothic architecture.

Meanwhile, one further test of this explanation of the twelfth-century English perception of the Gothic style will help to validate it and also to show why English architecture developed as it did through the middle of the thirteenth century. That test is to apply the positive and negative aspects of this definition of the Gothic style to subsequent buildings in England. To begin with the latter, the negative aspect is that the French tendency toward the development of skeletal structure was regarded as nonessential to the Gothic style. Flying buttresses received very little consideration after Canterbury itself and even high ribbed vaults were deemed unimportant in most northern and some southern and western churches. Very few English churches dispensed with the thick wall and its clerestory passage. Vertical articulation at bay divisions became increasingly unimportant: the number of shafts was reduced or kept to a minimum and even those remaining were frequently corbeled out above the main arcade piers, conceding their purely decorative character. As a result, no development toward the formulation of skeletal structure took place in the first seven decades of English Gothic architecture. Continuing with the positive aspect of this definition, no one would deny that English architecture after Canterbury and Ripon was definitely Gothic, despite its structural conservatism. Although more influence by far was exerted by Canterbury than by Ripon—because it was ecclesiastically much more important, because the pilgrimage of St. Thomas brought vastly many more people to see it, and because it was completed virtually as it was intended—each church had planted the Gothic seed in its respective region and in these regions the development of the Gothic style proceeded largely from the examples they set. The special Gothic quality in English architecture was projected by the features employed for textural articulation, each of which was exaggerated in the decades after the 1170s.[17] A brief survey of important instances will suffice to demonstrate the point.[18]

For the most part the basically columnar pier was employed. In the north the shaft-bundle version was predominant and its form did not vary a great deal nor did it easily lend itself to exaggeration, except when it was employed for crossing piers, as at Whitby Abbey (pl. 70), soon after 1225, or when it was articulated as if it had more than twelve shafts, as at Rievaulx Abbey (ca. 1230). But the application of detached shafts, in contrasting Purbeck marble, to the columnar piers of Canterbury, resulted in exaggerated compositions like that of the Chichester retrochoir (after

---

[17] Geoffrey Webb (in *Architecture in Britain: The Middle Ages*, The Pelican History of Art (Harmondsworth, 1956) 77) raised this issue in his comparison of Lincoln Cathedral to Canterbury. See also Newman ("Introduction," *North East and East Kent*, 45) for a mention of techniques in relation to decoration.

[18] Discussions of the stylistic development of English Gothic architecture vary primarily only in the degree of detail and in points of emphasis. Those which constitute the principal body of modern literature on the subject are Bony, "French Influences," 1-15; Webb, *Architecture in Britain*; Kidson, *English Architecture*, and the introductions to the relevant volumes of Nikolaus Pevsner's *The Buildings of England* especially those covering Yorkshire, Kent, Somerset and Lincolnshire.

1186) (pl. 85) and in the adoption of the most extravagant Canterbury types as the standard for the Lincoln nave (after 1210) (pl. 86).[19] Meanwhile, the independent Gothic tradition in the west of England produced in Wells Cathedral (ca. 1185), (pl. 73) some compound piers that were completely sheathed in slender, attached shafts. Almost everywhere the pier was articulated by or composed of a group of slender shafts which related the scale of the pier as a whole to the molding of the arch it supported.

Elsewhere on the elevation, slender shafts, whether single or in clusters and whether detached or attached, were provided as responds to arches and as vertical articulation, even in unvaulted interiors. Their structural significance is slight; most rise from string-courses or corbels. However, in every region their application was maximal—most strikingly in the middle story of three-story elevations, where the number of splayed jambs was multiplied—both in each opening and in the number of locations within a given structure. In the North, representative examples within the tradition of Ripon (that is, with a round arch embracing a pair of pointed arches) are the nave of Jedburgh Abbey (ca. 1200) (pl. 72), the choir and transepts of Hexham Priory (ca. 1210), and the choir of Whitby Abbey (ca. 1225) (pl. 70). In the South, the retrochoir of Chichester (ca. 1186) (pl. 85), and the nave of Lincoln (begun ca. 1210) (pl. 86), elaborated the Canterbury choir triforium in a similar fashion. Others, such as the new choir of Rochester Cathedral (ca. 1200), employed numerous detached shafts as the most conspicuous decorative element. And in the distinctive Gothic tradition of western England, the interior of the Wells Cathedral north porch (ca. 1210) and the exterior of the west facade (1220s), both used detached shafts with a copiousness unrivaled in earlier work and never exceeded afterward.

The use of molded arches and the complexity of arch moldings proliferated almost everywhere in proportion to the use of shafts. Indeed, as the slight importance of the French structural system to English architecture receded further in successive decades, when even rational cogency in the system of surface articulation was no longer honored, the wall became actually thicker than in the first Gothic buildings. Consequently, main arcades and triforium arches acquired additional orders, each of which was embellished with multiple-roll moldings separated by shadowy hollows. Soffit rolls became standard features; hence main arcades especially acquired a V-profile which transformed them into deep embrasures covered with plastic lines. Spectacular examples abound in every region among the churches already cited, such as Jedburgh nave (pl. 72), Whitby choir and transepts (pl. 70), Lincoln (pl. 86), Salisbury, Worcester choir and Wells (pl. 73). Vaulting arches were molded to a similar degree, although they remained slender, consonant with the minimal vertical bay-

---

[19] Bony, "French Influences," 10; and *Idem.*, "Origines des piles anglaises gothiques à fûts en délit," *Gedenkschrift Ernst Gall* (Munich and Berlin, 1965), 95–122.

division shafts which served as their responds. The principle of elaboration was applied to the vaults chiefly in the proliferation of ribs, beginning in the Lincoln Cathedral nave (ca. 1210) (pl. 86), where tiercerons and ridge-ribs were added, and continuing elsewhere somewhat later with the introduction of liernes. The result of this development was that vault articulation became a decorative pattern similar in nature to that on the elevation.

More specialized forms of decorative elaboration were also inspired by Canterbury and Ripon. From the former, the introduction of polychromy through the application of contrasting Purbeck marble shafts (pl. 82) spread rapidly throughout the country and was soon extended also to capitals and string-courses. Notable examples are the Temple Church in London, Rochester choir, Salisbury, Worcester choir, and Beverley, begun sequentially between ca. 1185 and ca. 1230. The mixture of other varieties of stone, as in the Lincoln nave (pl. 86) followed closely upon the fashion for Purbeck marble. From Ripon, on the other hand, came syncopated rhythms of articulation, as in its revised nave elevation (fig. 10). While a slightly earlier instance already existed in the Worksop Priory nave (ca. 1180–1190), the Ripon elevation does not seem to have been derived from this composition and, moreover, was most likely the one that set the example for English master builders. Syncopation showed up shortly after the revision of the Ripon nave (ca. 1185–1190) in the nave of Nun Monkton (ca. 1200) and in decorative blind arcades and triforium arcades, respectively, in the Lincoln choir aisles (ca. 1192) (pl. 87) and in the Worcester choir (ca. 1224) and at Beverley (ca. 1230). These two different specialized types of decoration both enhanced the contrast between the decorative system and the ashlar walls, contributing thereby to the expression of vitality in the decorative order of architecture and increasing its dazzling effect on the viewer. But of overriding significance is the fact that all the decorative articulating elements of English elevations—the piers and shafts and the arch moldings—were accentuated and elaborated in the decades after the 1170s.

From three different angles—comparative formal analysis, close textural reading of a document, and observation of changes in the course of development—the perception of the Gothic style in twelfth-century England can be defined as the application of particular techniques to the elements of textural articulation in order to achieve a new decorative effect. The effect was metaphysical in import, creating an illusion of organic vitality that could be associated with the feeling of spiritual uplift afforded by mystical states of mind. It is easy to imagine a medieval ecclesiastical patron conceiving such a desideratum but, described as an abstraction, it would be difficult to achieve. However, it is clear that the desired effect had been recognized in certain formal elements, especially in certain combinations of elements, and that the techniques employed to make these elements would recreate the effect in every situation where they were applied. Whatever the specific circumstances in which this discovery first occurred, the concept once formulated could be easily understood by any builder and readily applied both in the process of design and in the actual construction. While many factors were brought into play in the design of a building of the Gothic mode, including all manner of structural and spatial concerns, the one indispensible ingredient was the manner of creating its decorative system.

The twelfth-century church of Ripon Minster shared with Canterbury the role of introducing this new concept of architectural design into England. In its revised form Ripon was a less complete exemplar of the Gothic mode; but its use of the decorative system in elevations provided an equally persuasive demonstration of the optical properties conferred on masonry by the systematic application of the relevant techniques.

## The Place of Ripon in English Gothic Architecture

As the first Gothic building in the North, Ripon did not serve the same function that Canterbury did in the South. Canterbury, because of its completeness as an aesthetic statement and because of its ecclesiastical importance, served as a model to which designers returned time and again for inspiration, even when it was no longer new. Ripon, on the other hand, initiated a movement that was continually evolving; accordingly, it was directly influential only at the beginning and then only in terms of its modified scheme. Because of its highly particularized program, not much of Ripon's plan was adaptable to other churches. Among the features of this plan, the high flat east end did prove to be readily transferable, appearing in numerous churches of the thirteenth century and even of the fourteenth.[20] Behind it, of course, was the prestige of York Minster's late Romanesque example, but the version of Ripon was more up-to-date. As in the case of the plan, the elevation was highly specialized and some parts, such as the transepts with compound piers between the eastern chapels, became permanently outdated almost at once when the design of Byland Abbey was formulated with columnar piers between the transept chapels. Similarly, the elevation with a middle story articulated as a low false-gallery was taken up only at Byland; but the motif of the round arch embracing two pointed arches was firmly planted in the North, being repeated at Byland, Old Malton, Lanercost, Hexham, Jedburgh, and Whitby. Likewise, the stylistic quality of the decorative system of shafts and arch-moldings rapidly evolved. At Ripon, the visual effect had the same restrained but supple quality found in French early Gothic architecture and it was passed on to Byland. Thereafter, however, the decorative system became more elaborate, its articulation increasingly crisp and sharp—to some sensibilities, cold and hard. Curiously, this evolution began in Ripon itself, where, in the clerestory of the transept west wall (pl.

---

[20] Examples, beginning ca. 1200 and extending well into the fourteenth century, include Hexham Priory; Jervaulx, Rievaulx and Whitby Abbeys; Beverley Minster; Ely, London, and Lincoln Cathedrals; Selby and Guisborough Abbeys; Carlisle Cathedral; and York Minster.

22) round arch moldings were displaced by plain, chamfered, arch faces. And this development continued to evolve from the crossing tower (pl. 30) and nave clerestory to the west front (pls. 34, 36, 38). Indeed, even the rationalized quality of the decorative system began to disintegrate with the Ripon nave and the Byland elevations and this trend continued through the middle of the thirteenth century.

Ripon was originally designed to be rather eccentric in layout and structure but to be articulated on the surface in the most orthodox manner of the latest style. Because it was so radically modified during construction its intended formal expressiveness was considerably distorted. As a result, the Gothic style in the north of England, albeit introduced in a normal version, was, by French standards, rapidly transformed into a somewhat bizarre provincial tradition. Even so, this tradition did carry in it the Gothic aesthetic and Ripon Minster was the instrument through which the new mode was transmitted to the northern region.

# APPENDIX

### GRANT OF MONEY FROM ARCHBISHOP ROGER TO BUILD RIPON MINSTER

Ro[gerus] Dei gratia Eboracensis archiepiscopus, Apostolicae sedis legatus, omnibus sanctae matris ecclesiae filiis salutem. Notum facimus universitati vestrae quod dedimus operi Beati Wilfridi de Ripon, ad aedificandam basilicam ipsius, quam de novo inchoavimus, mille libras veteris monetae. Ut autem haec nostra donatio firma et illibata permaneat, ne quis eam infringere praesumat auctoritate qua fungimur prohibemus. Si quis autem contra prohibitionem nostram venerit, auctoritate Dei Patris Omnipotentis, Sanctae Mariae Virginis, et Beatorum Apostolorum Petri et Pauli, ac Sancti Wilfridi, et (nostra), excommunicetur, et a liminibus sanctae Dei ecclesiae sequestretur (*Memorials of Ripon* 1:97).

### INDULGENCE FROM ARCHBISHOP GRAY TO ALL WHO VISIT THE CHURCH OF RIPON AND THE TOMB OF ST. WILFRID

Universis sanctae matris ecclesiae filiis praesentes literas visuris vel audituris, Walterus Dei gratia Eboracensis archiepiscopus, Angliae primas, salutem in Domino. Quoniam summa veneratione digna sunt corpora corum in terris, quorum nomina felici titulo scripta sunt in coelis, nos, ad supplicationem et instantiam dilectorum filiorum canonicorum Riponensium, anno Dominicae incarnationis millesimo ducentesimo vicesimo quarto, corpus sancti patris et ejusdem ecclesiae patroni, Wilfridi, a veteri capsa in novam sedem die Natalis Domini transtulimus, et corpus ipsum totum, nullo majore vel minore osse vel articulo, ut pro certo credamus, deficiente; caput autem ipsius Sancti duximus exterius servandum, et honorifice collocandum, ut ex ejus visione et fides fidelium roboretur, et devotio augeatur. Volentes igitur honorem ipsius beatissimi patris ampliare, et saluti animarum in ipsius venerationem providere, de misericordia Dei confisi, omnibus qui ad eundem Sanctum venerandum, et ecclesiam Riponensem honorandam et promovendam accesserint, vel alio modo per alios, si praepediti fuerint, visitaverint, confessis et vere poenitentibus, de injuncta sibi poenitentia triginta dies relaxamus. Hoc videlicet proviso, ut haec indulgentia triginta dierum a die translationis Sancti per nos factae duret usque ad diem Epiphaniae completum. In festis vero tam suae Depositionis quam Translationis primo per Beatum Oswaldum factae duret per octo dies, ut qui . . . eosdem dies ipsum Sanctum adierint, vel quocunque modo pia devotione visitaverint, ejusdem indulgentiae plenum consequentur effectum. Universitatem igitur vestram monemus attentius et exhortamur in Domino, quatenus ob salutem animarum vestrarum talem circa ipsius Sancti venerationem exhibere studeatis devotionem, ut, ipsius intervenientibus meritis, aeternam a Deo sperare possitis remunerationem. Datum apud Ottele, duodecimo kalendas Februarii, anno gratiae praedicto, pontificatus nostri anno decimo (*Memorials of Ripon*, 1: 49–50).

# APPENDIX II

### Gervase's Description of Canterbury

Dictum est in superioribus quod post combustionem illam vetera fere omnia chori diruta sunt, et in quandam augustioris formae transierunt novitatem. Nunc autem quae sit operis utriusque differentia dicendum est. Pilariorum igitur tam veterum quam novorum una forma est, una et grossitudo, sed longitudo dissimilis. Elongati sunt enim pilarii novi longitudine pedum fere duodecim. In capitellis veteribus opus erat planum, in novis sculptura subtilis. Ibi in chori ambitu pilarii viginti duo, hic autem viginti octo. Ibi arcus et caetera omnia plana, utpote sculpta secure et non scisello, hic in omnibus fere sculptura idonea. Ibi columpna nulla marmorea, hic innumerae. Ibi in circuitu extra chorum fornices planae, hic arcuatae sunt et clavatae. Ibi murus super pilarios directus cruces a choro sequestrabat, hic vero nullo interstitio cruces a choro divisae in unam clavem quae in medio fornicis magnae consistit, quae quatuor pilariis principalibus innititur, convenire videntur. Ibi caelum ligneum egregia pictura decoratum, hic fornix ex lapide et tofo levi decenter composita est. Ibi triforium unum, hic duo in choro, et in ala ecclesiae tertium. Quae omnia visu melius quam auditu intelligere volenti patebunt. Hoc tamen sciendum est quod novum opus altius est veteri quantum superiores fenestrae tam corporis chori quam laterum ejus a tabulato marmoreo in altum porriguntur. . . . Haec autem dicta sunt ut utriusque operis, novi scilicet et veteris, differentia possit agnosci.

# BIBLIOGRAPHY

## I. Collections of Transcribed Documents

Dugdale, William. *Monasticon Anglicanum: A History of the Abbies and other Monasteries, Hospitals, Friaries, and Cathedral and Collegiate Churches, with their dependencies, in England and Wales.* John Caley, Henry Ellis, and the Rev. Bulkeley Bandinel, eds. 6 vols. in 8. London: 1817–1830.

Fowler, J. T., ed. *Acts of Chapter of the Collegiate Church of SS Peter and Wilfrid, Ripon, A.D. 1452 to A.D. 1506.* The Publications of the Surtees Society, 66. London: 1874.

Fowler, J. T. *Memorials of the Church of SS Peter and Wilfrid, Ripon.* The Publications of the Surtees Society, 74, 78, 81, 115. London: 1881, 1884, 1886, 1908.

Leach, Arthur Francis, ed. *Memorials of Beverley Minster: The Chapter Acts Book.* The Publications of the Surtees Society, 108. London: 1903.

Leland, John. *Joannis Lelandi antiquarii De Rebus Britannicus Collectaneorum,* 1, pt. 2. Thomas Hearne, ed. Oxford: 1715.

Panofsky, Erwin. *Abbot Suger on the Abbey Church of St.-Denis and Its Art Treasures.* Princeton: 1946.

Raine, James, ed. *The Fabric Rolls of York Minster.* The Publications of the Surtees Society, 35. London: 1858.

Raine, James, ed., *The Historians of the Church of York and Its Archbishops.* 3 vols. London: 1886.

Shirley-Price, Leo, ed. and trans. *Bede: A History of the English Church and People.* Harmondsworth: 1955.

Stubbs, William, ed. *The Historical Works of Gervase of Canterbury.* 1. Rolls Series, Vol. 73. London, 1879.

## II. General Works on Architecture or History

Boase, T. S. R. *English Art, 1100–1216.* Oxford History of English Art. Oxford: 1953.
Bond, Francis. *The Chancel of English Churches.* London: 1916.
———. *An Introduction to English Church Architecture from the Eleventh to the Sixteenth Century.* 2 vols. London: 1913.
Bruyne, Edgar de. *Etudes d'esthétique médiévale.* 3 vols. Bruges: 1946.
Clapham, Alfred. *English Romanesque Architecture after the Conquest.* London: 1934.
———. *English Romanesque Architecture before the Conquest.* London: 1931.
Colvin, H. M. *The History of the King's Works.* 3 vols. London: 1963.
Frankl, Paul. *Gothic Architecture.* The Pelican History of Art. Harmondsworth: 1962.
Jackson, Thomas Graham. *Gothic Architecture in France, England, and Italy.* 2 vols. Cambridge: 1915.
Jantzen, Hans. *High Gothic, The Classic Cathedrals of Chartres, Reims, Amiens.* Translated by James Palmes. Letchworth: 1962.
Kidson, Peter. Part 1, *A History of English Architecture.* London: 1965.
Knowles, David. *The Episcopal Colleagues of Archbishop Thomas Becket.* Cambridge: 1951.
Newman, John. *North East and East Kent.* The Buildings of England, Nikolaus Pevsner, ed. Harmondsworth: 1968.
Pevsner, Nikolaus. *North Somerset and Bristol.* The Buildings of England. Harmondsworth: 1958.
———. *Yorkshire: The North Riding.* The Buildings of England. Harmondsworth: 1966.
———. *Yorkshire: The West Riding.* The Buildings of England. Harmondsworth: 1959.
——— with Hutchinson, John. *Yorkshire: York and The East Riding.* The Buildings of England. Harmondsworth, 1972.
Prior, Edward S. *A History of Gothic Art in England.* London: 1900.
Sharpe, Edmund. *Architectural Parallels.* London: 1848.

Stephen, Leslie, and Lee, Sidney, eds. *Dictionary of National Biography*, 17 vols. London: 1917 (with addenda to 1966).
Webb, Geoffrey. *Architecture in Britain: The Middle Ages*. The Pelican History of Art. Harmondsworth: 1956.

### III. Specialized Works on Architecture

Aubert, Marcel. "Airaines," *Congrès archéologique de France, Amiens* 99 (1936): 459–467.
Aylmer, G. E., and Cant, Reginald, eds. *A History of York Minster*. Oxford: 1977.
Baillie Reynolds, P. K. *Castle Acre Priory, Norfolk*, Ministry of Works Guide. London: 1952.
Bilson, John. "The Architecture of the Cistercians, with Special Reference to Some of Their Earlier Churches in England," *Archaeological Journal* 66 (1909): 185–280.
———. "The Architecture of Kirkstall Abbey Church, With Some General Remarks on the Architecture of the Cistercians," *Publications of the Thoresby Society* 16 (1907): 73–140.
———. "Beverley Minster," *The Antiquary* 27 (1893): 23 ff.
———. "Beverley Minster," *Architectural Review* 3 (1897): 197 ff.
———. "The Norman School and the Beginnings of Gothic Architecture. Two Octopartite Vaults: Montivilliers and Canterbury," *Archaeological Journal* 74 (1917): 1–35.
———. "Ripon Minster," *Archaeological Journal* 79 (1922): 362–65.
Bony, Jean. "French Influences on the Origins of English Gothic Architecture," *Journal of the Warburg and Courtauld Institutes*, 12 (1949): 1–15.
———. Letter quoted in Pierre Héliot, "Les oeuvres capitales du gothique français primitif et l'influence de l'architecture anglaise," *Wallraf-Richartz Jahrbuch* 20 (1958): 98–99.
———. "Origines des piles gothiques anglaises à fûts en délit," *Gedenkschrift Ernst Gall*. Munich and Berlin: 1965, 95–122.
Brakspear, Harold. "Bardney Abbey," *Archaeological Journal*, 79 (1922): 1–92.
Branner, Robert. *Burgundian Gothic*. London: 1960.
Browne, John. *The History of the Metropolitan Church of St. Peter, York*. London: 1847.
Craster, O. E. *Llanthony Priory, Monmouthshire*, Ministry of Works Guides. London: 1963.
Deshoulières, François. "Bertaucourt-les-Dames," *Congrès archéologique de France, Amiens* 99 (1936): 125–33.
Enlart, Camille. *Monuments religieux de l'architecture romane et de transition dans la région picarde*. Paris: 1895.
Fergusson, Peter. "The Late Twelfth-Century Rebuilding at Dundrennan Abbey," *Antiquaries Journal* 52 (1973): 232–43.
———. "Roche Abbey: The Source and Date of the Eastern Remains," *Journal of the British Archaeological Society* 34 (1971): 30–42.
———. "The South Transept Elevation of Byland Abbey," *Journal of the British Archaeological Association*. 38 (1975): 155–76.
Gilyard-Beer, R. *Fountains Abbey, Yorkshire*. Ministry of Works Guides. London: 1970.
Hallet, Cecil. *The Cathedral Church of Ripon, A Short History of the Church and A Description of Its Fabric*. Bell's Cathedral Series. London: 1901.
Hearn, M. F. "On the Original Nave of Ripon Cathedral," *Journal of the British Archaeological Association* 35 (1972) 39–45.
———. "Postscript: On the Original Nave of Ripon Cathedral," *Journal of the British Archaeological Association* 139 (1976): 93–94.
Héliot, Pierre. "Lillers," *Congrès archéologique de France, Amiens*, 99 (1936): 576–92.
———. "Les ouvres capitales du gothique français primitif et l'influence de l'architecture anglaise," *Wallraf-Richartz Jahrbuch* 20 (1958): 85–114.
Hiatt, Charles. *Beverley Minster*. Bell's Cathedral Series. London: 1898.
Hodges, Charles Clement. *The Abbey of St. Andrew, Hexham*. Edinburgh: 1888.
Hope, William Henry St. John. "The Abbey of St. Mary-in-Furness, Lancashire," *Transactions of the Cumberland and Westmoreland Antiquarian and Archaeological Society*, 16. 1909: 221–302.
———. "Fountains Abbey," *Yorkshire Archaeological Journal* 15 (1900), 269–402.
———. "Kirkstall Abbey," *The Publications of the Thoresby Society*, 16 (1907): 1–72.
Jones, W. T. "Durham Castle," *The Victoria History of the Counties of England, Durham*. 3. London: 1963, 78–82.
Kaines-Smith, S. C. "The Furness Abbey," *Victoria History of the Counties of England, Lancashire*. 8. London: 1914, 287 ff.

Kent, J. A. P. *The Pictorial History of Selby Abbey*. The Pitkin "Pride of Britain" Books. London: 1968.
Lambert, Elie. "L'Ancienne abbaye de Saint-Vincent de Laon," *Academie des Inscriptions et belles-lettres, comptes rendus des séances de l'année 1939*, 124–38.
———. "La Cathédrale de Laon," *Gazette des Beaux Arts* 130 (1926): 361–84.
Lefevre-Pontalis, Eugène. *L'Architecture religieuse dans l'ancien diocèse de Soissons*. 2 vols. Paris: 1894.
Lovegrove, E. W. "The Cathedral Church of St. David's," *Archaeological Journal* 83 (for 1926, pub. 1929): 254–83.
Macmahon, K. A. *The Pictorial History of Beverley Minster*. The Pitkin "Pride of Britain" Series. London: 1967.
Meer, Frederic van der. *Atlas de l'ordre cistercien*. Paris and Brussels: 1965.
Micklethwaite, J. T. "On the Crypts at Hexham and Ripon," *Archaeological Journal* 39 (1882): 347–54.
———. "Something about Saxon Church Building," *Archaeological Journal* 53 (1896): 293–351.
Peers, C. R. *Byland Abbey, Yorkshire*. Ministry of Works Guide. London: 1934.
———. "Peterborough Minster," *The Victoria History of the Counties of England, Northamptonshire*, vol. 2. London: 1906, 431–46.
———. "Recent Discoveries in the Minsters of York and Ripon," *The Antiquaries Journal* 11 (1931): 113–22.
———., and Brakspear, Harold. "Winchester: Hospital of St. Cross," *Victoria History of the Counties of England, Hampshire and the Isle of Wight*, 5. London, 1912, 59–66.
Phillips, Derek. "Excavations at York Minster, 1967–73," *Friends of York Minster, 46th Annual Report, 1975*. York: 1976.
Quekett, John and Cheetham, F. H. "Durham Cathedral: Detailed Description of Church," *Victoria History of the Counties of England, Durham*, 3. London: 1928, 96–123.
Salet, Francis. *La Madeleine de Vézelay*. Melun: 1948.
Scott, George Gilbert. "Ripon Minster," *Archaeological Journal* 31 (1874): 309–18.
———. "The Transition from the Romanesque to the Pointed Style in England," *Archaeological Journal*, 32 (1875): 347–68.
Seymour, Charles, Jr. *Notre-Dame of Noyon in the Twelfth Century*. New Haven: 1939; republished as *La cathédrale Notre-Dame de Noyon au XIIe siècle*. Droz and Geneva, 1978.
Thompson, A. Hamilton. "Southwell Minster," *Transactions of the Thoroton Society*, 15 (1912): 15–62.
Walbran, John Richard. *A Guide to Ripon, Harrogate, Fountains Abbey, Bolton Priory and Several Places of Interest in Their Vicinity*. 5th ed. Ripon: 1851.
Wander, Stephan. "Westminster Abbey: A Case Study in the Meaning of Architecture." Ph.D. Dissertation, Stanford University, 1974. Ann Arbor Microfilms, 1975.
Whittingham, A. B. "Bury St. Edmunds Abbey: The Plan, Design and Development of the Church and Monastic Buildings," *Archaeological Journal* 108 (1951): 169–76.
Wilkinson, W. E. *The Pictorial History of Ripon Cathedral*. The Pitkin "Pride of Britain" Books. London: 1969.
Willis, Robert. *The Architectural History of Canterbury Cathedral*. London: 1845.
———. *The Architectural History of York Cathedral*. London: 1846.
———. "On Foundations of Early Buildings, Recently Discovered in Lichfield Cathedral," *Archaeological Journal* 18 (1861): 1–24.

1. Ripon Minster, east end.

2. Ripon Minster, choir, looking east.

3. Ripon Minster, choir, west bays of north elevation.

4. Ripon Minster, choir, east bays of north elevation.

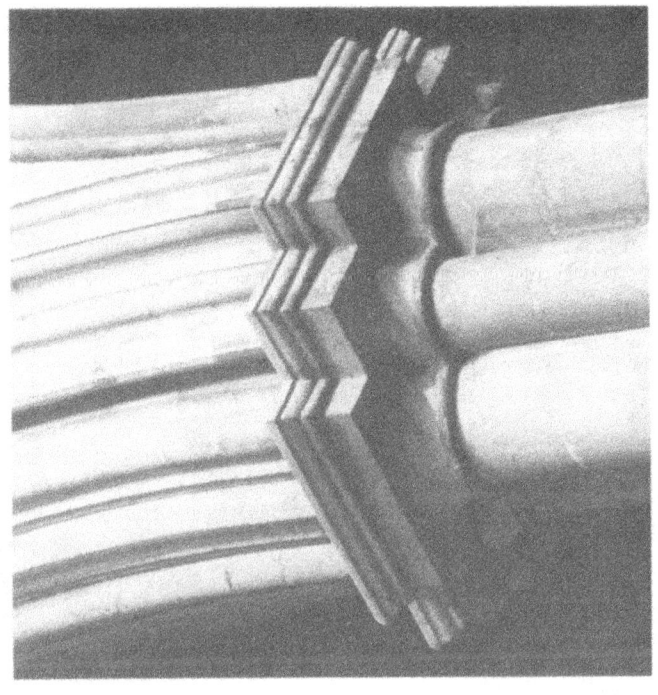

6. Ripon Minster, choir, capital of first freestanding pier of north elevation (with impost replaced in the late thirteenth century).

5. Ripon Minster, choir, second freestanding pier of north elevation.

8. Ripon Minster, choir, scar of original plinth on east bay of south aisle wall, at the juncture with the chapter house apse.

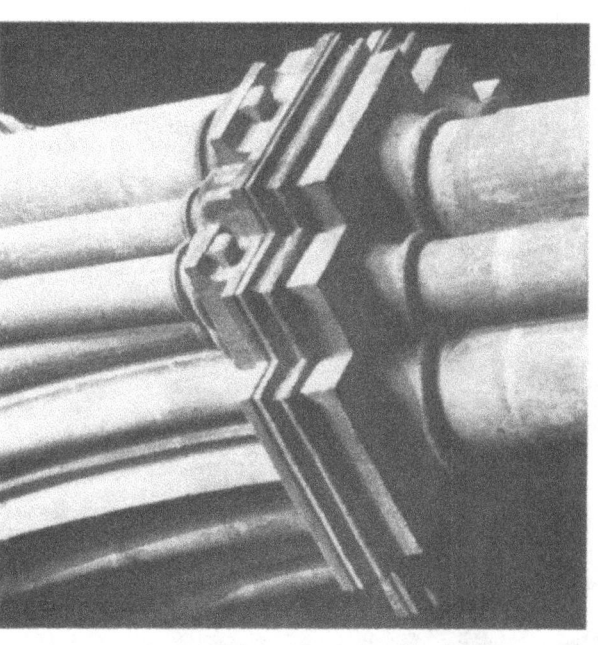

7. Ripon Minster, choir, capital of third freestanding pier of north elevation.

10. Ripon Minster, choir, north flank showing set-back late thirteenth-century bays to left.

9. Ripon Minster, choir, detail of east wall showing scar of relieving arch.

11. Ripon Minster, choir, triforium arcade in the fourth bay of the north elevation.

12. Ripon Minster, vaults in north choir aisle.

13. Ripon Minster, vault respond shafts in south choir aisle.

14. Ripon Minster, chapter house south flank.

16. Ripon Minster, juncture of chapter house and south transept showing continuous courses of ashlar masonry.

15. Ripon Minster, chapter house apse.

17. Ripon Minster, chapter house, vaults of undercroft, showing inserted ribs.

18. Ripon Minster, chapter house, vaults of upper chamber.

19. Ripon Minster, north transept east flank.

20. Ripon Minster, north transept, east elevation.

22. Ripon Minster, north transept, clerestory arcade in west elevation.

21. Ripon Minster, north transept, eastern chapel vault (inner bay).

23. Ripon Minster, north transept, west elevations.

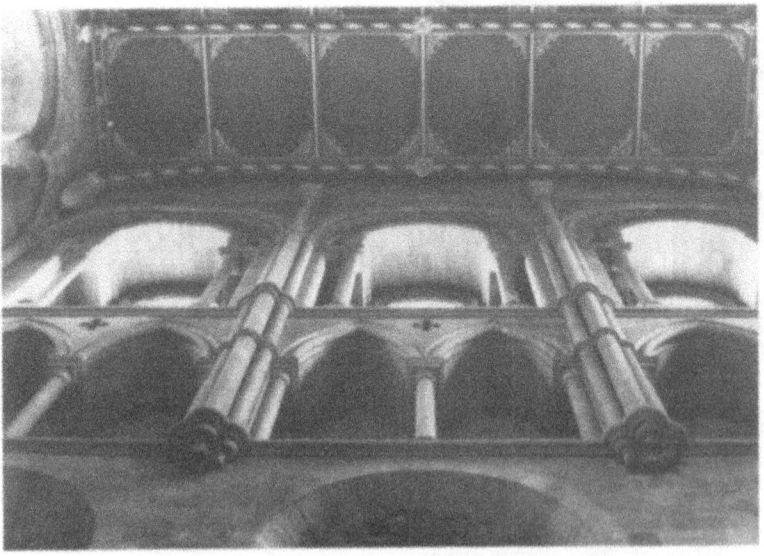
24. Ripon Minster, north transept, north elevation showing detached shafts and revised arch decoration.

25. Ripon Minster, south transept facade.

26. Ripon Minster, south transept west flank.

27. Ripon Minster, south transept south elevation.

28. Ripon Minster, south transept west elevation.

29. Ripon Minster, south transept eastern chapels, showing cluster of detached shafts for vault responds.

30. Ripon Minster, crossing, showing lantern tower.

31. Ripon Minster, crossing seen from nave, showing original crossing pier.

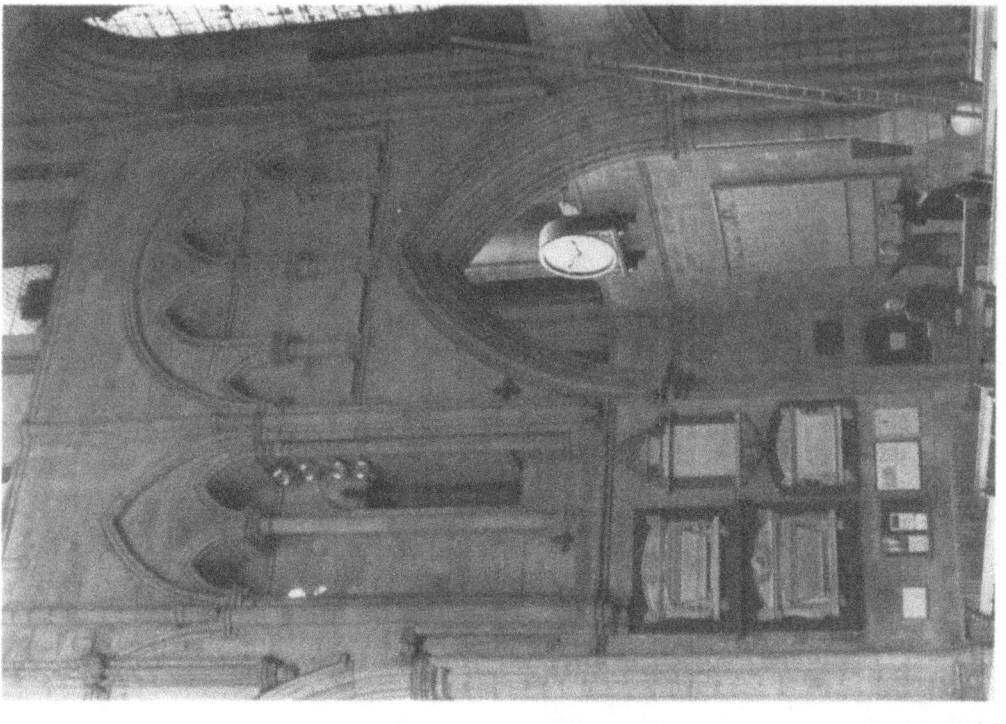

33. Ripon Minster, nave south elevation, west bays, lower stories.

32. Ripon Minster, nave, looking east.

34. Ripon Minster, nave south elevation, west bays, upper stories.

35. Ripon Minster, nave north elevation, west bays.

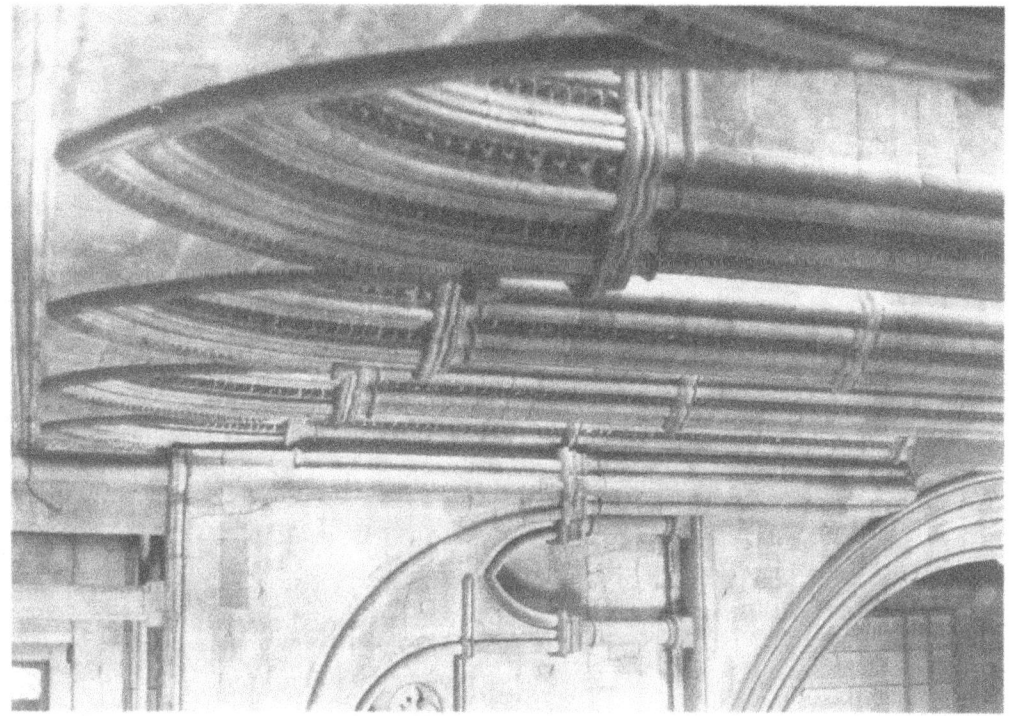

37. Ripon Minster, juncture of south and west elevations.

36. Ripon Minster, south west tower, blind arcade behind triforium of nave west bay.

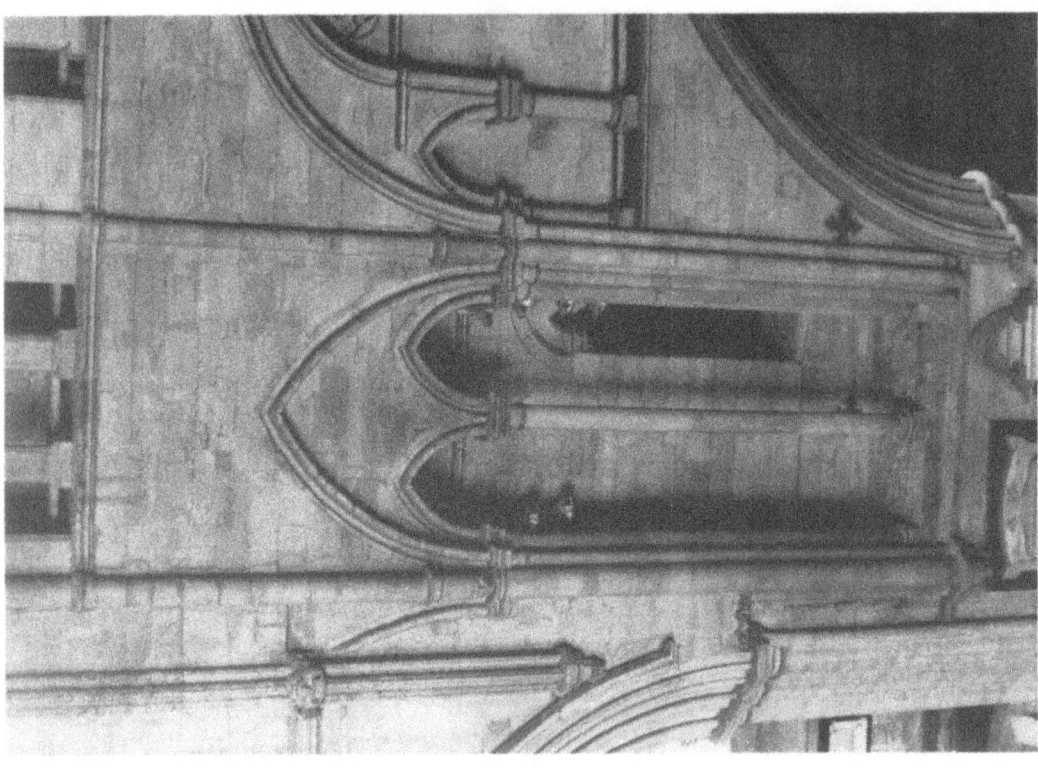

39. Ripon Minster, nave south elevation, penultimate bay.

38. Ripon Minster, south west tower, arch opening from the nave.

41. Ripon Minster, nave north elevation, east bay.

40. Ripon Minster, nave south elevation, east bay.

43. Ripon Minster, juncture of nave south flank and south west tower, showing original wall buttress (located in south aisle of the early-sixteenth-century nave).

42. Ripon Minster, nave north flank, buttress scar (located in north aisle of the early-sixteenth-century nave).

45. Ripon Minster, west front, south tower interior.

44. Ripon Minster, west front, south tower from the south.

47. Ripon Minster, west front, juncture of north tower and nave north flank, showing continuous courses of ashlar masonry up to the top of the nave wall buttress.

46. Ripon Minster, west front, juncture of north tower and nave north flank at plinth, showing continuous courses of ashlar masonry above the plinth.

49. Ripon Minster, west front, north tower showing corbel table which corresponds to the original ceiling level in the nave.

48. Ripon Minster, west front, north tower north east face showing lack of correspondence between ashlar masonry courses of the left and right window jambs.

51. Ripon Minster, west front, north tower, showing corbel table at the top of the upper story.

50. Ripon Minster, west front, north tower from the northeast.

52. Ripon Minster, west front, facade.

54. Preuilly Abbey, choir east elevation.

53. Fountains Abbey, south transept, windows of eastern chapels.

55. Laon Cathedral, choir, looking east.

56. Roche Abbey, north transept, east elevation (with remains of west elevation plinth in foreground).

58. Noyon Cathedral, south transept, east elevation.

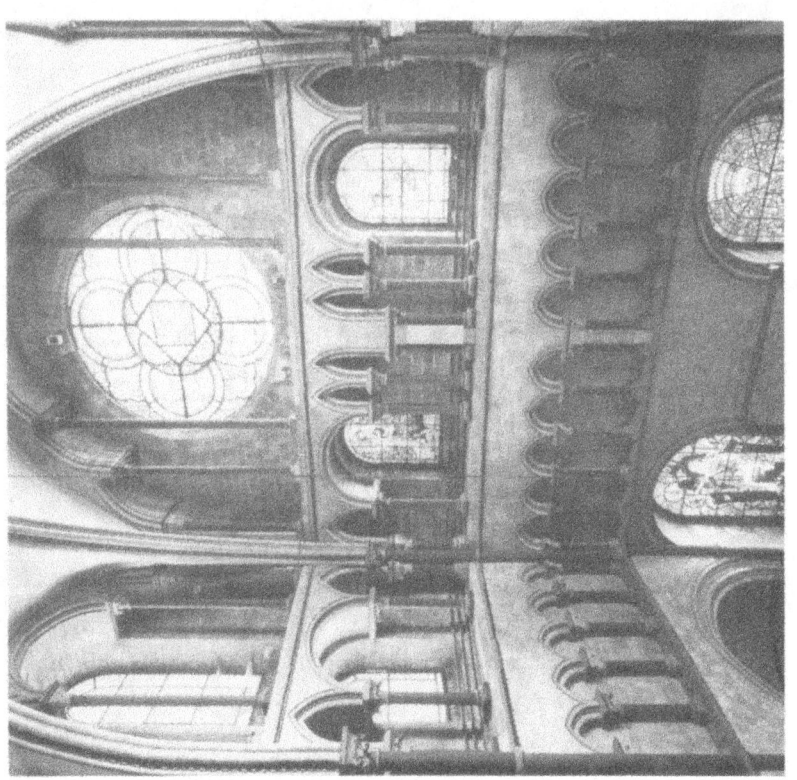

57. Canterbury Cathedral, south (east) transept, upper stories.

59. Selby Abbey, west front before the remodeling of 1935, but with modern gable.

61. Kirkstall Abbey, nave, north elevation.

60. Kirkstall Abbey, north transept, east elevation.

63. Byland Abbey, south transept, east elevation, detail of main arcade.

62. Roche Abbey, nave, north elevation, remains of pier.

64. Byland Abbey, south transept, east elevation upper stories.

65. Byland Abbey, choir, aisle vault responds.

67. Byland Abbey, south transept east elevation, remains of pier.

66. Byland Abbey, south transept, eastern chapel vault arches.

69. Furness Abbey, south transept east elevation, detail of main arcade.

68. Furness Abbey, south transept east elevation.

70. Whitby Abbey, choir, looking north.

72. Jedburgh Abbey, nave, looking west.

71. Lanercost Priory, detail of north choir elevation.

73. Wells Cathedral, nave, south elevation.

74. Bertaucourt-les-Dames, nave, south elevation, pier.

76. Soissons Cathedral, south transept, detail of main arcade.

75. Bellefontaine Chapel, arcade of north aisle chapel.

78. Laon Cathedral, north transept vaults.

77. Laon Cathedral, north transept east elevation.

80. Noyon Cathedral, south transept east flank.

79. Laon Cathedral, north transept, wall-passage at gallery level in north elevation.

81. Lillers Abbey, nave south elevation.

82. Canterbury Cathedral, choir.

83. Canterbury Cathedral, choir aisle, Romanesque capital.

84. Canterbury Cathedral, Trinity Chapel main arcade, Gothic capital.

85. Chichester Cathedral, retrochoir.

86. Lincoln Cathedral, nave, looking east.

87. Lincoln Cathedral, north choir aisle, blind arcade.

# INDEX

Airaines Priory, 111
Amblény Church, 123
Amiens (Old) Cathedral, 118
Angers Cathedral, 84
Angoulême Cathedral, 84
Arbroath Abbey, 105
Arras Cathedral, 113

Bardney Abbey, 72, 105, 106–07
Barfreston Priory, 17, 20
Beauvais, St. Etienne Collegiate Church, 17, 20
Bede, 93, 95
Bellefontaine Priory, 110, 111
Bertaucourt-les-Dames Church, 73, 105, 108, 119, 123
Béthizy-Saint-Pierre Church, 110
Beverley Minster, 16, 17, 76, 88, 89, 105, 133, 134
Buildwas Abbey, 64, 65, 68, 74
Bury St. Edmunds Abbey, 85, 90
Byland Abbey, 1, 10, 20, 23, 36, 64, 65, 67–74, 75, 81, 105, 107, 108, 112, 113, 115, 134, 135

Cambrai Cathedral, 113, 123
Canterbury Cathedral: Gothic choir, 1, 20, 23, 24, 31, 36, 64, 73, 76, 81, 92–93, 95, 113, 115, 119, 120, 121, 122–35; Romanesque choir, 88, 90, 92, 95, 97, 100; treasury, 110–111
Carlisle Cathedral, 134
Cartmel Priory, 105
Châlons-sur-Marne Collegiate Church, 123
Chartres Cathedral, 39, 119
Chichester Cathedral, 16, 23, 39, 81, 113, 123, 131, 132
Cistercian architecture, 5, 6, 19, 63–74, 75, 85, 105, 106, 107, 109, 117
Coulonges Church, 110
Crézancy Church, 110
Cuthbert, St., 93, 95

Daméry Church, 113
Dhuizel Church, 123
Dommartin Abbey, 105
Dundrennan Abbey, 64, 105
Durham: Castle, 72; Cathedral, 84, 90, 93, 95, 117

Eadmer of Canterbury, 93, 94
Eddius Stephanus, 94

Ely Cathedral, 16, 17, 33, 76, 87, 124, 134
Ernulf, prior, then bishop, of Rochester, 82, 92

Fécamp Abbey, 33
Fountains Abbey, 17, 64, 67, 105
Furness Abbey, 64, 65, 67, 68, 73, 74, 105, 107

Geoffrey Plantagenet, archbishop of York, 76
Gervase of Canterbury, 6, 73, 125–30, 137
Gothic style, 1–2, 5, 6, 63, 66, 80, 100, 102, 109, 113, 121, 122–35
Gournay-en-Bray Abbey, 82
Gray, Walter, archbishop of York, 76, 77, 94, 96, 136
Guisborough Abbey, 134
Gundulf, bishop of Rochester, 82

Hereford Cathedral, 16, 35
Hexham Priory, 16, 17, 23, 44, 73, 95, 105, 113, 132, 134

Jedburgh Abbey, 73, 105, 113, 132, 134
Jervaulx Abbey, 64, 105, 134
John of Beverley, St., 93

Kelso Abbey, 73
Kirkham Priory, 85
Kirkstall Abbey, 17, 19, 36, 64, 65, 67, 68, 74, 105, 106, 107, 108, 118, 120

Lanercost Priory, 73, 113, 134
Laon: Cathedral, 1, 12, 16, 19, 20, 80, 115–121, 123; St. Vincent Abbey, 112
Lillers Collegiate Church, 112
Lincoln Cathedral, 21, 23, 36, 76, 105, 124, 132, 133, 134
Llanthony Priory, 39, 76, 86
London: (Old St. Paul's) Cathedral, 134; St. Bartholomew Priory in Smithfield, 123; Temple Church, 133

Noirlac Abbey, 19
Norwich Cathedral, 33, 98, 124
Nouvron-Vingré Church, 110
Noyon Cathedral, 1, 44, 113–16, 119, 120, 123; bishop's chapel, 17
Nun Monkton Priory, 133

# INDEX

Old Malton Priory, 72, 105, 113, 134
Oswald, St., 96, 97, 100

Paris, Nôtre-Dame Cathedral, 119, 123
Paulinus, St., 92, 95
Pershore Abbey, 16, 35
Peterborough Abbey (now Cathedral), 31, 33, 84, 113, 124, 126
Preuilly Abbey, 19, 20

Reims, St.-Remi Abbey, 123
Rievaulx Abbey, 16, 17, 131, 134
Ripon master, 111, 119, 120–21, 124
Ripon Minster: altars, 13, 95, 98–100; arch moldings (including soffits), 103, 110, 125; building materials, 11; buttresses (pilaster), 24, 28–30, 44–45, 47, 50; capitals (molded, 29, 38, inverted-bell, 12, 68, 74, 104, 106, stiff-leaf, 76, waterleaf, 64, 74, 106); chapter house 9, 12, 26–32, 54, 55, 60, 78; choir (including east end), 9, 11, 19, 21, 54, 55, 60, 77, 78, 80, 99, 100, 105, 111, 121, 122, 134; choir aisles, 9, 12, 24, 60, 64, 99, 107; clerestory, 9, 16, 21–24, 32, 37, 39, 40, 41, 44, 45, 49, 54, 55, 65, 113, 115, 134; corbel table, 28, 50; crossing, 9, 37, 54, 55, 99; crossing (lantern) tower, 9, 42, 44, 54, 55, 60, 77, 134; crypt, 1, 96–97, 99; Lady Chapel (Lady Loft), 25, 30–32, 60; main arcade, 81, 104–11; main arcade piers, 12, 23, 102, 104, 111 (attic-bases, 12, 64, 104; capitals, 12, 68, 74, 104, 106; imposts, 12, 21, 62, 104; plinths, 12, 106; shaft-bundle type, 12, 64, 68, 74, 104–108, 119); nave, 9, 33, 37–47, 54, 55, 60, 80, 87, 134; oculus windows, 17–21, 35, 36, 52, 54, 65, 118; Oswald's putative church, 98; plan, 9, 11–19, 86, 87, 95, 99, 134; plinth on exterior, 10, 26, 49, 64; shafts cut *en délit*, 21, 32, 36, 48, 116, 119, 123; transept chapels, 9, 26, 37, 60, 69, 78, 80, 84, 87, 98, 110, 134; transepts, 9, 16, 32–37, 54, 55, 60, 77, 78, 110, 111, 134; triforium, 16, 21, 23, 33–36, 37, 39, 40, 41, 42, 44, 45, 46, 49, 50, 54, 55, 60, 65, 72, 111–12, 118; wall passages, 33–35, 50, 72–73, 80, 115; wall shafts, 2, 12, 16, 21, 45, 74, 102, 103, 104, 116, 119; west front (facade) 27, 47–52, 54, 55, 60, 79, 86; west towers, 37, 42, 46, 47–52, 54, 55, 79, 99; Wilfrid's church, 1, 5, 96–98; vaults, 2, 9, 12, 21, 24, 29, 30, 32, 33, 36, 54, 55, 60, 102, 104, 109, 110, 116–117

Roche Abbey, 1–2, 19, 35–36, 64–68, 74–75, 105, 107, 108, 118, 120
Rochester Cathedral, 82, 92, 95, 132, 133
Roger of Pont l'Eveque, archbishop of York, 1, 2, 63, 68, 76, 77, 79, 80–101, 122–23, 134
Romsey Abbey, 33, 124

St. Albans Abbey (now Cathedral), 76
Saint-Denis: Abbey, 17, 101, 123, 128; shrine of, 101
Saint-Omer, St. Bertin Abbey, 82
Salisbury Cathedral, 16, 76, 124, 132, 133
Santiago Cathedral, 99
Selby Abbey, 51, 105, 134
Sens Cathedral, 1
Silvacane Abbey, 19
Soissons Cathedral, 73, 123
Southwark Priory (now Cathedral), 76, 105
Southwell Minster (now Cathedral), 17, 76, 88, 105, 123

Tewkesbury Abbey, 31
Theobald, archbishop of Canterbury, 89
Thomas à Becket, St., archbishop of Canterbury, 88–93; pilgrimage in honor of, 122, 131
Thomas of Bayeux, archbishop of York, 86, 94
Thomas II, archbishop of York, 88, 94
Thurstan, archbishop of York, 94
Tintern Abbey, 117
Toulouse: Cathedral, 85; St. Sernin Collegiate Church, 99
Tynemouth Priory, 76, 113

Valenciennes Cathedral, 113, 123
Vaux-de-Cernay Abbey, 20
Veuilly-la-Poterie Church, 110
Vézelay Abbey, 113

Waverley Abbey, 117
Wells Cathedral, 23, 51, 52, 81, 86, 132
Westminster Abbey, 87, 89
Whitby: Abbey, 16, 17, 72, 131, 132, 134; Synod of, 1, 93
Wilfrid, St., 1, 93–101; pilgrimage in honor of, 94, 95, 98–99, 122; relics of 96, 98, 100
William, St., archbishop of York, 93, 94, 96
William of Sens, 124, 125, 128, 130
William the Englishman, 124
Winchester: Cathedral, 31; St. Cross Hospital, 16, 82, 117
Worcester Cathedral, 17, 132, 133
Worksop Priory, 133

York: Archbishop's Chapel, 17; Minster, 66, 75, 82–90, 95, 96, 99, 100, 113, 134; St. Mary's Abbey, 66

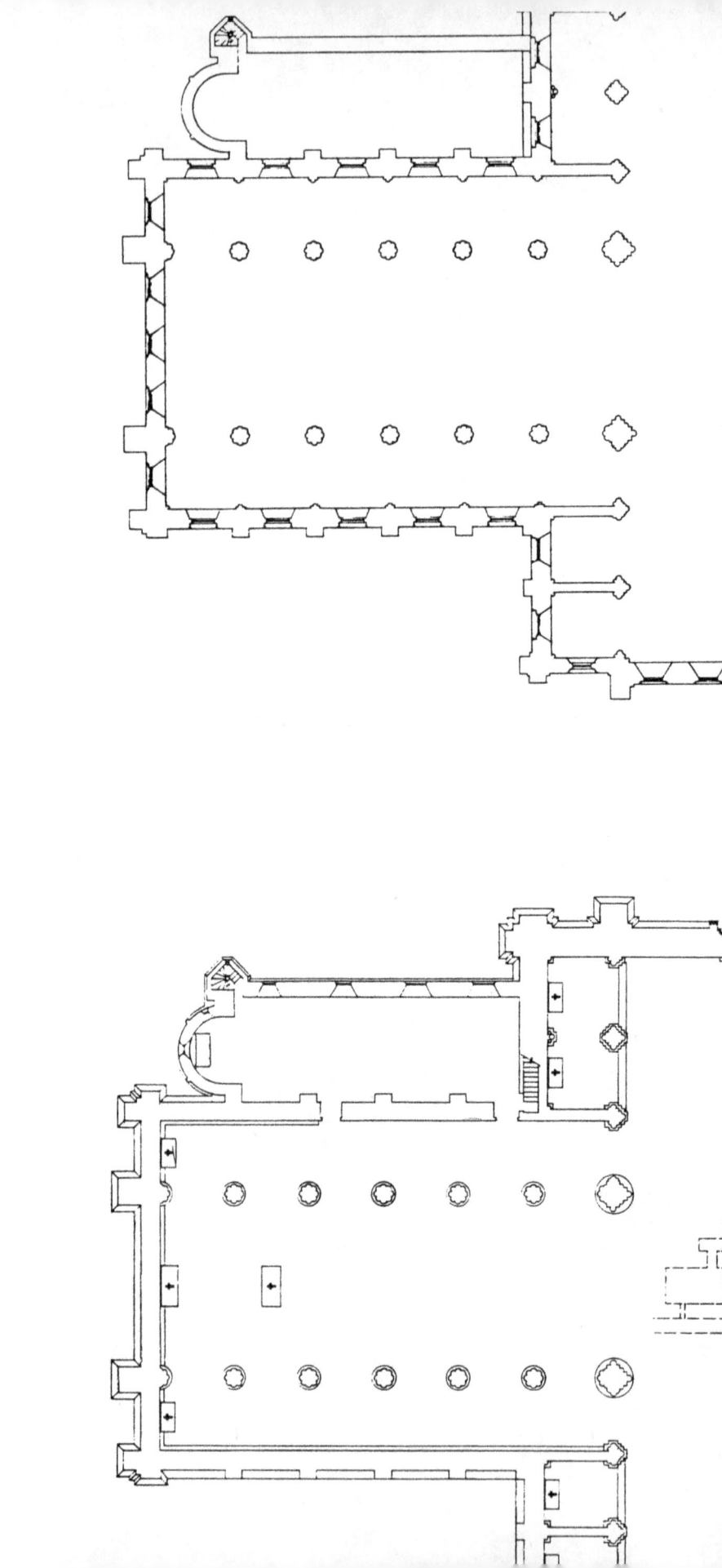

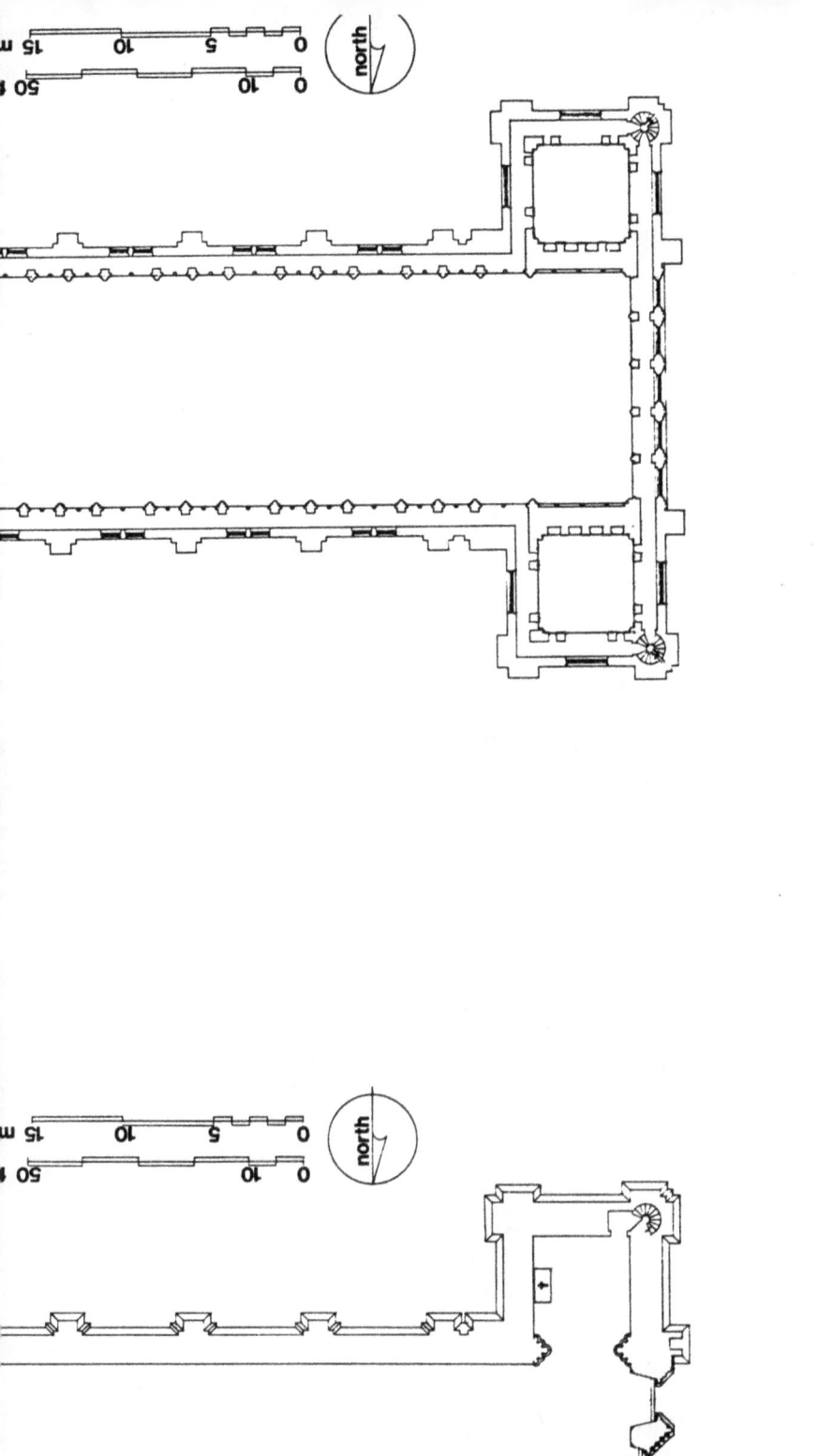

www.ingramcontent.com/pod-product-compliance
Lightning Source LLC
Chambersburg PA
CBHW080924100426
42812CB00007B/2366